Peter the Great
Transforms Russia

Third Edition

Edited and with an Introduction by
James Cracraft
University of Illinois at Chicago

D. C. HEATH AND COMPANY

Lexington, Massachusetts   Toronto

PROBLEMS IN EUROPEAN CIVILIZATION SERIES

Acquisitions Editor: James Miller
Production Editor: Anne Rebecca Starr
Designer: Alwyn R. Velàsquez
Production Coordinator: Mary J. Taylor
Text Permissions Editor: Margaret Roll

Cover: Peter I at the Battle of Poltava. Oil on canvas painted by J. G. Dannhauer, 1710s. (Russian Museum, Leningrad)

Published simultaneously in Canada.

Printed in the United States of America.

International Standard Book Number: 0-669-21674-7

Library of Congress Catalog Card Number: 90-81300

10 9 8 7

Preface

Marc Raeff graciously suggested that I assume from him editorship of the Heath volume on Peter the Great, which has long been a staple among teachers and students of Russian and European history. I am further indebted to him for his advice in planning this new volume and for agreeing to write its concluding essay. In recognition of these and his many other contributions to the study of Russian history, the volume is gratefully dedicated to him.

My thanks are also due to Reef Altoma, my former research assistant at the Russian Research Center, Harvard University, for translating three new selections from Russian; and to Cherylean Crockett, assistant in the History Department of the University of Illinois at Chicago, for help in preparing the volume for the publishers. Finally, I would like to acknowledge Professors John T. Alexander of the University of Kansas and David L. Ransel of Indiana University, Bloomington, for their suggestions in revising the text.

It should be noted that apart from necessary abridgement the readings gathered here have been slightly edited to achieve consistency in terminology and transliteration. The latter generally follows the modified Library of Congress system used by the *Slavic Review*, the journal of the American Association for the Advancement of Slavic Studies: except that Russian soft signs are dropped throughout the volume and the double-"i" ending of proper names is rendered as "y" (for example, Kliuchevsky, not Kliuchevskii). Dates are given in accordance with the Julian (or Old Style) calendar adopted in Russia by decree of Peter the Great on January 1, 1700, thereby abandoning the Russian tradition of calculating time "from the creation of the world." In the eighteenth century, this calendar was twelve days behind the Gregorian (or New Style) calendar that was gradually superceding it in Europe (to be adopted in Russia, at last, in 1918). Thus the great battle of Poltava, the turning point in Peter's long war with Sweden, took place on July 8, 1709 (New Style), but on June 27, 1709 (Old Style), the date that will be found here.

J. C.

Contents

Chronology of
Events

1645–1676	Reign of Tsar Aleksei Mikhailovich, father of Peter I
1649	Promulgation of *Ulozhenie* (law code)
1666–1667	Russian church schism
1667	Peace of Andrusovo with Poland, ceding eastern Ukraine to Russia; confirmed by treaty of 1686
1667–1671	Rebellion led by Stenka Razin
1672	Birth of Peter I, first son of Tsar Aleksei by his second wife
1676–1682	Reign of Tsar Feodor III, older half-brother of Peter I
1682	Ivan V (second half-brother of Peter I) and Peter proclaimed co-tsars, with sister Sophia (Sofia) as regent
1687	Formation by Peter I of Preobrazhenskii guards regiment
1689	Tsarevna Sophia deposed, party of Peter I takes power Peter marries Evdokiia Lopukhina
1690	Birth of Tsarevich Aleksei
1695–1696	Russian conquest of Azov; beginnings of Russian navy
1696	Death of Ivan V; Peter I now sole ruler in name as well as fact Preobrazhenskii Prikaz given jurisdiction over political offenses
1697–1698	Peter I's "Grand Embassy" to Europe
1698	Suppression of the royal musketeers (*streltsy*) in Moscow
1700	Beginning of the Northern (Swedish) War; Russian defeat at the siege of Narva

	Death of Patriarch Adrian; no successor named
	Adoption of the European (Julian) calendar
1701	Opening of the school of mathematics and navigation in Moscow
1702	Manifesto of Peter I welcoming foreigners to Russia
	Publication of the first Russian newspaper
1703	Foundation of St. Petersburg
1705–1706	Uprising in Astrakhan
1707–1708	Rebellion led by Bulavin
	Introduction of the "civil" alphabet
1708	Beginning of local government reform
	Russian victory over the Swedes at Lesnaia
	Revolt of Hetman Mazepa
1709	Battle of Poltava
1710	Russian capture of Viborg, Riga, and Reval
1711	Foundation of the Senate
	Russian defeat by the Turks at the battle on the Pruth
1712	Peter solemnizes his marriage (in 1707) to second wife, Catherine
1713	Transfer of the capital to St. Petersburg
	Russian invasion of Finland
1714	Russian naval victory over the Swedes off Cape Hango
	Foundation of the Naval Academy in St. Petersburg
1716	Publication of the *Military Statute*
1716–1717	Peter's second trip to Europe
1718	Introduction of the collegial administration system
	Trial and death of Tsarevich Aleksei
1719	Further reform of local government
1720	Establishment of the Main Municipal Council
	Publication of the *General Regulation* and the *Naval Statute*
1721	Publication of the *Ecclesiastical Regulation*; foundation of the Holy Synod
	Peace of Nystadt (Nystad) with Sweden, ending the Northern War
	Peter I proclaimed emperor
1722	Promulgation of the new succession law and the Table of Ranks
	Appointment of the procurator-general

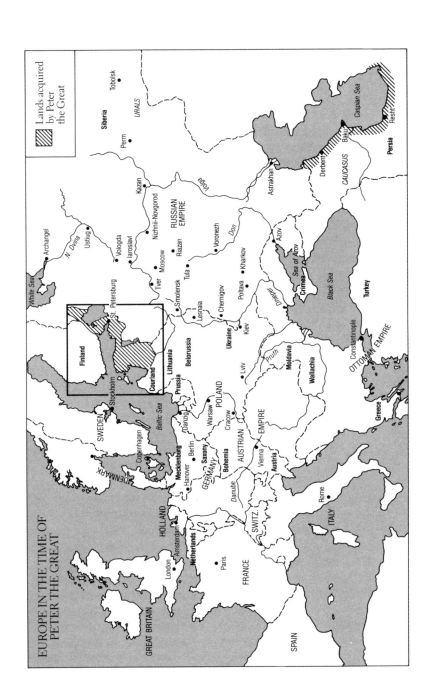

EUROPE IN THE TIME OF
PETER THE GREAT

Lands acquired
by Peter
the Great

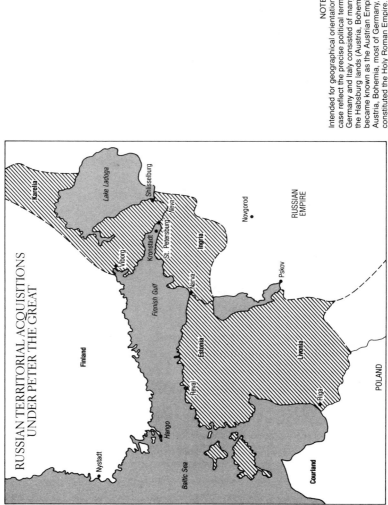

RUSSIAN TERRITORIAL ACQUISITIONS
UNDER PETER THE GREAT

Karelia

Lake Ladoga

Shlisselburg

Viborg

Kronstadt

St. Petersburg

Neva

Finland

Finnish Gulf

Hango

Nystadt

Baltic Sea

Narva

Ingria

Novgorod

RUSSIAN
EMPIRE

Pskov

Reval

Estonia

Livonia

Riga

POLAND

Courland

NOTE

Intended for geographical orientation, these maps do not in every case reflect the precise political terminology of 1725. For example, Germany and Italy consisted of many small independent states, and the Habsburg lands (Austria, Bohemia, Hungary, etc.) officially became known as the Austrian Empire only in 1804. Until 1806, Austria, Bohemia, most of Germany, and northern Italy nominally constituted the Holy Roman Empire.

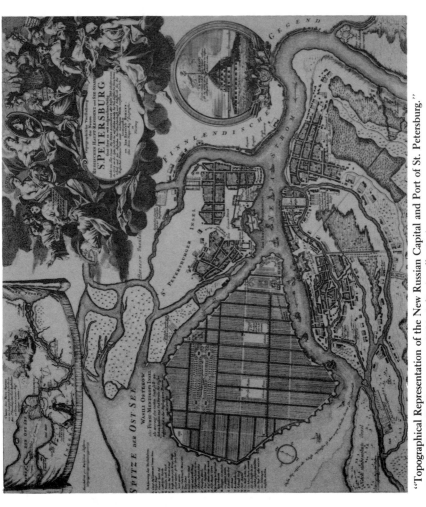

"Topographical Representation of the New Russian Capital and Port of St. Petersburg."
Engraving by J. B. Homann, ca. 1720. (editor's collection)

Introduction

Peter I (1672–1725), tsar and first emperor (1682–1725), the "father" and great reformer or "transformer" (*preobrazovatel*) of his country, remains the most famous ruler of Russia before the twentieth century. Indeed the legend of "Peter the Great," which was born in his own time and has since spread around the world, has tended to obscure for later generations the actual history of his reign. Not only historians but also novelists, playwrights, poets, filmmakers, and visual artists of every kind have contributed to the creation and dissemination of the Petrine legend — as did Peter himself. He was the first Russian ruler to grasp the potential of the new art emanating from the Renaissance in Europe and to commission numerous paintings, engravings, sculptures, and medals of himself which promptly projected his imperious image to countless observers both at home and abroad. Peter was also concerned to set the historical record straight, and in his later years commissioned and personally helped to edit a history of his reign based on official documents. This was another first for Russia.

The legend of Peter the Great is perhaps best encapsulated in Alexander Pushkin's celebrated poem, *The Bronze Horseman* (1833). The poem's title, like much of its lengthy text, refers to the great equestrian statue of Peter erected by Catherine II and still a prominent landmark of the city founded by him — then known as St. Petersburg, now as Leningrad.

> *He's awesome in the surrounding mist!*
> *What thoughts conceals his brow!*
> *What power in him is bound,*
> *And what fire in this his horse!*
> *Where dost thou gallop, proud steed,*
> *And where thy hooves to touch the ground?*
> *Oh mighty lord of Fate!*
> *Was it not thus that Russia too*
> *Was seized by thee with iron bridle,*
> *And to the chasm sped? . . .*

Pushkin's "chasm" may be interpreted as that which separated the past from the future, old Russia from the new, and Russia from Europe — meaning the dynamic economies, societies, and cultures particularly of

Sweden and Germany, the Netherlands and Britain, France and Italy. It was a chasm that Peter was determined to bridge. In fact, Europeanization, or Westernization, became the dominant policy of his reign, as the readings which follow make abundantly clear. Europeanization under Peter was at once a policy and a goal, and entailed a wide-ranging effort to bring Russia into closer political and economic contact with Europe while transforming it, internally, into a richer, stronger, more efficient state. Thus Pushkin's poem evokes not only the awesome image of the Petrine legend, but also the overriding purpose as well as the historical achievement of the Petrine regime. Moreover, the full text of *The Bronze Horseman* hauntingly conveys the profound ambiguity of the Petrine legacy in Russia, that great question of costs versus benefits which has been so hotly debated by generations of Russian thinkers in contemplating their country's past. Even now it is again being urgently asked in Russia whether Peter the Great is, or is not, an appropriate model, example, or precedent to follow for would-be reformers of the Soviet system.

These are among the major themes addressed in the readings that make up this book. They have been selected from the works of eighteen historians, Russian and non-Russian, with three considerations in mind: (1) the readings should, taken together, illuminate the main developments, accomplishments, and failures of Peter's reign in Russia; (2) they should, singly and together, show the variety of opinion that exists among historians in assessing the Petrine achievement; and (3) they should also, in some measure, indicate the range of methods and approaches adopted by historians in studying this crucial period in Russian and, by extension, European history.

In other words, no effort has been made to include in this book views of Peter the Great that are merely polemical, notably eccentric, or otherwise unhistorical — views that have usually been advanced over the years by non-historians. Nor have excerpts been taken from the highly detailed studies of aspects of Peter's reign published (mainly in Russian) by specialists addressing other specialists, since to do so would have required extensive editorial comment aimed at clarifying for general readers the relevance and importance of such contributions. Unfortunately, this consideration has eliminated a number of specialized works of interest by Soviet historians — works which are sometimes also characterized by a simplistic Marxist approach as well as by excessive nationalism. There are encouraging signs that these features of conventional Soviet scholarship are now being abandoned by younger Soviet historians, and we look forward to the day when more Soviet work will be worth the effort of translating and editing for inclusion in a book like this. Meanwhile, the two excerpts from general works by leading Soviet historians that are printed here will convey something of the conventional Soviet pattern.

Attentive readers will notice that several main conclusions emerge from the readings gathered here, conclusions which are virtually uncontested by historians. These are, first and foremost, that Russia under Peter I became a major European power; second, that Petrine Russia underwent radical internal reform; third, that Peter himself was a truly extraordinary ruler; and fourth, that Peter's reign, all told, had a lasting impact on Russia and, indeed, the world. But attentive readers will also notice that several major questions recur in the readings. To what degree were Peter's policies anticipated by his predecessors and particularly by his father, Tsar Aleksei? To what extent were the Petrine reforms borrowed from, and dependent on, foreigners and foreign models? How successful, on their own terms, were these reforms — and if they were not, why not? How far was Russia transformed under Peter I, or even revolutionized? Of course, these questions along with the great question of costs versus benefits mentioned earlier cannot be fully resolved here, and especially when they involve moral judgments deriving as much or more from philosophy and religion as from history. On the other hand, such questions cannot even be properly posed without a careful study of history. This book's overall purpose is to provide its readers with expert guidance both in studying the Petrine period of Russian history and in reaching at least tentative answers to these basic questions.

Variety of Opinion

Peter's program of reform [was] bequeathed to him by his predecessors. The first place among those predecessors unquestionably belongs to Peter's father. . . . . He created a favorable atmosphere for the reform movement.

V. O. Kliuchevsky

It was not Peter's arbitrary will nor historical chance that predetermined Russia's rise but the objective necessity of its socio-political development. At first intuitively and later consciously, Peter expressed na-

tional needs and energetically accelerated what was dictated by the objective course of history.

N. N. Molchanov

Of no ruler in the history of Europe can it be said with greater truth that his work was the outcome of his own essential character.

M. S. Anderson

It is impossible to agree with the thesis prevalent among Soviet historians that the use of the Swedish administrative system as a prototype for the Russian reforms was generally characterized by a "creative reworking" . . . [and] that the Swedish influence was very limited. . . . Not only was the framework of the [Petrine] administrative structure borrowed from Sweden, but the internal organization and activities of the various administrative organs were also patterned on their Swedish counterparts.

Claes Peterson

The establishment of a large standing army, which Peter initiated, constitutes one of the critical events in the history of the Russian state. . . . For a country as poor as Russia, the maintenance of such an armed force represented an immense burden. To enable it to carry the load, Peter had to revamp the country's fiscal, administrative and social structures, and, to some extent, transform its economic and cultural life as well.

Richard Pipes

When the full history of Peter's opposition has been written, our picture of a basically benign, enlightened, or at least progressive regime — of an era of great reform — will be fundamentally modified.

James Cracraft

While the main purpose of Russian development [under Peter] was to modernize the economy, and, in fact, much of Russia's social and political framework, that is, to bring it closer to Europe in some of its most significant respects, it was by the force of the selfsame development that Russia was being forced in other, no less significant respects away from Europe, towards the despotisms of the Orient with their service states, which involved enslavement of the population by the state.

Alexander Gerschenkron

Against this background, the efforts by Peter the Great to modernize Russia appear genuinely heroic.

Arcadius Kahan

What was the legacy of Peter? . . . First and most obviously, he transformed Russia's foreign relations. Henceforward Russia played her part as one of the main participants in European history.

B. H. Sumner

No revolution is ever complete, and in this sense Peter I's reign was a revolution, if only in the self image and consciousness of Russian society and culture.

Marc Raeff

Stylized portrait of Tsar Aleksei Mikhailovich. Reproduced from a royal manuscript compiled in Moscow in 1672. (Harvard College Library)

Russia Before Peter the Great

M. S. *Anderson*

Modernization and Resistance

The degree to which Russia before Peter I was undergoing modernization — or Europeanization (or Westernization) — has long been disputed by historians. Some have asserted, at one extreme, that nearly everything of importance which occurred during Peter's reign was solidly based on precedent: that Peter merely carried forward a program of reform which in all its essentials had been inaugurated under his predecessors, particularly his father, Tsar Aleksei (reigned 1645–1676). Other historians, expressing a view that goes back to the entourage of Peter himself, have seen the first emperor as the virtual creator of modern Russia — and thus as the "greatest leader in Russian history," in the words of S. M. Soloviev (1820–1879), who is generally considered Russia's greatest historian. In this selection, Professor M. S. Anderson, of the University of London, tries to steer a middle course. Summarizing the work of numerous scholars in the field,

From M. S. Anderson, *Peter the Great*, 1978, pp. 9–24. Reprinted by permission of Thames and Hudson Ltd.

Anderson concludes that although Russia before Peter came to power was "rapidly developing," the "old Russia, isolated, self-sufficient, fearing and despising foreigners, dominated by traditional pieties, hostile to individualism and incapable of conceiving of real change, was far from dead."

The Russia into which Peter was born was already in some ways a part of Europe, or rapidly becoming one. It differed radically, nonetheless, from the states and societies to be found further west. Though much smaller in terms of territory than it was to become under Peter and his successors, it already covered a gigantic area. In the west it was severed from the Baltic by Sweden's possession of Finland, Ingria and Estonia. The great fortress-city of Smolensk, only 150 miles west of Moscow, bitterly contested for many years, had been finally wrested from the Poles as recently as 1654, and not until 1667 was Poland forced to surrender Kiev. Moreover, Russia had no outlet on the Black Sea, from which it was separated by hundreds of miles of largely uninhabited steppe as well as by the Moslem Nogais and Tatars of the Khanate of the Crimea, a vassal-state of the Ottoman Empire since the later fifteenth century. Its only usable coastline, on the White Sea in the far north, where the new port of Archangel had been established at the end of the sixteenth century, was blocked by ice for much of the year. In the Caucasus, though its influence was growing, Russia as yet held no territory. It had nevertheless, in spite of these still restricted European frontiers, already shown both the desire and the capacity for territorial growth on a great scale. In the 1550s Ivan IV (Ivan the Terrible) had made a gigantic forward step by conquering the Tatar Khanates of Kazan and Astrakhan, thus gaining control of the whole course of the Volga. From the 1580s onwards the exploration and conquest of Siberia had been pushed ahead with remarkable speed, so that by the 1630s Russian adventurers had already reached the shores of the north Pacific. Long before Peter's birth, therefore, his country had become, in mere size, a giant who dwarfed all the states of Europe.

This enormous territory was as yet undeveloped or only inadequately developed, and almost everywhere very thinly populated. In the north, vast tracts of tundra and forest supported only hunters, fur-trappers and a little primitive and precarious agriculture. The potentialities of Siberia, in the main still peopled only by native tribes, were almost completely unexploited, as indeed they were to remain until the present century. Even in central Russia, in the areas around Moscow whose expansion had produced the huge territorial aggregation which Peter inherited, the population was scanty and the level of economic development low by European standards. It is impossible to say with any accuracy what the total population was; perhaps a figure of 10–12 million for the second half of the seventeenth century is the most plausible. Some signs of economic growth were visible. From the sixteenth century onwards, with the emergence of larger and to some extent unified markets, a tendency for different areas to specialize in the production of different commodities had become more marked. Thus iron was smelted and worked in the northwest and around Tula, south of Moscow; linen and canvas were also produced in the northwest, grain most abundantly in the middle Volga valley and the area south of Moscow; and salt was an important product on the White Sea coast, in the Perm area and on the lower Volga. But the overwhelming impression is still one of potentially enormous resources exploited very inadequately if at all.

To some extent this was a matter of geography. Great distances and an extreme "continental" climate, with severe winters, burning summers and a shorter growing season for crops than in western Europe, were in themselves barriers to economic progress. For each grain of wheat or rye sown only three of four were harvested; this was far lower than the standard yield in the more advanced areas of Europe. Such a scanty yield meant that the overwhelming majority of the population had to till the ground if any kind of organized society were to survive. These natural obstacles, however, were reinforced by man-made ones. The rulers of Russia had forged a form of government more completely autocratic, in both form and substance, than any to be found in Europe. The services rendered to the country by the autocracy were real. From the time of the Grand Duke Ivan III of Muscovy (1462–1505), a line of rulers had struggled, with considerable success, to unify Russia, to extend its territory and to defend it against the enemies — Poles, Tatars, Swedes — who confronted it across exposed and badly-defined frontiers. Military defense and territorial growth demanded strong and centralized, if necessarily ruthless, government. But rule of this kind involved an increasingly complete monopoly by the ruler and

the central government of initiative and decision-making of all significant kinds. New decrees in the seventeenth century still began with the
traditional formula, "the tsar has decreed and the boyars have assented";
but in fact members of old boyar families and the "feudal" influences
they represented were by the later part of the century becoming less
important than an inner ring of personal advisers of the tsars. Many of
these were drawn from relatively minor landowning families, though
they were often promoted to the rank of boyar. The disappearance
under Peter of the Boyar Council (*Duma*) was merely the culmination
of a development which had begun a good deal earlier. The obse-
quiousness which even the greatest nobles showed to the tsar, describing
themselves as his "slaves" and prostrating themselves before him, together with their acceptance of humiliating corporal punishments,
showed how little they possessed the outlook of a European *noblesse*,
with all that this implied in terms of a sense of personal honor. In the
first decades of the century it had seemed that the Assembly of the Land
(*Zemskii Sobor*) might become a permanent feature of Russian government and even a check on the tsar's autocracy. This was a representative
body made up mainly of representatives of the service class, the "serving
men" who provided the tsars with most of their army and their rudimentary administration and who were normally rewarded for their services with grants of land. It also included, however, spokesmen of the
town merchant class, and for a moment seemed to be on the point of
gaining real power. But after the early 1650s the Assembly ceased to be
called together; instead the government, for its own purposes and at its
own convenience, summoned only occasional meetings of particular
and limited social groups — merchants, serving men, or the representatives of Moscow. From this quasi-parliamentary direction no effective
tempering of tsarist autocracy was to be hoped for. Even the officials
through whom the tsar ruled were kept under continual scrutiny,
guided by meticulous instructions and deprived as far as possible of all
powers of initiative. Seventeenth-century Russia was thus a society in
which there was no secular institution able or even willing to challenge
the autocracy of the monarch. In it any display of independence or
initiative, whether on a class or an institutional basis, was distrusted and
discouraged.

It was largely through the landholding service class that the tsars,
ruling an overwhelmingly agrarian society, made their authority effective. Whether as officials, as soldiers, or in a few cases as diplomats, it

was members of this group who staffed the state machine. Often poor, very often uneducated, they frequently depended heavily on government service for a livelihood. The tsar in his turn could not govern without their help. The result was a partnership which, although not always easy, proved lasting and for centuries gave a distinctive tone and flavor to almost every aspect of Russian life. Most landlords still held their estates only on a life tenure in return for service. In practice, however, the distinction between an estate held on these conditions (*pomestie*) and one held by the more prestigious hereditary tenure (*votchina*) was now becoming increasingly formal and unreal, since service was exacted irrespective of the type of tenure. More important, the government by the second half of the seventeenth century was in effect guaranteeing to the landlord, by the extension of serfdom, a secure supply of peasant labor. In 1649 a new law code (*Ulozhenie*) bound the peasant holding land from a lord permanently to the estate on which he worked. Henceforth it was impossible for him legally to move without a certificate of permission from the lord. This legislation, the climax of a long process of cutting down peasant freedom of movement which had begun in the fifteenth century, consolidated the position of serfdom as the most fundamental and most pervasive of all Russian social institutions. Free peasants still existed in considerable numbers; and even the many affected by the *Ulozhenie* retained significant rights — they could sue in the law courts and could own movable property. Their legal position was still much superior to that of the slaves (*kholopy*) who formed the lowest stratum of society. Nevertheless by the second half of the century the largest single element in the population of Russia was made up of unfree peasants paying dues to their lord in labor or kind. Given the situation in which Russia found itself, the need to pin down a scanty population in a huge undeveloped country and force it to support the service class of soldiers and officials essential for defense and the workings of even a primitive administrative machine, some development of this kind was perhaps inevitable. Heavy losses of population in the later sixteenth and early seventeenth centuries, and perhaps also the territorial growth of the Russian state from the 1550s, were powerful forces tending in this direction. In a sense, it can be argued, the peasant was enserfed not to the land or to the person of the landowner but indirectly to the state. In the last analysis he worked for the state, with the landlord as an intermediary; and Peter's policies and the thinking behind them intensified this aspect of the situation. But serfdom, however inevitable, was being extended and made more rigid in Russia at a time when it was contracting and becoming less important in much of Europe. It therefore tended to mark the country, in the eyes of foreigners, as backward and semibarbaric; and in the long run serfdom was to become one of the most intractable obstacles to constructive change.

Nothing showed more clearly the social and economic gulf which separated Russia from the more developed parts of Europe than the weakness and unimportance of its towns. Even if settlements of as few as 1,000 inhabitants are regarded as towns, it is probable that less than a twentieth of the population was urban. Moscow was an exception. It had a population of 150,000–200,000 and impressed foreign visitors as one of the greatest cities in the world; the German Adam Olearius, who saw it in the 1630s, thought it numbered as many as 40,000 houses. No other city except Astrakhan, hundreds of miles away on the Caspian, held even a tenth as many people. But townsmen were slowly coming to make up a larger fraction of the total population. An enumeration of 1678 showed an increase of 24 percent in their numbers over an earlier one of 1652, though the figures are unreliable and hard to interpret. Yet the urban population remained proportionately much smaller than in Europe. It was subject not merely to the epidemics which afflicted towns everywhere in this period (plague is said to have killed almost 80 percent of the taxpaying population of Moscow in 1654–1655) but also to devastating fires which frequently ravaged towns built overwhelmingly of wood. Moscow, for example, suffered great fires in 1626 and 1648; the old and still important provincial city of Iaroslavl in 1658, 1659, and 1680.

The smallness and vulnerability of Russian towns partly explain the complete subjection to the central government which had for long been characteristic of them. Their social structure was complex: but even the richest merchants, the *gosti* (of whom there were in all no more than 300–400), did not enjoy the relative independence of the bourgeois of western Europe. Unlike his equivalent in the West, the Russian townsman enjoyed no taxation privileges. In so far as he was called on to take any share in local administration he did so under the control of the provincial governor, the *voevoda*, and not as a member of a self-governing urban community. When he acted in this way he was performing, usually reluctantly, a service to the state, not exercising a right. Nor had he much more freedom of movement than the serf in the countryside. The increasingly inflexible structure of Muscovite society demanded that, to ease the collection of taxes, he should remain as bound to his town as the serf was to the estate upon which he worked. In 1665 a new searching-out of runaway townsmen was ordered by the government; and in 1674 Iaroslavl and Vologda petitioned successfully for the forcible return to them of former inhabitants now living in Moscow. Not until 1699, as a result of Peter's rather unsuccessful effort of that year at urban reform, did the town population acquire, at least for a time, the right to move freely. Moreover, although Russian merchants showed a certain amount of enterprise as far as trade with foreign countries was concerned, their efforts during the seventeenth century to branch out into industry were nearly always unimportant and small scale. Nor do we find any contributions to Russian cultural life from the merchant class of the kind made in western Europe. Even the wealthiest Russian traders owned few, if any, books; and those they did possess seem largely to have been conventional works of religion.

Seventeenth-century Russia was thus a highly rigid and restrictive society; and at the same time it was singularly lacking in institutions through which the people might exercise some initiative and some control of their own lives. It was a society still in many ways unformed, disjointed, full of contradictions. Side by side with increasing official efforts to immobilize more and more of the population and end free movement went large scale flight to the frontier areas of the south and the east, where the effective authority of Moscow was slight or nonexistent. Among the Cossacks of the Ukraine (semi-independent communities made up originally of refugees from Russian or Polish rule) or in the largely non-Russian areas of the Urals, fugitive serfs, religious dissidents, anyone in flight from the oppressive authority of Moscow, might hope for refuge. While the central government sought to assert its control by minutely detailed legislation, and opposition was severely punished, there was a stubborn undercurrent of popular resistance which often expressed itself in anarchic violence. It is significant that the brigands, who created one of the most intractable of the problems facing the tsar's government, were the heroes of many folk-tales; oral epics (*byliny*) often credited them with magical powers such as invulnerability to bullets. And Peter himself had to issue frequent decrees (for example, in 1699, 1714, 1716, 1719, and 1724) forbidding the giving of shelter to bandits and prescribing severe punishment for those who did so. Resentment of bondage, of government exactions, of oppressive administration, broke out most spectacularly in the revolt which, under the leadership of Stenka Razin, set aflame a great area of southeast Russia in 1667–1671. Razin, a Cossack, dreamed of introducing the free Cossack form of government into the tsardom itself; but in practice this amounted merely to a desire "to take Moscow and to beat to death all you boyars and landlords and the government men." In spite of its lack of constructive or well-defined objectives, however, this famous uprising (which was also sympathetically reflected in the folksongs and tales of the period) showed with frightening clarity the potentially explosive popular grievances and anger which simmered, barely concealed, under the surface of seventeenth-century Russia.

The greatest and most far reaching of all conflicts in the two decades before Peter's birth was, however, a religious one. From a remarkable churchman, Patriarch Nikon, came the one serious effort of the age to create a power able to counterbalance the autocracy of the tsar. Head of the church in Russia in 1652, at the early age of forty-seven, Nikon introduced over the next fifteen years a series of liturgical and ritual reforms — making the sign of the cross with three fingers instead of two and singing three hallelujahs instead of two were the most important — which had the effect of aligning Russian Orthodoxy with that of Constantinople. These changes, which also involved the repudiation of ancient and revered liturgical works if they differed from Greek originals, horrified and infuriated a great body of nationalist religious conservatives in Russia. Nikon, a learned man and a passionate reformer, stood for a more critical and intellectually questioning attitude than that hitherto dominant in the Russian church. His reforms implied a recognition that, as Russia's contacts with the outside world developed, its religious life must be put on a firmer intellectual basis than the blind acceptance of tradition. Nevertheless his opponents were often sustained by a fanatical loathing of "Greek innovations" and a determination to adhere to practices felt to be sanctified by time. (In fact, the making of the sign of the cross with two fingers, the most emotionally charged of all the points in dispute, had been prescribed only as late as 1551, by a church council held in Moscow.) The result was a deep and unbridgeable cleavage between different aspects of Orthodoxy in Russia.

Simultaneously Nikon put forward far-reaching claims on behalf of the church against the ruler. For several years after his appointment as Patriarch he dominated the young Tsar Aleksei (1645–1676), receiving

the title of Great Sovereign (*Velikii Gosudar*) which was normally reserved to the ruler alone, and asserting the supremacy of ecclesiastical
over secular power and the derivation of the latter from the former.
Conflict soon followed. The growing subjection of church to state in
nonecclesiastical affairs and efforts (in the *Ulozhenie* of 1649) to prevent
the accumulation of still more land in the hands of clerics aroused his
particular anger. In 1658 Aleksei deprived Nikon of his title of Great
Sovereign; but it was not until the end of 1666 that a church council in
Moscow, attended by representatives of the patriarchates of Alexandria,
Antioch, Constantinople, and Jerusalem, finally deprived him of the
patriarchate. This council reiterated the traditional subjection of the
church to the tsar in all secular matters, thus clearly rejecting Nikon's
claims in this sphere; but in 1667 it confirmed his ritual and liturgical
reforms and excommunicated those who refused to accept them. This
decision formalized and made permanent the schism (*raskol*) which had
been developing for many years. The adherents of the old practices
(*raskolniki* or *starovertsy*, or "Old Believers") were henceforth driven
increasingly to regard the tsar and his ministers not merely as mistaken
in their policies but as the very agents of Antichrist himself.

The schism was thus more than a religious or even spiritual struggle. Its outcome marked the victory of an attitude to church affairs
which was critical, and at least to some extent rational, over one which
was traditionalist and essentially uncritical. The effects of this victory
spilled over from the purely religious sphere into other aspects of Russian life, slowly eroding old conservative certainties and accelerating the
pace of change. It is true that these effects were felt in full only by a
small segment at the top of society; but that segment was strong enough
to change the course of the country's history, in spite of the adherence
of a great mass of ordinary folk to the intense and narrow pieties, the
traditional values and certainties, of the past. It is an exaggeration to say
that the *raskol* marked the end of the old Russia; but it was the beginning of the end.

Seventeenth-century Russia was thus a society in many ways profoundly
different from those of western and even eastern Europe. Yet contacts of
many kinds — political, economic, cultural — with Europe now were
of long standing. In the later decades of the century particularly they
were increasing in frequency and importance.

Foreign policy, and above all relations with Russia's western neighbors and with the Ottoman Empire on the south, were coming to assume, as the century went on, an importance hitherto unprecedented in the Russian official scheme of things. The *Posolskii prikaz* (Office of Embassies), the chief government organ for the conduct of foreign affairs, had roots going back to the early days of the Muscovite state. It had first been given definite form under Tsar Ivan IV, in 1549. But the growing scale and significance of Russia's foreign relations in the seventeenth century can be seen in a tendency for its functions to expand and its official importance to increase. Until 1667 it was normally controlled by a senior official with the high rank of *dumnyi diak*; but in that year A. L. Ordin-Nashchokin, who had just been raised to the higher rank of boyar, became its head. The rise in its status can be seen more strikingly in a growing tendency in the later years of the century for the official who directed it to be also keeper of the seals of state, required to give validity to decrees or orders of the tsar. Its functions, moreover, were much wider than the mere conduct of foreign policy in a strict sense. Foreign trade, the post office (postal services between Moscow and several European capitals had begun in the 1660s), the import of foreign newspapers and books, were all under its control. It kept records of all the European reigning families. It was also well provided with experts in foreign languages; in the later seventeenth century it could normally muster perhaps twenty *perevodchiki* (translators) and twice as many *tolmachi* (interpreters). In the 1660s it began the regular compilation and circulation of *kuranty*, handwritten digests of information obtained from foreign newspapers. Its officials were chosen on the basis of education and specialized knowledge and not on that of favoritism or social standing (a school for the training of young recruits was set up in 1660), and from their ranks were invariably selected the heads of Russian missions to foreign rulers. Before reaching the rank of *diak* (that most frequently held by the head of a Russian mission abroad) an official of the *Posolskii prikaz* would normally have served in such missions in a subordinate capacity on numerous occasions, sometimes for as long as a year at a stretch. In other words, the *prikaz* was not merely an agency for the conduct of foreign policy whose efficiency has perhaps been rather underestimated in most conventional accounts of seventeenth-century Russia: it was also a channel for the entry of foreign ideas, techniques, and culture in general. Many European terms relating to diplomacy and international law, for example, had entered the Russian language and were in use by the *Posolskii prikaz* long before the reign of Peter and the Europeanization with which it is conventionally associated.

Throughout the seventeenth century, however, there were no permanent Russian diplomatic missions stationed in the capitals of Europe. Instead such missions were sent only intermittently, often merely when some crisis or turn of events made them necessary; and it was quite normal for the same mission to visit a series of courts in turn, staying only briefly in each. Apart from their intermittent and impermanent character, diplomatic missions from Moscow suffered from other difficulties. The almost total ignorance of the Russian language in the courts and capitals of Europe sometimes created problems. Thus in 1673, after Prussian protests, the Russian government had to agree to provide in future Latin or German translations of any documents which its envoys might bring to Berlin. The not uncommon Russian practice of paying diplomats in kind, by providing them with furs and other goods to sell abroad, sometimes inspired condescending amusement, or even outright contempt, in the capitals of Europe. When in 1687 a Russian embassy to Paris and Madrid publicly sold goods in this way in France, the diplomats concerned were accused by an official observer of "forgetting, so to speak, the quality of ambassadors to act as retail traders, and preferring their individual profit and interest to the honor of their masters."

Nevertheless, minor difficulties of this kind could not conceal the fact that the international significance of Russia was perceptibly increasing. In the first half of the seventeenth century, in the aftermath of the "Time of Troubles" (the period of internal collapse and foreign occupation which in 1605–1613 temporarily destroyed the country as an effective political organism), its weight in the affairs of Europe had been slight indeed. Gustavus Adolphus, the warrior-king of Sweden, had seen as early as the 1620s Russia's potentialities as an ally against Poland and the powers of the Counter-Reformation. In 1630 he had established a Swedish resident in Moscow to exploit these potentialities. No other major ruler or statesman of the period, however, found it necessary to pay Russia much attention. In the Treaty of Osnabrück, one of those which in 1648 ended the Thirty Years War in Germany, it was referred to merely in passing as one of the states "allied and adhering" to Sweden. (This fact, unknown to the Russian government at the time, was later, under Peter, made a grievance against Sweden during the Great Northern War.) By the later decades of the century Russia's growing military strength and more active interest in the politics of Europe had made considerable changes in this position. In particular its accession to the Holy League of 1686, which united it with Poland, Venice, and the Habsburg Emperor Leopold I in a long struggle against the Ottoman Empire, meant its formal emergence, more clearly than ever before, as a factor in international affairs, and the recognition of this fact by other states. History and geography confronted Russia with different and competing foreign policy objectives. Its inability to achieve them all simultaneously compelled it to choose between them. Ordin-Nashchokin, perhaps the most intelligent and open-minded figure in Russian foreign policy during the seventeenth century, was throughout his career (after successfully holding a number of provincial governorships he was head of the *Posolskii prikaz* between 1667 and 1671) a strong advocate of alliance with Poland, which he regarded as Russia's natural ally against Sweden and the Turks. To him the most important of all possible acquisitions was that of a secure outlet on the Baltic, the outlet which Ivan IV had sought unsuccessfully and at great cost during the long Livonian War against the Swedes and Poles in 1558–1582. But other views were equally possible. It could be argued (as by his successor as head of the *Posolskii prikaz*, A. S. Matveev) that the gaining of territory in the Ukraine at the expense of the Poles was more significant than that of a coastline and ports on the Baltic; while in the 1670s and 1680s the need to defend Russia against a partially rejuvenated Ottoman Empire and its vassal-state, the Khanate of the Crimera, and perhaps to overrun the latter and obtain an outlet on the Black Sea, came to bulk larger than ever before in the thinking of statesmen and officials in Moscow. The traditions of Russian external relations were, however, until the last decades of the century, much more anti-Polish and anti-Swedish than anti-Turkish. Ottoman dominance of the Black Sea littoral was not resented as a bridling of Russia's economic development, and a seizure of territory formerly Russian, in the way that Swedish possession of Ingria and Livonia was. Nor (in spite of devastating raids by the Crimean Tatars, during one of which Moscow was taken and burned in 1571) had an Ottoman army ever threatened the permanent conquest of much of Russia as the Poles did during the later years of the Times of Troubles. Yet by 1686 Russia was a partner in a great anti-Turkish alliance; and in 1687 and 1689 it made unsuccessful efforts to invade and conquer the Crimea, so long a thorn in its flesh. The last quarter of the century, in other words, made it increasingly clear that Russian expansionist energies would in future be directed in the main either westwards against Sweden, in a renewed effort to force an entry to the Baltic, or southwards against the Turks. Poland, so formidable a threat for so long, was now much too far gone in decay to be in itself a serious danger. The treaty of 1686, which gave Russia final possession of Kiev and much of the Ukraine, marked the end of the Russo-Polish struggles which for two centuries had been the most permanent feature of international relations in eastern Europe. But both Sweden and the Ottoman Empire remained dangerous antagonists. To fight them simultaneously with any hope of success was impossible. Russia, if it were to expand and end the isolation from which it still suffered, must decide at whose expense this was to be achieved.

The economic as well as the diplomatic relations between Russia and the European states were growing in scale and importance in the later seventeenth century. From early in the century the importance of the English merchants who, since the 1550s and the beginnings of trade with western Europe via the White Sea, had been the most active element in commercial relations between Russia and the outside world, declined sharply. But this was more than compensated for by a growth of trade with other parts of western Europe, notably with the Dutch Republic, now commercially the most advanced and successful state in the world. Russian raw materials — pitch, tallow, leather, grain, furs — formed the basis of a rapidly growing Dutch trade carried on both directly through Archangel and indirectly through such Swedish Baltic ports as Narva and Riga. By the 1690s there were over 300 Dutch merchants in Russia; while the whole European colony in Moscow numbered well over 1,000. The later years of the century saw a considerable expansion of commercial contacts with the outside world (for example, in the signature of a trade agreement with Prussia in 1689). All over Europe merchants and governments continued to be attracted by the century-old hope that through Russia it might be possible to develop a lucrative trade in luxury goods with Persia and perhaps even with China. Nor should it be forgotten, as it often tends to be, that Russia was at least to some extent an active partner in these commercial contacts with the outside world. Its merchants had traveled and traded abroad, at least in Sweden, Livonia, and Denmark, since the sixteenth century. The peace of 1661, which ended a sharp five-year struggle with

Sweden, increased their numbers, so that twenty years later there were about forty Russians trading in Stockholm.

Underlying and accompanying the growth of political and economic relations between Russia and Europe was a corresponding expansion of European influences of many kinds — military, technological, artistic, intellectual — in Russian life. These influences already had a long history. In the later fifteenth century there had been a considerable influx into Russia of Italian artists and experts of various sorts: an Italian was for some time in charge of the Russian coinage, and Italian architects such as Fioravanti, Ruffo, and Solario built churches and palaces in Moscow. A hundred years later the country was host to a number of foreign mercenary soldiers; the first European work on military affairs to reach Russia, the *Kriegsbuch* of Leonhard Fronsperger (first published in Frankfurt-am-Main in 1566), made its appearance there during the Time of Troubles. The seventeenth century, especially in its second half, was marked by a rapid growth in these military influences. In 1648, in what seemed a potentially revolutionary situation, Tsar Aleksei thought of placing his personal bodyguard under the command of a Dutch colonel; and during the great struggle with Poland in 1654–1667 there was a rapid formation of new regiments organized on more or less western European lines. By 1663 some 60,000 men were in units of this kind. Such a development was made possible only by the large-scale import of foreign officers. The Austrian ambassador, Mayerberg, spoke in 1661 of an "innumerable multitude" of foreign soldiers in Russia: he knew of over a hundred generals and colonels from different parts of Europe who were serving there. An official list of 1696 gives the names of 231 foreign cavalry officers and 723 infantry ones (down to and including the rank of ensign). In the 1630s the first large-scale production of arms in Russia began in a new foundry at Tula built by Dutch experts.

Perhaps the most convincing index of the spectacular growth in the numbers and importance of foreigners in Russia is the fact that, whereas the law code of 1589 mentioned them in only one of its articles, the more famous (and admittedly much more extensive) code of 1649 referred to them in over forty. European influences on material life and in the provision of expert professional knowledge generally were concentrated in and symbolized by the German (or Foreign) Suburb (*Nemetskaia sloboda*) of Moscow. The establishment of this foreign settlement just outside the capital, in 1652, was the result of a marked growth of antiforeign feeling in the middle years of the century. Unable, as they would have preferred, either to expel foreigners from the country altogether or to convert them forcibly to Orthodoxy, religious conservatives had to be content with the modified victory represented by confining them to a limited area of the capital. Marked out as strangers and therefore dangerous by being forbidden to wear Russian clothes, forbidden also to sell wine, beer, or tobacco to Russians, the inhabitants of the German Suburb (who in the 1670s and 1680s numbered in all perhaps some 1,500) lived largely cut off from the life around them. Nevertheless, they were the one substantial element of relatively advanced technical and professional knowledge in the country: the Suburb included workshops, mills, a paperworks, an ironworks, and a glassworks.

Technology, new industrial methods and techniques, new forms of tactics and military organization, came from Europe, above all from the Dutch Republic and Germany. From Poland in the later decades of the seventeenth century came other influences, less material but, for some time at least, equally important. The union of a large part of the Ukraine with Russia in 1654, and the acquisition of much former Polish territory in 1667, greatly strengthened such influences. These conquests were followed by a considerable movement of Belorussian and Ukrainian craftsmen to Moscow and the production there of large quantities of Polish luxury goods, while in the last quarter of the century well over a hundred Polish books were translated into Russian — a degree of cultural borrowing from Russia's western neighbor never before approached. From the Polish-Lithuanian Commonwealth there was even some infiltration into Russia of foreign, above all Italian, musical influences, notably with the arrival in Moscow in about 1681 of Nicholas Diletskii from the University of Vilnius. It was at the top of society that the influence of Polish culture showed itself most clearly. In the 1660s Tsar Aleksei began to sit on a new Polish-designed throne which, significantly, bore a Latin inscription. His successor, Tsar Feodor, ordered the wearing of Polish dress at court, was a patron of Diletskii and in 1680 married the daughter of a Polish nobleman from Smolensk. From Poland the Russian nobility acquired a taste for heraldry and genealogy and began to equip itself for the first time with coats of arms of the kind which had for so long been a preoccupation of the nobility of Europe.

More important was the pronounced Ukrainian influence which

was developing within the Orthodox church in Russia by the middle of the century. Through scholars from the Ukraine who had been exposed to Catholic and Uniate influences (above all those educated at the great Kiev Academy, where much teaching was in Latin), foreign and even to some extent secular forces entered Russian religious life on an unprecedented scale.[1] So marked was the leading role of the Ukrainians that in 1686 the Patriarch of Jerusalem, Dositheus, was moved to urge that "in Moscow the old order of things should be preserved, so that there should not be igumens [i.e. abbots] or archimandrites of the Cossack people [i.e. Ukrainians], but Muscovites."

Ukrainians were also very prominent as teachers and as tutors of the sons of the greater Russian nobles; from their ranks were drawn most of the orators who, on holidays and festivals, made speeches praising traditional heroes and well-doers. Simeon Polotskii, who came to Moscow from the Ukraine in 1663 and was by 1667 teaching several members of the ruling family, was the greatest scholar of the age in Russia. A prolific writer, he composed stage plays, wrote speeches for the tsar and high officials and produced polemical works on religious subjects, as well as carrying on an extensive correspondence on literary questions with other scholars in Moscow and the Ukraine. In his works can be seen the first reasonably clear statement in Russia of the idea of the state as a secular institution, one originating not merely in the divine will but in a natural human tendency to associate in groups and communities. The ruler, whom the need for security compelled these communities to choose for themselves, was not merely to lead his subjects to virtue but to safeguard their material welfare in this world. This emphasis on the tsar's inescapable secular responsibilities was one which was later to appeal strongly to Peter, though there is no evidence that Poloskii or any other theorist influenced him much on this point. Ukrainian intellectual influences, however, were always deeply suspect in the eyes of devout Russians as likely to be tainted with Catholicism. The result was an effort to weaken them by importing Greek scholars who could provide Russia with the modern teaching which was now clearly needed but whose Orthodoxy was not open to the same suspicions. The statute for a college which would combine the study of Latin and Greek with

---

[1] The Uniate Church, whose adherents were numerous in the eastern parts of the Polish-Lithuanian Commonwealth, used a Slavonic liturgy but acknowledged the authority of the Pope. — Ed.

the teaching of religion along Orthodox lines, the Slavonic-Greek-Latin Academy, was approved by Tsar Feodor and Patriarch Joachim in 1682; but it was only in 1687, after suitable Greek scholars had been brought to Moscow to run it, that it began to function. Kievans and their Russian pupils were excluded from it, and it soon became the main focus of the struggle between Greek and "Latin" (Ukrainian) intellectual influences which was to be a feature of the next decade.

It is easy to see these widely differing stimuli from the West mainly in terms of the material and the external. It is tempting to describe them in terms of trivialities such as the placing for the first time of weathervanes on Russian churches, or even of more significant developments. . . . Yet this would be to take a superficial and short-sighted view. As has already been seen, the great schism of the 1650s and 1660s had strained as never before the spiritual and psychological unity of Russia. Henceforth, individuals were no longer to be submerged as in the past in an all-pervasive structure of impersonal unanimity and anonymous piety. One great scholar, S. F. Platonov, has spoken of an "emancipation of personality" in Russia during the second half of the seventeenth century; and it now becomes possible for the first time for the historian to receive, from letters, autobiographies, and similar materials, the impression of distinct and recognizable individuals. Ordin-Nashchokin; A. S. Matveev; F. M. Rtishchev and G. K. Kotoshikhin, two of the most interesting and original of the statesmen of the period; Prince V. V. Golitsyn, the favorite and chief minister of Tsarevna Sophia during her years as effective ruler of Russia in 1682–1689: all these are examples. One of the most striking testimonies to the new feeling for the individual, the new willingness to consider him in his own right and not merely as a member of a social order or a religious communion, is the beginnings of portrait painting. An interest now begins to be visible, for the first time in Russian history, in the realistic representation by the artist of an individual sitter. Nikon himself sat for his portrait to the Dutch painter Daniel Wuchters, who in 1667 was engaged as official artist to the tsar and his family. A few years later the officially sponsored *Book of Titled Figures* was published. This contained sixty-five portraits of rulers, foreign as well as Russian, which in their relatively lifelike character mark a clear break with the impersonal and nonrealistic representation of saints which had hitherto dominated Russian painting.

Allied with this new secular individualism was the birth of the modern theater in Russia. As early as 1660 Tsar Aleksei had shown his eagerness to obtain from Europe experts skilled in the production of plays. A decade later Matveev was maintaining a private theatrical troupe led by a German, Johann Gottfried. The first secular dramas to be staged in Russia were probably those written and produced in the autumn of 1672 by Johann Gregory, the pastor of one of the foreign churches in Moscow. Two years later, without arousing any popular protest, Aleksei attended a performance of a "comedy" on the Biblical story of Esther (though he took the precaution of consulting his confessor beforehand on the permissibility of his behavior). Even within the church a slowly growing willingness to give more freedom to the individual and more scope to his talents can be seen in the tentative introduction of church preaching of the type normal in Europe. The duty of a pious Orthodox man, according to centuries-old assumptions, was not to glorify his petty individual abilities by delivering sermons of his own concoction but to submit absolutely to the great stream of unchanging tradition of which the church was the guardian. Any weakening of this attitude was a sure sign of intellectual and psychological change.

The Russia of Peter's childhood, adolescence, and early manhood was thus rapidly developing. The great territorial gains made during the 1650s and 1660s and the ending of the Polish threat pointed to a future of further growth and increasing power. Though peasant agriculture, unchanging in its techniques and based on a labor-force increasingly made up of serfs, was overwhelmingly the most important form of economic activity, foreign technology was beginning to reveal possibilities of industrial growth on a scale hitherto unknown. The grip of the church on intellectual life, hitherto almost total, was still complete as far as the ordinary man was concerned. But it was slowly beginning, at least in the capital and among the upper ranks of society, to relax. The old Russia, isolated, self-sufficient, fearing and despising foreigners, dominated by traditional pieties, hostile to individualism and incapable of conceiving of real change, was far from dead. The attitudes which it embodied were still unchallenged among the vast majority of the population. But some of its foundations were now, if not undermined, at least partially eroded by new ideas, new possibilities and widening horizons. To see Peter, as many of his contemporaries came to and nearly all writers of the eighteenth century did, as bursting upon a Russia still languishing in medieval obscurantism and hopeless stagnation, is a gross error. Long before his birth, forces of change and possibilities of new growth had been evident. He strengthened these forces and in some cases diverted them into important new channels; but he did not create them.

V. O. Kliuchevsky

Tsar Aleksei

V. O. Kliuchevsky (1841–1911), still probably the most widely read historian of Russia, was professor of Russian history at Moscow University from 1879 until 1910. His famous *Course in Russian History,* from which this excerpt is taken, was based on his students' lecture notes and first published not long before his death. Himself a specialist on Muscovite (pre-Petrine) Russia, Kliuchevsky's pen portrait of Tsar Aleksei, father of Peter I, is considered something of a masterpiece. It might be noted that one of his former students, P. N. Miliukov, whose own work is excerpted later in this book, pointed out in an obituary of his teacher that Kliuchevsky's somewhat idealized depiction of the "pious" Tsar Aleksei owes something to his background as the son of a country priest and to his lifelong attachment to the old Russian way of life.

One of the two conflicting currents that agitated Russian society in the seventeenth century was driving it back to the old order of things, and the other was drawing it forward to dim and alien horizons. These mutually opposed tendencies gave rise to vague feelings and aspirations in the community at large, but in men who were in advance of it, those moods and strivings became clear-cut ideas to be carried out in practice. The study of such representative types will help us to understand more fully the kind of life that had bred them. They focused in themselves, as it were, and vividly exemplified interests and characteristics of their

From V. O. Kliuchevsky, A *Course in Russian History: The Seventeenth Century,* ed. Alfred J. Rieber, trans. Natalie Duddington (Chicago: Quadrangle Books, 1968), pp. 342–53.

environment that escape notice in everyday life, where they only occasionally come to the surface as accidental individual peculiarities leading nowhere. I shall draw your attention to some of the men who stood in the forefront of the reform movement preparatory to Peter's work. The results achieved by this movement can be plainly seen from the fact that those men's aims and ideas became an integral part of Peter's program of reform, bequeathed to him by his predecessors.

The first place among those predecessors unquestionably belongs to Peter's father. He typifies the first stage of the reform movement, when its leaders had as yet no intention of breaking with the past and shattering the existing order of things. Tsar Aleksei Mikhailovich's attitude might be described as that of a man who firmly rested one foot on the native Orthodox ground and lifted the other to cross the boundary — and permanently remained in this uncertain position. He belonged to the generation that was driven by necessity to look with care and anxiety at the heretical West in the hope of finding there means to overcome domestic difficulties without giving up the ideas, customs, and beliefs of his pious ancestors. His was the only generation that thought it possible. Neither the preceding nor the succeeding generations shared this view. In former days people were afraid to borrow even purely material comforts from the West, lest by doing so they impair the ancestral moral tradition cherished as a sacred heritage. Later on, this tradition was readily abandoned by many in order to relish Western comforts all the more.

Tsar Aleksei and his contemporaries valued their Orthodox tradition no less than their ancestors had done. But for some time they were convinced that one could "wear a German coat and even watch a foreign entertainment while keeping intact such feelings and ideas as pious fear at the very thought of breaking fast on Christmas Eve before the first star appeared in the sky."

Tsar Aleksei was born in 1629. He went through the whole course of old Russian education in "literary learning," as it was then called. According to custom, at the age of six he was set to learn the alphabet from a textbook specially compiled for him at the request of his grandfather, Patriarch Filaret, by the Patriarch's secretary, on the familiar pattern of old Russian elementary "readers." It contained the alphabet, the usual abbreviations, the Commandments, a short catechism, and so on. The tsarevich was taught, as was the custom of the Moscow court, by the secretary of one of the government departments. After a year the elementary reader was replaced by the Book of Hours, which after about five months was replaced by the Psalter. After another three months the study of the Acts of the Apostles was begun; after six more months the boy was taught to write. When he was nine years old the choirmaster of the palace choir began instructing him in the *Oktoikh,* a book of liturgical chants, and some eight months later he taught him the Holy Week chants, particularly difficult musically. At ten the tsarevich had finished the whole course of old Russian secondary education. He could easily read the hours in church and successfully join in the singing of the hymns and the canons. He had mastered the order of church services to the smallest detail, and could vie in this matter with any specialist from a monastery or even a cathedral.

In former days a tsarevich would probably have stopped at this, but Aleksei was being educated at a time when people were becoming aware of a vague but persistent urge to go further, to probe the mysterious realm of Hellenic and Latin wisdom, which pious Russian scholars of an earlier period timidly passed by, protecting themselves by a spell and the sign of the cross. The Germans, having found their way into the ranks of the Russian army with their newfangled devices, wormed themselves into the palace nursery as well. As a child Aleksei already had a toy horse of German workmanship, German pictures bought at the vegetable market for about a ruble and a half in our currency, and even a suit of armor made for him by a German craftsman, Peter Schalt. At the age of eleven or twelve the tsarevich possessed a library of about thirteen volumes, most of them presents from his grandfather, tutors, and instructors. The books were chiefly copies of the scriptures and liturgical texts, but among them was a grammar printed in Lithuania, a book on cosmography, and a lexicon, also printed in Lithuania. The person in charge of Aleksei's education was one of the foremost Russian boyars, Boris Ivanovich Morozov, who was greatly attracted by European ways. He introduced the method of visual demonstration into the tsarevich's course of study and familiarized him with certain subjects by means of German engravings. He brought a still more daring innovation into the tsar's palace by dressing Tsarevich Aleksei and his brother in German fashion.

In his mature years Tsar Aleksei combined in a most attractive way the good qualities of an old-time Russian, loyal to old traditions, with a liking for useful and pleasant novelties. He was a pattern of piety — of the decorous, orderly, disciplined piety that the religious feeling of old

Russia had so assiduously cultivated for centuries. He could rival any monk in the arts of praying and fasting. On Sundays, Tuesdays, Thursdays, and Saturdays in Lent and during the fast before Assumption the tsar had only one meal a day, consisting of cabbage, mushrooms, and berries without dressing. On Mondays, Wednesdays, and Fridays he did not eat anything during the fasts. In church he sometimes stood for five or six hours on end, made a thousand and sometimes fifteen hundred prostrations a day. He was a truly devout worshiper in the old Russian style, and fully and harmoniously combined spiritual and physical exertion in seeking salvation.

This piety had a powerful influence both on Tsar Aleksei's political ideas and on his relations with people. Son and successor of a sovereign whose power was limited, Aleksei was an autocrat and firmly held the exalted view of a tsar's authority worked out by the old Muscovite community. The ideas of Ivan the Terrible[1] find an echo in the words of Tsar Aleksei: "God has blessed and appointed us tsar, to rule and judge with fairness our people in the east and west and south and north." But the way in which he wielded his autocratic power was softened by his gentle piety and profound humility; he strove to remember his humanity. In Tsar Aleksei there was not a trace of proud self-confidence, of the touchy, suspicious, jealous love of power that afflicted Ivan the Terrible. "It is better to perform one's tasks with contrition, zeal, and humility before God than do it forcefully and with haughty conceit," he wrote to one of his provincial governors. Kindliness combined with authority helped him to be on good terms with his boyars, to whom he assigned a large part in the administration. To share his power and act together with them was his customary rule, and not a sacrifice or an annoying concession to circumstances. "And we, the great Tsar," he wrote in 1652 to Prince Nikita Odoevsky, "daily pray to the Lord God and His Most Pure Mother and all the saints that the Creator should accord it to us, the great Tsar, and you, the boyars, to be of one mind and rule the people in fairness and justice to everyone."

There has come down to us a characteristic little note of Tsar Aleksei's giving a short summary of matters to be discussed in the Boyar Council. This document shows that the tsar prepared himself for the council sittings. He not merely listed the questions he submitted to the

---

[1] Tsar Ivan IV, reigned 1533–1584. — Ed.

boyars for discussion, but put down what he himself proposed to say and noted how this or that question was to be settled. About some matters he had made inquiries and written down figures, about others he had not yet formed an opinion and did not know what the boyars would say; on some points he held an undecisive opinion, which he was prepared to give up in case of objections. But on certain questions he had firmly made up his mind and would staunchly defend his decision before the council. These were questions of simple justice and conscientious service. It was rumored that the *voevoda* of Astrakhan allowed the Kalmuks to keep Orthodox captives they had seized. The tsar decided to write to him "with threats and mercy," and if the rumor proved to be true to put him to death, or at any rate to cut off his hand and banish him to Siberia. This little note shows better than anything else the tsar's simple and straightforward attitude to his councilors, as well as the serious attention he paid to his duties as a ruler.

In some cases, however, the morals and customs of the time proved stronger than the tsar's good qualities and intentions. In old Russia a man in authority easily forgot that he was not the only person in the world and failed to recognize that his will had limits beyond which lay other people's rights and the universally binding rules of decorum. Old Russian piety had a somewhat restricted field of action. It nurtured religious feeling but did little to control the will. Quick, lively, and impressionable, Aleksei was hotheaded, easily lost self-control, and gave too much rein to his hands and tongue. On one occasion the tsar, whose relations with Patriarch Nikon were already strained, quarreled with him in the cathedral on Good Friday about a church rite, and angered by the patriarch's arrogance, swore at him, using a coarse expression common in those days among highly placed Muscovite people, including the patriarch himself.

On another occasion the tsar was visiting his favorite monastery, the newly restored St. Savva Storozhevsky, to attend a festive service commemorating the holy founder of the monastery in the presence of the Patriarch of Antioch, Makarios. During the solemn matins the cantor, before beginning to read from the life of the saint, intoned as usual, "Give the blessing, Father." The tsar leaped up from his chair and shouted, "What are you saying, you clodhopper? A patriarch is present! You should say 'My lord,' not 'Father!' " During the service the tsar moved about among the monks, telling them what to read and how to sing. If they made mistakes, he rudely corrected them. He acted as if he were a churchwarden, lighted, trimmed, and extinguished candles before the icons, and kept talking to the patriarch, who stood next to him. He behaved in church as though he were at home with no one looking on. Neither the tsar's natural kindness nor the thought of his high office and others' efforts to be pious and decorous raised him above the rudest of his subjects. Religious and moral feeling was powerless against undisciplined temperament, and even good impulses found unseemly expression.

The tsar's explosive temper was chiefly roused by actions that were morally repulsive, especially those that showed conceit and arrogance. Observation of life had taught him that "pride will have a fall." In 1660 Prince Khovansky was defeated in Lithuania and lost almost the whole of his army of 20,000. The tsar asked the boyars in council what was to be done. I. D. Miloslavsky, the tsar's father-in-law, who had never taken part in a campaign, suddenly declared that if the tsar favored him and made him commander in chief, he would soon bring the king of Poland to Moscow as prisoner. "How dare you," the tsar shouted at him, "you lowborn churl, boast of your military skill! When did you lead a regiment? What victories have you won?" And he leaped up from his seat, slapped the old man's cheek, pulled his beard, and pushed him out of the council chamber, banging the door after him.

The tsar would flare up at a braggart or a bully, perhaps even use his fists if the culprit was close by, and certainly swear at him to his heart's content. Aleksei was past master of the kind of picturesque abuse of which only the wrathful but unresentful Russian good nature is capable. The treasurer of St. Savva's Monastery, Father Nikita, having taken a drop too much, had a fight with the *streltsy*[2] who lodged at the monastery, gave a beating to their officer, and ordered their clothes and arms thrown out of the place. The tsar was indignant. He was on the verge of tears and walked about like one dazed, as he put it. He could not resist writing a furious letter to the unruly monk. The very form of address is characteristic: "From the Tsar and Grand Prince Aleksei Mikhailovich of All Russia to the enemy and hater of God and betrayer of Christ, destroyer of the holy miracle-worker's house and friend of Satan, cursed enemy, futile scoffer, and wicked crafty reprobate, Treasurer Nikita."

---

[2] Musketeers, or royal guard. — Ed.

But the wave of the tsar's anger subsided at the thought, which never left him, that no one in the world was sinless before God and that tsars and their subjects were equals before His judgment seat. At the height of passion Aleksei tried not to forget that both he and his guilty subject were human. "Let me tell you, you limb of Satan," he wrote in his letter to Nikita, "that only you and your father, the devil, care for and value your worldly honor, but to me, sinner that I am, the honor of this world is like dust, and unless we fear God, you and I and all our heartfelt thoughts are of little value before Him." The autocrat, who could blow Father Nikita off the face of the earth like a speck of dust, says further in his letter that he will tearfully pray to St. Savva graciously to defend him against the ill-natured treasurer: "In the world to come God will judge between you and me, but here I have no other means of defense against you."

The tsar's good nature and mildness and his respect for a subject's human dignity greatly attracted both his own people and foreigners, and earned him the name of "the gentle tsar." Foreigners never stopped marveling at the fact that this tsar who wielded absolute power over his people, who was accustomed to complete servitude, never attempted to deprive anyone of life or property or honor (this was said by the Austrian ambassador Meyerberg). Other people's bad actions affected him painfully, chiefly because they laid on him the distasteful duty of imposing punishment. His anger did not last long and was a momentary flash that never went further than threats and a blow. The tsar was the first to approach the victim with apologies and seek reconciliation, trying to appease him by special kindness.

One day the tsar, who suffered from obesity, called in a German doctor to bleed him, which gave him relief. From his habit of sharing every pleasure with other people, he offered his courtiers the same treatment. The only person to refuse was Streshnev, the tsar's maternal uncle, who said he was too old. The tsar flared up and gave the old man several blows. "Is your blood more precious than mine? Do you think you are better than anyone else?" But soon the tsar was doing his utmost to mollify the injured party, and scarcely knew what presents to send him to appease his anger and make him forget the insult.

Aleksei liked everyone around him to be content and cheerful. He could not bear to think that someone was annoyed with him, or murmuring against him, or ill at ease with him. He was the first to relax rigid court etiquette that made relations with the sovereign so strained and cumbersome. He condescended to joke with his courtiers, paid informal visits to them, invited them to evening parties, treated them to drinks, and took an interest in their home life. One of his best features was his ability to put himself in other people's shoes, to understand and take to heart their joys and sorrows. Tsar Aleksei's warm letters of condolence to Prince Nikita Odoevsky on the occasion of his son's death and to Ordin-Nashchokin, whose son escaped to Poland, show how delicately considerate and morally sensitive his sympathy for other people's grief made him, in spite of his uncertain temper.

In 1652, when Prince Nikita Odoevsky was serving as *voevoda* in Kazan, his son died of fever almost before the tsar's eyes. The tsar wrote to the old father to comfort him, and among other things he said in his letter: "You shouldn't grieve overmuch, our dear prince, but of course one can't help grieving and shedding tears, and indeed it is right to weep, but within reason, so as not to offend God." He gave a detailed account of the unexpected death, poured out a flood of comforting words to the father, and at the end of the letter could not resist adding one sentence more: "Prince Nikita Ivanovich, do not grieve, but trust in God, and rely on me."

In 1660 Ordin-Nashchokin's son, a very promising young man, fled from Russia. Foreign tutors had turned his head with their stories of Europe. The father was dreadfully embarrassed and overcome with grief. He informed the tsar of his misfortune himself, and asked to be dismissed from his post. The tsar could understand this kind of situation and wrote a warm letter to the father defending him against his self-accusations. He said, among other things: "You ask to be dismissed; but what could have made you ask that? Excessive sorrow, I think. Your son has done a silly thing, but there's nothing extraordinary about it; it was just foolishness on his part. He is young, he wanted to have a look at God's world and at what is happening there. Just as a bird flies hither and thither and having had enough of it flies back to its nest, so your son will recall his nest and his spiritual attachment, and soon return to you."

Tsar Aleksei Mikhailovich was the kindest of men, a good Russian soul. I am prepared to say that he was the best representative of old Russia — at any rate, I know of no other who produced a more favorable impression — but certainly not on the throne. He was too passive a character. Whether by nature or owing to his upbringing, his chief qualities were those that are most valuable in everyday intercourse and bring so much light and warmth into home life. But with all his moral sensitiveness, Tsar Aleksei lacked moral energy. He loved his fellow men and wished them well because he did not want his quiet personal joys disturbed by their distress and complaints. He was, if one may put it so, something of a moral sybarite, one who loves the good because it gives him pleasant sensations. He was little able and little disposed to introduce anything on his own initiative, or stand up for it, or carry on a long struggle. He appointed to important posts both gifted and honest public servants and men of whom he himself had a very poor opinion. Unprejudiced and impartial observers carried away contradictory impressions of him, which went to form the general verdict that the tsar would have been the kindest and wisest of rulers had he not listened to bad and stupid advisers. There was no trace of the fighter in Tsar Aleksei. Least of all was he able or willing to urge people forward, to direct them and drive them on, though he liked sometimes "to discipline" — that is, to give a beating to — "an inefficient or unscrupulous servant."

Contemporaries, even foreigners, recognized his rich natural endowments. Receptivity of mind and love of learning helped him to acquire considerable knowledge by the standards of his time, both of theological and of secular writings. It was said of him that he was "familiar with many philosophical sciences." The spirit of the needs of the moment provoked thought, posed new problems. This was reflected in Tsar Aleksei's literary inclinations. He liked writing and wrote a great deal, perhaps more than any other tsar after Ivan the Terrible. He tried to record his campaigns and actually made attempts at writing verse. A few lines in his handwriting have been preserved, which may have seemed to the author to be poetry.

But most of his literary remains are letters to various people. In these letters there is much simpleheartedness, gaiety, and sometimes genuine sadness. They show subtle understanding of everyday human relations and sensitive appraisal of the trifling details of life and of commonplace people, but there is no trace of the bold, quick flights of thought or of the irony in which Ivan the Terrible's letters abound. Tsar Aleksei's writings are pleasant, wordy, sometimes lively and imaginative, but on the whole rather colorless, subdued, mild, and slightly mawkish. The author was evidently a man of an orderly disposition and not one to be carried away by an idea or ready to disturb the existing order for the sake of it. He was willing to follow all that was good, but only to a certain point, so as not to disturb the comfortable equilibrium either in himself or in his surroundings. His moral and intellectual makeup was reflected to perfection in his comfortable-looking, indeed rather portly, figure, his low brow, fair skin, puffy rosy cheeks framed by a well-trimmed beard, light-brown hair, mild features, and gentle eyes.

And it was this tsar who was caught in the whirlpool of internal and foreign events of the gravest importance. It so happened that in his reign social and ecclesiastical questions and many-sided relations, old and new, with Sweden, Poland, the Crimea, Turkey, and the Ukraine, came to the fore all together, out of their historical turn, forming an inextricable knot and requiring immediate solution. And towering above them all stood the question that was the key to the whole situation: Should Russia remain faithful to her native past, or take lessons from foreigners? Tsar Aleksei settled this question in his own fashion. So as not to choose between antiquity and innovations, he did not break with the old and did not reject the new. Habits, family ties, and other relations bound him to the conservative camp. Needs of the state, personal sympathies, and responsiveness to everything that was good drew him to the side of the intelligent and energetic men who wanted to change the old ways in the interests of national welfare. The tsar did not hinder the reformers; indeed, he supported them; but the first forceful objection from the conservatives made him draw back. Under the influence of new ideas the tsar departed in many respects from the traditional order of life. He drove about in a German carriage, took his wife hunting with him, took her and his children to see foreign amusements — theatrical performances with music and dancing — and treated his boyars and his father confessor to too many drinks at his evening parties, at which "a German blew trumpets and played organs." He engaged as tutor for his children a learned monk from Kiev whose teaching went far beyond the Book of Hours, the Psalter, and the *Oktoikh*, and included Latin and Polish. But Tsar Aleksei could not stand at the head of the new movement, give it a definite direction, find the right men and show them the way and the methods of action. He was not averse to plucking the flowers of foreign culture, but he did not want to soil his hands with the rough work of planting it in Russian soil.

And yet in spite of his passive disposition and his good-naturedly hesitant attitude to the questions of the day, Tsar Aleksei greatly helped the success of the reform movement. His striving, often illogical and unsystematic, for something new and his gift for smoothing out differences and settling things amicably accustomed timorous Russian minds to influences coming from alien lands. He provided no leading ideas about improvements to be introduced, but he helped the first reformers to come forward with their own ideas and made it possible for them to feel free to use their powers. He opened a fairly wide field of activity to them, and while giving no plan and indicating no direction for the reforms to follow, he created a favorable atmosphere for the reform movement.

The Admiralty, St. Petersburg. Engraving by A. I. Rostovtsev, 1717. (Harvard College Library)

II Peter's Great Achievements

M. S. Anderson

Poltava and Europe

The battle near the town of Poltava, in the Ukraine, which took place on June 27, 1709, between the forces of Peter I and those of Charles XII, king of Sweden (reigned 1697–1718), has been accounted one of the most decisive battles in world history. In this excerpt, M. S. Anderson explains why. As he says, the victory at Poltava was the key to a process whereby Russia for the first time became politically a part of Europe, a position it was never to lose. Anderson also indicates that the victory greatly enhanced Peter's own prestige, "sometimes amounting to adulation," in Europe.

Indeed the Russian victory over Sweden in the prolonged Northern War — which began with Russia's defeat at Narva in 1700, reached its turning point at Poltava, and was finally concluded, by the Treaty of Nystadt (or Nystad), in 1721 — was one of several undoubted achievements of Peter's reign, resulting as it did in the emergence of Russia as a major European power. Other such undoubted achievements included Peter's

From M. S. Anderson, "Russia Under Peter the Great and the Changed Relations of East and West," in J. S. Bromley, ed. *The New Cambridge Modern History*, vol. 6: *The Rise of Great Britain and Russia*, 1971, pp. 733–40. Reprinted with the permission of Cambridge University Press.

foundation of St. Petersburg and his creation of the Russian navy, each the subject of subsequent readings.

Poltava is an unmistakable turning point in Russia's relations with the rest of Europe. Until the catastrophic defeat of Charles XII in the Ukraine, Peter and his country had occupied a relatively minor place in the calculations of European statesmen.

It is true that Russia's entry into the Northern War had brought her into closer political contact than ever before with other states. The Maritime Powers,[1] anxious to end the war and so use Swedish troops in their imminent struggle with France, offered mediation in 1700 to both Peter and Charles. Such offers, repeated more than once in after years, were consistently accepted by the tsar and as consistently refused by the king of Sweden, flushed with success and inspired by the idea of a righteous vengeance to be exacted from the states which had attacked him. Charles's stubbornness, however, served to increase the interest which the anti-French powers were now compelled to take in events in the north. In 1702, for example, Keyserlingk, the Prussian representative at Moscow, proposed that Peter should ally with the [Austrian] emperor and the Maritime Powers, while in May and June 1707 A. A. Matveev, the very able Russian minister at The Hague, was in London negotiating for a possible Russian adhesion to the Grand Alliance — negotiations not finally abandoned until autumn 1708. Meanwhile, France had also hoped to obtain Swedish troops for the Spanish Succession War. When Peter and Augustus II of Saxony-Poland met at Birże early in 1701, the French ambassador to Poland, du Héron, proposed a peace with Charles XII: then Russia, Poland, Sweden, and Turkey should all join France in a great coalition against the emperor and the Maritime Powers. A year later, Patkul, the Livonian nobleman who had done so much to create the anti-Swedish coalition of 1699–1700, suggested an alliance of France with Russia, Denmark and "other northern states." In the spring of 1707, hard pressed by the Swedish victories in Poland and mounting discontent at home, Peter offered to supply Louis XIV with a considerable body of troops in return for his mediation to end the Northern War. Louis accepted this proposal. But

---

[1] Primarily Britain and the United Netherlands. — Ed.

Charles XII's demand for the restitution of all former Swedish territory, together with Peter's equally adamant refusal to give up his newly created St. Petersburg, meant that there was as yet no real possibility of peace. These negotiations, however, never seemed of really fundamental importance to the English or French statesmen concerned, none of whom attached any great significance to Russian support. In February 1706, Torcy refused to make a bid for the tsar's goodwill even at the comparatively trivial cost of returning two Russian ships seized by Dunkirk privateers; at the end of August, he rejected a proposal for a commercial treaty with Russia on the grounds that the war precluded any development of trade between the two countries. Similarly, in England, Godolphin argued in 1707 that the Northern War "may be without much affecting our war, unless the Turk takes the advantage, when Muscovy and Poland can give him no diversion, to fall upon the Emperor and the Venetians."

Poltava, which transformed Charles XII from a conqueror into a fugitive, revolutionized the whole position. It made possible a resurrection of the anti-Swedish coalition of 1699–1700, thus threatening Britain and the Netherlands with the recall of the auxiliary troops they had hired from Denmark and Saxony. It destroyed the position of Stanislas Leszczyński and made Russian influence dominant in Poland.[2] It opened the prospect of Russian occupation of much of the Baltic coastline and even of northern Germany. In these ways it enormously increased Peter's influence in Europe, besides endowing him with the prestige which military success alone could give. "Now," wrote Urbich (the Russian minister in Vienna) to Leibniz in August 1709, "people begin to fear the Tsar as formerly they feared Sweden." The philosopher agreed that "it is commonly said that the Tsar will be formidable to all Europe, and that he will be a kind of northern Turk," and a few weeks later advised his employer, the elector of Hanover, to take pains to keep on good terms with Peter. In 1710, during the negotiations with Britain and France at Geertruidenburg, Torcy suggested that the Spanish Succession War should be ended by Russian mediation; he hoped, as he admitted, to use Peter for French purposes. Poltava had thus produced an immediate recognition of Russia's new standing in European affairs. It also made clear that the other states of northern Europe had now far

---

[2]Leszczyński was the Swedish-backed claimant to the Polish throne. — Ed.

more to fear from her than from the decaying empire of Sweden. In 1711 a Prussian diplomat proposed that Denmark, Prussia and Augustus II should form an alliance, which might later be joined by Charles XII, to restrain the now menacing expansion of Russian power. This was only one of a number of similar suggestions put forward in the years following the Russian victory.

Active intervention in the north by the major Western powers was nevertheless impossible until 1713 or later. The British government indeed regarded with uneasiness the conquest of Livonia, the eruption of Russian troops into Germany, the growth of Russian naval power in the Baltic, and the possibility that Peter might soon come to monopolize the supply of some types of naval stores; but until peace had been made with France its hands were tied. . . . In 1714, with the accession of a king who was already, as elector of Hanover, a member of the anti-Swedish alliance, the prospect of British action to restrain Russian expansion became still more remote.[3] The United Netherlands also, linked to Russia by the desire of many Amsterdam merchants to preserve and extend their profitable trading connections there, were unlikely to offer her any effective opposition. Louis XIV and his ministers, though strongly influenced by the pro-Swedish tradition still powerful in France, had hoped to use Russia against the victorious coalition, believing in particular that Peter might be persuaded to support the Hungarian nationalists under Rákóczi against the emperor. After Poltava, therefore, Peter was able to complete the conquest of Livonia without interference, while Denmark, Hanover, and Prussia expelled the Swedes from all their German possessions.

It was also during this period that Peter undertook the most spectacular and dangerous adventure of his reign, the Turkish campaign of 1711. The war declared by the Porte in November 1710 had not been sought by the tsar, whose hands were still tied by the need to consolidate his conquests on the Baltic and make peace with Sweden. The Russo-Turkish war of 1711 was the work of Charles XII, of Poniatowski[4] and his other agents at Constantinople, and above all of the khan of the Crimea. Peter would have been willing to accept mediation by one of the great powers in order to avoid the dispersal of his energies by a conflict on his southern borders: not until March 1711 was a formal and

---

[3] Reference is to George I, king of England (reigned 1714–1727).—Ed.
[4] Polish statesman. — Ed.

public declaration of war issued in Moscow. Once declared, however, war was pressed forward with energy. The tsar now dreamed of a victorious advance to the Danube, supported by a general revolt of the Balkan Christians against Muslim rule. The offensive was nevertheless a catastrophic failure. The loss of Russia's new and hard-won foothold on the Black Sea[5] was a bitter blow, but the outcome of the campaign was less disastrous than at one time seemed likely. It did not result in the destruction of Peter's army or the loss of his personal liberty, and it left him free to complete the overthrow of Swedish power in the Baltic. Not even the belated return of Charles XII in 1714 from exile in Turkey could prevent this taking place. With the fall of Wismar in 1716, the last of Sweden's continental possessions had been lost; by the summer it seemed that a Russo-Danish army, supported by British and Dutch squadrons, was about to land in southern Sweden.

The crisis which followed — the sudden decision of the tsar to abandon the invasion, the quartering in Mecklenburg during the winter of 1716–1717 of much of the Russian force which had been collected for it, the alarm of Peter's allies, and the consequent dissolution of the anti-Swedish coalition — this was the most serious diplomatic complication in which Russia had yet been involved. The events of 1716, by the very intensity of the anti-Russian feeling they stimulated in Britain, Denmark, and Hanover, made it clear — more, perhaps, even than Poltava — that Russia was now politically a part of Europe. The fears of complete Russian domination of the Baltic and of north Germany then aroused were slow to die down. Peter appears to have thought of seeking compensation in Livonia, or at the expense of Hanover, for the tyrannical duke of Mecklenburg, who had been expelled by his estates with the support of a Hanoverian force; and in 1722 there were fears that the tsar might seize Mecklenburg and Danzig for himself. In the last years of his reign the possibility that his son-in-law, Duke Charles Frederick of Holstein-Gottorp, might be established as king of Sweden, with Russian backing, fed distrust in the chancelleries of western Europe. Disliked, feared, in some respects still despised, Russia could no longer be ignored. The strangeness and barbarity of many aspects of her national life, the incomprehensibility of her language, the superstitions of her church, could not disguise the fact that she now played a growing part in molding the policies of the European states.

---

[5] Reference is to the Russian conquest of Azov, etc., in 1696. — Ed.

Peter was soon to emphasize this in unmistakable manner. In 1717 he undertook a journey to the West, a journey which included visits to Hamburg and Amsterdam and culminated in Paris where, not surprisingly, the Gobelins factory and the *Jardin du Roi* held a peculiar fascination for him. He now appeared, however, no longer as a pupil traveling incognito in search of new ideas and techniques, but as a political innovator and military conqueror, to many eyes the greatest ruler of the age. At the same time, the results of this journey were negligible in terms of immediate political advantage. Peter hoped for a French alliance, an idea that was to influence much of his foreign policy until his death: "I come," he told Marshal Tessé, who had been appointed to negotiate with him, "to offer myself to France, to take for her the place of Sweden." This offer, made with typical frankness and wholeheartedness, was sterile. The French government, now bound to Britain by the Triple Alliance of 1717, was to some extent caught up in its hostility to Russia and remained obstinately loyal to Sweden, France's traditional ally. The Regent Orléans was unable to offer Peter either the subsidy or the guarantee of his conquests for which he asked. The tsar had to be content merely with the signature in August, at Amsterdam, of a treaty with France and Prussia by which the former agreed to mediate in the Baltic and make no new agreement contrary to Russian interests. Ineffective as it was, the treaty nevertheless constituted a still further recognition of Russia's new European status.

This was recognized in other ways. Diplomatic relations with the European states were now far more continuous and systematic than ever before. By the end of Peter's reign representatives of the major powers were established in Russia on a permanent basis, and a value unknown in the seventeenth century was attached to their negotiations and reports. On his side, Peter did much to accelerate this growth of contact. In 1699, with the dispatch of A. A. Matveev to The Hague, he inaugurated a Russian diplomatic service of a modern kind. Russian embassies to Europe ceased to be the short-lived, *ad hoc* episodes of the two preceding centuries. Furthermore, from 1707, Russia began to acquire for the first time a system of consular representation in Europe. By 1725 she was equipped with a diplomatic service comparable with that of any European state. The enhancement of her international standing can also be seen in the hitherto unheard-of-willingness of many ruling families to contemplate marriage alliances with the Romanovs. As early as 1701 Emperor Leopold hinted at a possible marriage of his son to

Peter's sister Nataliia, or to one of his nieces, though it is unlikely that this project was ever taken very seriously in Vienna. Of more practical importance was the marriage in 1710 of the tsar's niece Anna to the duke of Courland; she was the first Russian princess for two centuries to marry a foreigner, and six years later another niece, Catherine, became duchess of Mecklenburg. Tsarevich Aleksei married in 1711 Charlotte of Brunswick-Wolfenbüttel. Philip V of Spain appears to have considered marrying his son to a Russian princess in Peter's last years, when the tsar was able on more than one occasion seriously to suggest that one of his daughters marry into the French royal family — a striking demonstration indeed of how highly the standing of the Romanovs had improved. When, on the conclusion of a victorious peace with Sweden in 1721, he assumed the title of emperor, the gesture struck European statesmen as an appropriate assertion of Russia's new place in the world.

His position on the Baltic finally secured [by the Peace of] Nystad, Peter's last years were spent largely in pursuit of expansion in Asia. A regular caravan trade from Moscow to Peking had been organized since 1698, but no attempt was made to reoccupy the Amur valley — despite its proven value as a granary for the Russian colonies on the Siberian rivers — after the assertion of Manchu influence over it by the Treaty of Nerchinsk in 1689. Russian resources were not likely to be diverted to this region while they were strained in Europe, although Peter gave considerable support to missionary activity in Siberia and was much concerned to halt the abuses of the local Siberian administrators, not least in the interest of his treasury, which still drew a useful revenue from the profits of the state-controlled fur trade. From 1714 a series of somewhat unsuccessful missions — part military, part scientific — were sent to the khanates of central Asia, and in 1717 a commercial treaty was signed with Persia. In 1721, tempted after Nystad by the approaching collapse of the Safavi dynasty, Peter began a systematic campaign to seize Persia's Caspian provinces, rich in silk and apparently easy to conquer. Disease, difficulties of communication, lack of help from the Christians of Georgia, the threat of Turkish intervention, all made the war unexpectedly difficult and expensive. Nevertheless Derbent and Resht were occupied in 1722, Baku in 1723; and in 1724, after much complicated diplomacy, Russia found herself possessed of a long strip of territory on the west and south coasts of the Caspian. This, Peter's last conquest, proved neither valuable nor permanent. Russian troops stationed in the conquered area, much of which was never effectively occupied, continued to lose many men by disease; and in 1732, under the rule of Empress Anna, the territories acquired less than a decade earlier were abandoned.

Russia's new power naturally had intellectual and psychological repercussions abroad, requiring a drastic revision of the contemptuous indifference long current in Europe. Even before Poltava there were signs that Peter's activities were beginning to win the respect, if not the admiration, of European observers; the great Leibniz, deeply interested in Russia as a field for scientific and linguistic study and as an intermediary between the civilizations of Europe and China, had already been impressed by the opportunities which a largely undeveloped country appeared to present to such a ruler. It was, however, her military successes against Sweden which above all won for Russia the attention of Europe. Mainly for this reason, the second half of Peter's reign saw a steady increase in the output of books on Russia, and in the notice allotted to Russian affairs by European newspapers and periodicals. Peter himself understood the importance of a good press abroad. As early as 1703 he maintained at Paris an agent whose duty was to spread news of his victories and reforms, while the major German political journal of the time, the *Europäische Fama*, was strongly influenced by him and gave favorable publicity to what he did. It is true that knowledge of Russia and her tsar remained, even after Poltava, remarkably limited in some respects. As late as 1717, on his visit to Paris, a good many of the citizens who flocked to see Peter were uncertain even of his exact name or title. To the end of his reign, and indeed for long after, many of the most significant aspects of Russian life — the problems created by the consolidation and extension of serfdom, by bureaucratic inefficiency and corruption, by religious dissent — were almost a closed book to Europe. As yet no European writer had succeeded in presenting a truly balanced and realistic picture of Russian society. Nevertheless, it was widely felt that what had been the obscurantist and semibarbaric Muscovy was now beginning to belong to Europe in more than a merely political sense. This awareness is symbolized by the appearance of Russia in 1716, for the first time, in the list of European powers printed in the French *Almanach Royal*.

The growing respect thus felt for Russia reflected in large degree, of course, the admiration, sometimes amounting to adulation, lavished on her ruler personally. Even before Louis XIV died, Peter had become for many observers by far the greatest of living monarchs. His energy, his open-mindedness, his regard for knowledge (at least for certain types of knowledge), his self-sacrifice in the cause of national greatness — these qualities seemed irrefutable proofs of the benefits to be obtained from the rule of an intelligent and public-spirited autocrat. Peter appealed almost irresistibly to the growing taste of the Enlightenment for constructive rulers willing to follow the dictates of reason and nature. "His Piety is visible," wrote the chaplain of the British factory at St. Petersburg, "in his noble Attempt to reform the Manners of his People, his Resolution great in thwarting their Inclinations, and obliging them to relinquish their long-espoused Errors and superstitious Practices which they were born and bred in." His death produced a flood of laudatory comments and epitaphs, at least one of which, the eulogy delivered to the French Academy by Fontenelle, was profoundly to influence future Western views of his reign: this somewhat uncritical admiration was to be given even more influential form a generation later by Voltaire, notably in his *Histoire de l'Empire de Russie sous Pierre le Grand* (1759–1763). Whatever reservations Peter's contemporaries may have felt about welcoming Russia as a European state, they had none in his later years about accepting him as a great man. In spite of his brutalities, his over-confidence, his miscalculations and occasional catastrophic defeats, Peter's place in the pantheon of those who have "made history" was even then secure.

N. N. Molchanov

For the Greatness, Glory, and Might of Our Country

N. N. Molchanov, professor at Moscow State University, surveys in considerable detail, in the book from which this reading is taken, the diplomacy of Peter I. Here he summarizes his survey, whose main conclusions coincide closely with those reached by M. S. Anderson and other Western historians

From N. N. Molchanov, *Diplomatiia Petra Pervogo* [The Diplomacy of Peter the First], Moscow, 1984, pp. 422–28, 430–31. Published by Mezhdunarodnye Otnosheniia. Trans. by Reef Altoma.

who have written on the subject. But readers will notice the unmistakably proud, nationalistic, and defensive spirit of Molchanov's summary as well as his assertion, echoing current Soviet foreign policy, that Russia rightfully, indeed necessarily belongs to a common European homeland stretching from the Atlantic to the Urals. It will also be noticed that Molchanov treats Peter as a heroic exception to his otherwise blanket condemnation of Peter's successors on the Russian throne.

In the first quarter of the eighteenth century Russian diplomacy as reformed by Peter became an important factor in international relations. Based on the growing strengths of the Russian people, it resolutely competed with the experienced diplomatic services of the European powers which had been formed long before. Gradually, and especially after the victory at Poltava [1709], Petrine diplomats more and more successfully opposed these services, energetically defending Russia's national interests.

International relations of that time were characterized by two significant phenomena: in western Europe, England was on the rise, edging out France and entering the era of the so-called English predominance; and in the eastern portion of the continent Russia appeared as a new, young, and strong power. Before this, owing to Russia's weakness, backwardness, and isolation from the diplomatic circles of the West, the Dnieper River was considered the eastern border of Europe in terms of political relations. Now this border was moved back to its natural geographical limit — that is, to the Ural Mountains. International relations on our continent acquired a truly common European character.

But there was a striking difference in the rise of Russia and England. The English predominance took root gradually, over a period of centuries. It was predetermined by a long process of military, industrial, commercial, and cultural growth. In England, in the middle of the seventeenth century, a bourgeois revolution took place. The rise of Russia, by contrast, came about in an unusually short time. The Petrine reforms sharply intensified the country's development. Yet it was not Peter's arbitrary will or historical chance that predetermined Russia's rise but the objective necessity of her sociopolitical development. At first intuitively and later consciously, Peter expressed national needs and energetically accelerated what was dictated by the objective course of history. His work remains a truly heroic achievement for the greatness, glory, and might of our country. . . .

In truth, our country was at the edge of an abyss at that time. [Thus] in 1670 — that is, two years before Peter's birth — [the German philosopher] Leibniz worked out a plan for the creation of a European union which was to ensure eternal peace for the continent. As Leibniz saw it, the natural, aggressive energy of the European states was to be directed to other regions of the globe. Each of the major powers of the time received its zone of colonial expansion: North America was set aside for England and Denmark, Africa and Egypt for France, South America for Spain, the East Indies for Holland, and Russia for Switzerland. And so our country, like those of Africa, Asia, and America, was threatened with colonial servitude. Was Leibniz's plan a groundless dream? Unfortunately, for Russia at the end of the seventeenth century it was a cruel reality. Academician Tarle, on the basis of extensive research, came to the conclusion that the situation of Russia then "posed for all progressive and independent-minded people terrifying questions about the further preservation of the state and even about national self-preservation in the broader sense, should the country maintain its accustomed way of political and social life, its intransigently conservative ideology, and its rejection of any active foreign policy."[1] Fortunately, this did not happen, for Russia, raised to her feet by Peter and exerting all her strength, met the challenge.

But this was not done in order to conquer Europe. Having achieved only what was necessary for her natural development, Russia [under Peter] became an organic component of the European system of international relations. In this way the system itself attained the balance it was lacking.

In the fifth volume of the classic French *Universal History of Civilization*, published twenty years ago under the editorship of Maurice Cruze, it says this about international relations at the beginning of the eighteenth century: "European equilibrium required that no state be powerful enough to threaten the independence of the others. This doctrine was of long standing. It was adhered to by the French and the English. It explains English continental policies from the end of the Hundred Years War and the protracted struggle of the French royal

---

[1] E. V. Tarle (1874–1955), a leading Russian-Soviet historian. — Ed.

house against the Habsburgs." This policy of maintaining a balance of power was put into practice in Europe in the following centuries. . . .

Unfortunately for Europe, the theory of balance was often used only to conceal the attempts of various powers to establish their dominion. We need only recall the Napoleonic era, the pretensions of the Pan-Germanists, the policies of Bismarck and Kaiser Wilhelm II, the criminal adventurism of Hitler. In various and at times threatening historical circumstances the countries of Europe succeeded in preserving their independence from such pretensions, and this turned out to be possible thanks solely to the fact that Russia was the deciding factor in the European balance of power from the time of Peter. Only by taking into account this state of affairs can the role and place of Petrine diplomacy in the history of Europe be properly evaluated.

But above all, Peter's diplomacy secured for Russia the most important condition for her transformation: it included her in the European system. It established tighter, closer relations with countries that had outstripped Russia on the path of industrial, commercial, and cultural development. Peter's diplomacy helped her to receive from them the newest technology, more up-to-date weapons — from battleships to bayonets and the means for their production — and machine tools, equipment, and other products. All this gave a jolt to the enormous creative resources slumbering in the mass of the Russian people, constrained by the fetters of a backward sociopolitical structure and by the bonds of religious conservatism. Russia received a powerful impulse toward independent development in all spheres of life: from the manufacture of material products and objects of everyday necessity to the establishment of new cultural values in science, literature, and art.

However, the sharp expansion of ties with Europe also had negative consequences. The process of overcoming intra-European separatism — the provisional and partly separate development of the western and eastern parts of the continent — and of transforming regional ties into genuinely common European ones was neither simple nor painless, and could not be achieved by a single plan. Russia's entry into Europe scarcely resembled the appearance in a big, friendly family of a new member whom the elders welcome with tender care and hurry to help stand on his feet. The rapprochement of Russia with Europe proceeded in conditions of sharp struggle, for the rise of a new, active, and powerful state came up against fear of competition, fear of losing a privileged position, fear of a breach of the monopoly, fear of having to share something with a new participant in the common life of Europe. Russia had to acquire her right to a place in the European sun at the cost of a heavy military and diplomatic struggle.

Russia went to Europe with the goal of strengthening and consolidating her independence. But the various ties necessary for achieving this goal inevitably gave rise to new forms of dependence. A process of interdependence developed in which the maintenance of independence required a constant, patient, military and diplomatic effort.

It is no accident that in the historiography of the Petrine era questions and doubts arose in various forms concerning the rapprochement with western Europe brought about under Peter's influence. Did not Peter, in his enthusiasm for western Europe, place Russia in the service of foreign and hostile interests? Would it not have been better to maintain the secluded, isolated, grandiose existence of old Muscovy for the sake of preserving age-old Russian principles? In short, did the Petrine Europeanization of Russia turn out to be antinational and antipatriotic? Did Peter eliminate Russia's backwardness at the cost of losing Russia's distinctiveness and the celebrated "Russian soul"?

Here it is appropriate to listen to the opinion of a foreigner — of, for example, so versatile and competent a scholar as Roger Portal: "When the problem of foreign influence, of eliminating the lag behind the West, and of renouncing the past is posed in connection with Peter the Great, often the main issue is forgotten — namely, the fact that Russia was threatened by an economic colonization from which her government and merchants had to be protected. Thus in spite of the external appearance of imitating Western fashions and the summoning of foreign technicians, all of Peter's actions served to answer this threat. The lag behind Western states in Russia's material development at the end of the seventeenth century was such that it placed in question her very political existence. The whole of Peter's reign proceeded under the banner of national independence, and the spirit of this reign was a national spirit. . . . Not only did Peter not turn his back on the Russian past; he glorified its historical figures and their military victories; he always linked himself with the great tsars among his predecessors and strove to continue and add to their deeds. The word 'patriot' appeared [in Russian] under Peter the Great, who less than a quarter of a century after his death was considered a national hero."[2]

---

[2]Molchanov quotes from Roger Portal, *Pierre le Grand* (Paris, 1961). — Ed.

But while agreeing with this view one should not give way, as often happens, to the temptation to idealize Peter and his work. The giant cast in bronze, riding high on the rocky pedestal of his legendary monument, is only an idealized symbolic embodiment of Peter — his artistically generalized form.[3] In real life, in historical reality, in his actual work, he was an extremely complex, controversial, and at times incomprehensible human being. And this affected his diplomacy. Peter's domestic "reforms" proved even more multifaceted.

Often he would find himself in unexpected, ill-fated, and quite unwanted circumstances. Following the Peace of Nystadt, Peter organized a magnificent celebration in the capital; but as soon as it was over an awful flood inundated St. Petersburg. Having concluded the Northern War, Peter wanted to bring relief to the people; but from 1721 to 1724 Russia fell victim to severe crop failure, famine, and epidemics. He wanted to ensure the people's well-being; but thousands of peasants died as a result of harsh labor in the construction of canals, fortresses, and St. Petersburg. He wanted to distribute tax burdens justly; but he thereby strengthened social backwardness. He tried to make workers, educated officers, engineers, scholars, and administrators out of the nobility; but three decades after his demise, they began to free themselves from obligatory state service. For all his respect for progressive representatives of European civilization, Peter prudently did not entrust foreigners with the highest offices; nevertheless, he conferred on Russia an essentially German dynasty.

Peter was extremely anxious that the progressive transformation of Russia begun by him should be continued by his successors. For this he sacrificed his own son, personally enduring the agonizing reverses of the Aleksei affair.[4] But despite Peter's concern about the further transformation of Russia, the Russian throne was left to the mercy of fate; it became the plaything of fortune. A long period ensued during which, in place of Peter the Great at the head of the Russian Empire, a succession of persons who were at the very least mediocre, effectively incapable of statesmanship — and sometimes simply physical and moral degenerates — took turns on the throne. . . . That which had

---

[3] Reference is to the celebrated equestrian statue of Peter I — "The Bronze Horseman" — erected in St. Petersburg under Catherine II and still standing in Leningrad. — Ed.

[4] Reference is to the arrest and trial for treason of Peter's son and heir, Tsarevich Aleksei, for which see Part VI. — Ed.

given meaning to Peter's existence and activity — the interest of the state — yielded to the interest of preserving and strengthening the power of the ruling dynasty. Thus the entire post-Petrine rule of the Romanovs constituted an enormous step backward in comparison with the higher and more enlightened understanding of the tasks of absolute monarchy which characterized Petrine political thought. For Peter the use of foreign specialists served as a means of eliminating the backwardness of Russia while preparing and training native replacements. For his successors it was a means of preserving the supremacy of their dynasty. . . .

The attitude abroad toward Peter following his death is interesting. News of the emperor's demise provoked a huge response. Basically, it was an involuntary sigh of relief from the rulers of European countries who, especially after the Peace of Nystadt, trembled at the mention of his name. There was also rejoicing in Constantinople. It was hoped that the death of the menacing sovereign of Russia would produce confusion and internal disorder, and that the great country would return to its previous wretched and secluded existence on the backward periphery of Europe. To be sure, Peter's departure was abruptly reflected in the international situation of Russia. The first to feel this change were the Russian ambassadors who, under Peter, had grown used to the respect which was lavished on mighty Russia. Such respect sharply diminished as foreign diplomats reported from St. Petersburg that a governmental leapfrog around the Russian throne had begun, with various cliques and clans contending for power. However, certain Russian representatives abroad were gladdened by the disappearance of Peter's strict control and firm leadership. A golden age for profiteers had begun. If the chief Russian embezzler, Menshikov, ended up in power, these Russian diplomats would be less constrained and able to take bribes equal to those of their foreign colleagues.[5] Although the complete elimination of the Petrine diplomatic legacy was simply not possible, Russia's external policy gradually lost the monolithic firmness of Peter's grand designs and increasingly betrayed inconsistency and weakness.

The very fact that Russia proved capable of producing a figure of such stature as Peter — a ruler who strengthened Russia's power to a degree previously unthinkable — had an irreversible effect. Abroad it was feared, above all, that suddenly some worthy continuer of Peter's

---

[5] Alexander Menshikov, powerful favorite of Peter I and the dominant figure at court during the brief reign (1725–1727) of Peter's wife and successor, Catherine I. — Ed.

work might appear. It was feared even more that the biggest European power would increase its strength at the same dizzying pace as it had under Peter. This, unfortunately, did not happen; indeed, it could not happen. Although for Europe he remained an astounding and completely inexplicable historical phenomenon, when all is said and done Peter himself did not work miracles, but only boldly exploited objective processes and circumstances. As the Soviet historian K. N. Derzhavin put it: "To western Europe of the first quarter of the eighteenth century Russia and Peter the Great were not always understandable, but they clearly had to be taken into account in [assessing] world political problems of an unprecedented nature and scale. Peter's demise prompted an appraisal of his statesmanship, and the successes of Russia in the world political arena elicited fearful discussion of her future role in resolving the tangled problems of European political life. . . ."

James Cracraft

St. Petersburg

The city of St. Petersburg, renamed Petrograd in 1914 and Leningrad in 1924, has been one of the great cities of the modern world. Founded by Peter I, who also made it Russia's capital (which it remained until 1918), St. Petersburg proved to be among the most enduring of his achievements. An Italian visitor in 1739 called it "this great window recently opened in the north through which Russia looks on Europe." But it was always more than that. For St. Petersburg quickly became the main channel through which countless Europeans, bearing their values and their ways, poured into Russia, making the city the center of European civilization in the newly named (1721) Russian Empire.

The first of these two readings views the early history of St. Petersburg primarily in the light of the revolution in Russian architecture which it embodied. This "Petrine revolution in Russian architecture" was itself an-

From James Cracraft, *The Petrine Revolution in Russian Architecture*, 1988, pp. 173–76, 178–81, 243–44, 249, 266, 270. Reprinted by permission of The University of Chicago Press.

other notable achievement of the reign, a point also brought out in the reading that follows.

St. Petersburg the military base, the shipyard and port, the administrative capital and royal residence, the principal site and then the embodiment of the Petrine revolution in Russian architecture: St. Petersburg was built to order, the order of one man, Peter I. His decision that it should become such a center dates to soon after his forces conquered the site from the Swedes, in the spring of 1703. But a less auspicious setting in which to found a city is difficult to imagine.

In European urban history, as one specialist has noted, "the choice of a site was probably the most significant single factor shaping a city's growth pattern and urban picture." And

> *traditionally the demands to be met included a healthy climate; a year-round fresh-water supply; a fertile surrounding countryside; accessibility to trade routes; safety from floods, avalanches, and landslides; and safety from enemies. The last consideration, although not always decisive, generally was of primary importance to city founders.*

In violation of virtually every one of these principles, the site chosen for St. Petersburg was a marshy river delta, its maze of islands subject to frequent flooding, its damp climate wearying if not downright insalubrious, its extreme northern location — the northernmost of any major city in the world — unsettling in the prolonged darkness of its winter months and the extended daylight — the "white nights" — of its short summer. The Neva itself, from the beginning the city's principal waterway, is free of ice, and therefore navigable, an average of 218 days a year, or not much more than half the time. The soils of the immediate area are poor, its vegetation sparse; under a natural economy it never supported more than a few fishing hamlets. From a geopolitical perspective, moreover, its accessibility to major trade routes, and its defensibility, have always been problematic.

In 1703, to be sure, both the natural setting and the geographical position of St. Petersburg's site offered certain strategic advantages to a commander bent on controlling the area. Then too, under Swedish rule the fortified settlement of Nyenskans (in Swedish) or Nienshants (in Russian), located just to the south of the last big bend in the Neva,

Church of Sts. Peter and Paul, Peter-Paul fortress, Leningrad, built 1712–1732; Dominico Trezzini, architect. (photo by editor)

where the river turns west to flow rapidly into its delta, had become something of a regional trading center. Nyenskans/Nienshants, with its modern fort and outworks (German *Schanze* = entrenchment, redoubt, earthworks), its approximately 450 houses and Swedish, German, and Russian churches, was the nearest settlement of any size to the site where St. Petersburg would rise.

On or about May 2, 1703, Peter I renamed Nyenskans/Nienshants "Shlotburg" (compare German *Schlot* or "neck," referring no doubt to the nearby neck of the Neva). According to contemporary official sources, the tsar and his lieutenants then decided to look for a better place to fortify, which they soon found: a little island called "Lust-Eland" (in Swedish; "Janni-saari," or "Hare Island," in Finnish) located about four kilometers down river from Shlotburg, in the main channel of the Neva, roughly at the point where it separates into several branches, a spot accessible from the Finnish Gulf and Baltic Sea to the largest vessels then afloat. There, on May 16, 1703, the foundations of a fortress to be called "St. Petersburg" — *Sanktpeterburg* or *Sankt'piterburkh* in Russian (or russified German) — were laid.

There is some evidence that the new fortress only received this name on or about June 29, 1703, when its church was ceremoniously founded and dedicated to Sts. Peter and Paul, whose feast day it was. Our first dated reference to St. Petersburg is a notation on a letter sent to the tsar by one of his officials in Moscow, which indicates that the letter was "received in Sant-Piterburkh" on June 30, 1703. The Latin or Greek-based forms "Petropolis" and "Petropol" are also to be found in documents of July 1703, and of later dates. In any case, an edition of the Moscow *Vedomosti (Gazette)* published in August 1703 announced that "His Tsarish Majesty has ordered a fortified town to be built not far from Shlotburg, by the sea, so that henceforth all goods which arrive at Riga, Narva, and Shantsy should find a haven there, as should Persian and Chinese goods." In a letter of September 1704 to A. D. Menshikov, Peter I wrote that "in three or four days we will be in the metropolis, St. Petersburg [*v stolitsu, Piterburkh*]." That same autumn construction began on an "Admiralty [*Admiralteistvo*]" or fortified shipyard sited on the left or southern bank of the Neva, at a place just across and a little down river from the fortress.

A fortress and more, a fortified town; a harbor; shipyards; "the metropolis" (*stolitsa* could of course also be translated "capital" or "capital city"): within a year of choosing the site Peter I had obviously decided, for both strategic and commercial reasons, that a port city of some importance should rise on it and be called, in an oddly Germanic formulation, after his own patron saint. It is equally clear that for the next few years strategic considerations predominated in the city's development and that in this initial or outpost phase of its history it otherwise grew spontaneously — thus following, in these respects, traditional Russian norms.

By 1710 an up-to-date system of largely earthen defenses had been completed after Dominico Trezzini's designs,[1] a system consisting mainly of the six-bastioned Peter-Paul fortress (as it came to be called, after its church) with extensive outworks (most notably the *Kronverk*, or "Crownwork," located just behind it); the ramparts of the Admiralty complex; and the round bastion on Kotlin Island, out in the Finnish Gulf, protecting the seaward approach. By this time, too, a more or less permanent population of 8,000 laborers, soldiers, and others together with a seasonal population of that many again and more lived and worked and worshipped in some 16,000 houses, shops, and churches jurisdictionally divided into several *slobody*, again on the traditional pattern. Almost all of these buildings were small one-story wooden structures hastily and haphazardly erected by native builders along narrow crooked lanes, and were clustered in the vicinity of the fortress — on the large island immediately behind it — and on the left bank of the Neva, on either side of the Admiralty. The first masonry houses in St. Petersburg, belonging to Count G. I. Golovkin, Prince Menshikov, and the tsar (the Summer Palace), were begun only in 1710.

Peter I's direct concern with the construction of St. Petersburg's defenses dates to the city's very beginnings, as indicated: to the spring of 1703, when the foundations of the first Peter-Paul fortress, to be built of earth and wood, were laid. His concern with the rest of the town's development dates to 1706. In Peter's correspondence with various officials of the second half of that year we find him issuing instructions on how to build wharves, observing with pleasure the completion of some masonry construction in the center of town, and insisting that new buildings outside the fortress should be uniform in size and face the street, whether it was straight or curved — this a reflection of earlier directives to Moscow's residents. It was also in 1706 that Peter founded, in a house belonging to Ulian Akimovich Seniavin and located very

---

[1]Trezzini was a Swiss-Italian architect who had entered Peter's service in 1703. — Ed.

near his own, a Chancellery of Urban Affairs (*Kantseliariia gorodovykh del*) to coordinate all aspects of the building of St. Petersburg. Seniavin was named director of the chancellery, and Dominico Trezzini its chief architect. "Chancellery of Fortification Matters" might be a stricter translation of the Russian here, given the more limited meaning that the term *gorod* still generally bore; but "Urban Affairs" more accurately reflects the scope of the chancellery's activities, which in any case was renamed, in 1723, the Chancellery of Construction (*Kantseliariia ot stroenii*), the name historians use.

The St. Petersburg Chancellery of Construction played a critical part in training, examining, and certifying architects and other building specialists for the tsar's service. The chancellery also oversaw the annual conscription and deployment of thousands of laborers, the administration of all moneys levied for the construction of the city, and the purchase if not the actual production of huge quantities of building materials. By 1721 the chancellery was spending annually sums of between 300,000 and 400,000 rubles, a figure approaching 5 percent of total state revenue. Its architects and their assistants directed almost all of the principal works and drafted nearly all of the main projects; and anything of architectural significance undertaken elsewhere — at the Admiralty, for example — sooner or later required the chancellery's approval and cooperation. Above all, it was the chief agent of Peter I, whose written and oral instructions regarding the building and beautifying of the new capital came, after 1714, in a flood. . . .

In January 1725, when Peter I died, the Chancellery of Construction was under the immediate supervision of the emperor's personal office, a position it had been steadily attaining since 1711. By 1732 the chancellery had become a kind of ministry of construction setting building standards for the whole country, and so large and cumbersome that some of its responsibilities were given to several other offices, one concerned with fortification, another with naval construction, and a third with the imperial residences; but everything else — "churches, colleges, covered markets, hospitals, and any other buildings," especially governmental buildings — remained in the chancellery's domain. In the scope of its operations, as in the number of people it employed, the Chancellery of Construction had been without precedent in Russian history. It had served in effect as the chief administrative agency of the Petrine revolution in Russian architecture.

. . .

The annual conscriptions of laborers for the construction of St. Petersburg provide evidence of the scale both of the chancellery's operations and of the great project itself. . . . Such figures as we have indicate that between 1703 and 1725 anywhere from 10,000 to 30,000 ordinary workers labored *annually* on the construction of the new capital. These totals are the more impressive when set beside the maximum of a few thousand men known to have worked in any one season on any one project in pre-Petrine times; or beside even the total of 30,000 workers said to have labored over two years (1707–1708), under what was thought to be a military emergency, building new defenses for Moscow. At the same time, these figures tend to belie the allegations, originating in foreigners' travel accounts and acquiring thereafter the force of legend, that in these early years tens of thousands of workers — "60,000" in seven years, "100,000" in eight, "two-thirds" of the annual labor force — lost their lives in the construction of St. Petersburg. Luppov suggests reasonably enough that the total number of such deaths between 1703 and 1725 was in the thousands, and he points out that after 1710 if not before steps were taken to alleviate the situation by medical means.[2]

Equally impressive of the scale of St. Petersburg's construction under Peter I are figures relating to the production of building materials. Siniavin's reports to the tsar of 1709 and 1710, for example, indicate that 11 million bricks had been manufactured in and around St. Petersburg for use in building in 1710. This was an enormous sum for the time, greater by a factor of perhaps ten times than any comparable pre-Petrine figure; only the production in Moscow of 4 million bricks over a period of two years (1702–1703) for use in the renovation of the Smolensk fortifications even approaches it; and that total was not to be reached again by Moscow's brickworks — soon subordinated to those in St. Petersburg — until the 1760s. Moreover, after 1710 an annual production quota of 10 million bricks was in force in St. Petersburg, a quota that the local brickmakers at first found hard to maintain. The Chancellery of Construction again took the lead, and by 1712 its brickworks employed several thousand craftsmen and laborers. In 1719 the latter were put under the direction of a foreign specialist, Timothy Fonarmus, and soon were producing to order 12 million bricks and 3 million tiles a year. In addition, by 1725 other governmental as well as

---

[2] S. P. Luppov, Soviet historian of St. Petersburg. — Ed.

private works were producing annually up to 3 million bricks and 500,000 tiles in accordance with the chancellery's (with Dominico Trezzini's) specifications. And comparable advances had been made in the production of lumber, glass, lime, and cement (*tsement*), which was now being manufactured in Russia for the first time.

Yet for all of this remarkable progress the production of building materials fell far short of St. Petersburg's projected needs. What today is called "quality control" was one big problem, as contemporary European observers would notice. Wasteful construction methods meant that even with a total annual production of 15 million bricks no more than thirty masonry houses of any size could be built in a year — and probably fewer, in view of the priority enjoyed by military construction (and of the universal need for brick stoves). The production of tiles was such that only official buildings and the mansions of grandees could be roofed with them; people of lesser means had to make do with wooden shingles, which following established methods were easier to manufacture; but even then there were shortages. Glass remained a rare and expensive commodity, so that windows were paned in mica even in the houses of grandees, while the mass of the population employed animal bladders or rags. Cut stone was used in considerable quantities in the building of St. Petersburg especially after 1714, and limestone and even marble were quarried nearby; but for years the finest stone needed for decorating in the "new style" had to be brought from afar, at great expense. And there is some evidence that even the most basic commodities — bricks, for instance — were also imported, either to augment the local supply or to improve on it. Thus in May 1720 Peter I ordered that three ships recently purchased in Holland were to be loaded with "English bricks" before sailing to Russia.

Luppov considers it a "curious" yet "significant" fact, significant of the "success" in producing building materials which St. Petersburg had achieved, that fully 80 percent of the workers laboring under the Chancellery of Construction in 1709, and nearly 70 percent in 1714, were involved in the production and transport of building materials. But surely these figures testify equally to the extravagance, if not the folly, of attempting to build, virtually overnight, a new-style metropolis in the wilderness.

Peter I's direct concern with the development of St. Petersburg beyond its fortifications dates, to repeat, to 1706. Over the next few years this concern was shared, however, by building projects at Azov or in Moscow and by, above all, the manifold tasks of his ongoing war against Sweden. Indeed, there is ample evidence that Peter regarded his decisive victory over the Swedes at Poltava in June 1709 as a turning point not only in the war but in the city's history as well: "Now with God's help the final stone in the foundation of St. Petersburg has been laid," he wrote to Admiral Apraksin on the day of the victory. And after 1710 the city's rate of growth, as reflected in cadastral and other such records, sharply intensified. Its permanent population in 1710 of about 8,000 had tripled by 1717; and it had nearly doubled again — to approximately 40,000 — by 1725.

This rapid growth can be attributed directly to legislation by Peter I intended to enhance St. Petersburg's status as a commercial, industrial, administrative, and residential center. Beginning in 1712, for example, various ranks and categories of courtiers and administrators, members of the service nobility, and merchants were ordered to settle permanently in the city; while another series of decrees redirected Archangel's foreign trade to the new port and otherwise favored St. Petersburg's commercial development. In June 1714 a twice-weekly Moscow-St. Petersburg post was established; in 1718, Peter took steps to make St. Petersburg the ecclesiastical capital of his dominions; and in 1720, he ordered that its streets be cleared of unattended cattle. The range if not the arbitrariness of these and numerous similar measures is remarkable. But of more direct interest here are Peter's regulations concerning the actual construction, planning, and beautifying of St. Petersburg in the years of its rapid initial growth.

This effort began in earnest in 1714 and drew both on his earlier legislation governing building in Moscow and on, more heavily than ever before, European models and expertise. The decree that houses be built in conformity with plans to be obtained from Dominico Trezzini has been mentioned. At the same time (April 1714), plain wooden construction was prohibited everywhere in St. Petersburg in favor of wattle and daub (*mazanka*), roofs were to be made of tiles or shingles, and houses alone — not fences, stables, or sheds — were to face the street, all under pain of severe fines. In October 1714 it was repeated that houses were to be built of wattle and daub — "in the Prussian manner" — with foundations of stone; in November, that houses were to face the street, that stables and sheds were to be kept to the rear of the lot, and that houses were to be built following the specified (Trezzini's) plans. It was also decreed that persons arriving in St. Petersburg, whether by land or water, were to bring with them a certain quantity of stones suitable for building purposes, there being a shortage of same in the vicinity of the new city. The decrees were printed to insure wide circulation. It was in October 1714, and owing, it was said, to the shortage of skilled craftsmen available for work in St. Petersburg, that all further masonry construction was banned everywhere else in the tsar's dominions for an indefinite period of time.

Peter I's regulations of 1714 governing building in St. Petersburg and elsewhere were reiterated, strengthened by the addition of penalties, and in some points augmented in the years that followed. In fact, he would go much further. In 1715 and 1716, as noted earlier, he commissioned Trezzini and then Le Blond to draw up comprehensive plans for the city's development.[3] Both plans focused on Vasilevskii Island, which at the time was largely unsettled:[4] in 1716 St. Petersburg's buildings were concentrated on Petersburg Island (behind the fortress), on the easternmost tip of Vasilevskii Island, and around the Admiralty complex, on the left bank of the Neva. Contrary, then, to the city's initial and natural pattern of growth — outward from the fortress and particularly from the Admiralty complex, where the progressively higher ground could afford protection against the continual flooding — Peter embraced the idea of making the desolate and exposed Vasilevskii Island the center of St. Petersburg; and for the rest of his life he issued numerous directives to that end. The directives exude at times a maniacal air. For instance, a decree of April 9, 1719, ordered that from 700 to 1,000 large masonry houses were to be built on the Island along with 500 to 700 smaller ones, 300 to 500 smaller ones still, and so on; given the nexus of production quotas and building techniques mentioned above, whereby no more than thirty sizable masonry houses could be built annually, the order was exceedingly unrealistic. Yet it was issued again scarcely two years later, and equally without effect.

As things turned out, Peter's decision to develop Vasilevskii Island as the residential, commercial, and administrative center of St. Peters-

---

[3] J. B. A. Le Blond, French architect who worked in Russia (1716–1719). — Ed.

[4] According to a Dutch naval officer in Peter's service, Vasilevskii Island, uninhabited and nameless under the Swedes, was named after the Russian officer — Vasily — who commanded the first battery emplaced on it. Messages then were sent "to Vasily's Island." But it is also thought that the island had been so named, in Russian, since 1500, possibly after a fourteenth-century local landowner, Vasily Kazimer of Novgorod.

burg was to be largely frustrated. By the time of his death houses were finished on about a quarter of its assigned lots, and of these some 75 percent were wooden; while in the years immediately to follow the districts behind the Admiralty saw the most growth. Still, it is difficult not to admire the soaring ambition, the very impracticality of this legislation of Peter's last years. Gone is the preoccupation with fortification and fire prevention so characteristic of an earlier time. Instead, again and again we find an insistence on using "good builders," on following properly drawn plans, on building in a certain way not just to prevent fire but for the sake of "better construction" — on building, in what by the end of his reign had become a favorite phrase, "in accordance with architecture [*po arkhitekture*]." Build in St. Petersburg as it has been ordained, Peter commanded in April 1721, put up 595 streetlights, and do everything *po arkhitekture.* Luppov is right to suggest that behind Peter's sometimes conflicting measures for the planning and construction of St. Petersburg can be detected a striving to create a capital in keeping with contemporary European notions of the ideal city, and that in doing so he was guided by several basic principles: (1) to create a well-built city of masonry structures fronting on straight streets and broad boulevards intersected at various points by an integrated system of canals; (2) to make the numerous waterways, natural and artificial, the city's principal means of communication and the city itself, as far as possible, a seaward or coastal town; (3) to subject all building both in and around the city to strict regulation; and (4) to settle categories of people — soldiers, tradesmen, merchants, artisans, officials — in specific districts of the city, which should provide it in turn with major functional zones or quarters. . . .

The Petrine revolution in Russian architecture affected every aspect of the building art and sooner or later reached into every part of the Russian Empire, producing transformations in the built environment that would give it a more or less European — or "modern" — appearance. Initially a matter of necessity with respect to fortification and shipbuilding but essentially one of taste with regard to "civil" architecture, the revolution can be viewed as a process whereby the values and techniques of contemporary European architecture were deliberately brought to Russia, there to be so firmly implanted in the first decades of the eighteenth century that they determined the subsequent course of Russian architectural history. Ordinary domestic housing, parks and gardens, warehouses and wharves all came within the revolution's purview as did churches and palaces, official buildings of every variety, fortresses and other military structures, and ships — overwhelmingly naval ships — of every known kind. The Petrine architectural revolution was responsible for bringing to Russia everything from the idea of large-scale and detailed town planning to the art of applying plaster and alabaster modeling in the interior decoration of buildings. Scarcely any building or ensemble of buildings of any social importance would ever again be the same.

To recapitulate briefly, the revolution involved several distinct if interrelated steps. European architectural books and prints were collected in huge, entirely unprecedented numbers; Russian editions of various European architectural works were produced for the first time, as were engravings of Russian buildings in the "new style," engravings that were designed now by Russian as well as foreign artists; at least seventeen Russians were dispatched to Europe — mainly to Amsterdam and Rome — for the express purpose of studying architecture, something that had never been done before; and, most decisively, thousands of European experts were imported both to supervise or assist in the work of designing and building and to train, by precept and by example, their Russian pupils and assistants. Regular training in architectural theory as well as practice was established in Russia; and Russian builders, absorbing a whole new technical vocabulary of Dutch, Italian, English, German, French, and Latin terms, went on to apply their new knowledge in the construction of numerous buildings in what came to be called the St. Petersburg style — a new, local variant of the northern Baroque. . . .

With the foundation in St. Petersburg of the Imperial Academy of Fine Arts (1757), training in architectural theory and draftsmanship was definitively separated from the workshop or building site and given a central, authoritative, and privileged position in the preparation of builders in Russia. Not coincidentally, the profession of architect in Russia was acquiring new prestige, as it had elsewhere. Of students enrolled at the Academy already in 1758, nearly a third — eleven of thirty-eight — gave their social status (*chin*) as "of the nobility *[iz dvorian]*." Builders, like painters, were no longer drawn exclusively from the peasantry and townsfolk.

In 1764 the first class of the new junior school of the Imperial Academy of Fine Arts was enrolled: sixty boys, all six years of age. The idea was that if after nine years in the school any of its pupils was not judged sufficiently talented to move up to the Academy, he would remain to prepare for a trade such as metalworking or cabinetry. The architectural historian Pevsner thus finds two features of the St. Petersburg Academy that make it unique in the history of such institutions: (1) the combination of secondary school, trade school, and art academy under one roof, suggesting "a country where public education of all kinds was still undeveloped"; and (2) the amount of state control exercised, which can be explained, in Pevsner's view, "only by the particular coincidence of a nation grown up outside Western civilization being suddenly forced into it with an epoch in Western history in which absolutism and its commercial corollary, mercantilism, were ruling." Be that as it may, with respect to architecture and the decorative arts the St. Petersburg Academy of Fine Arts, like the 100 or more public schools of art established everywhere in Europe by 1790, served to disseminate, initially, the tenets of Neoclassicism. And in this way the Academy brought Russia firmly into the European mainstream.

The advance of Russian architecture under Catherine II (reigned 1762–1796) was the culmination of an extraordinary convergence of power and taste, one that had begun under Peter I and whose effects would reach still further into the future. For by the end of Catherine's reign, to take only the most obvious instance, the Russian government had directed the planning or replanning and renovation of more than 400 cities and towns, producing a deliberate uniformity of urban design throughout the Russian Empire. The purpose of this gigantic enterprise, in Catherine's own words, was to give the Russian built environment a "more European appearance." . . .

Nor was it only a matter of cities and towns, or of architecture at the upper levels of society. More slowly than in the urban centers, to be sure, and by a process that is far more difficult to trace, the Petrine architectural revolution reached into the villages of rural Russia, where a necessarily preliminary process of nucleation appears to have been in progress since well before the eighteenth century. As recently as 1550, it seems, some 90 percent of agricultural settlements were composed of fewer than five households, with about 70 percent of the total containing no more than one or two. But steadily in the later sixteenth and the seventeenth centuries, and on into the eighteenth, these tens of thousands of tiny isolated agricultural settlements were consolidating into larger villages—villages whose layout did not reflect, we can be

sure, any fixed or "regular" plan. The mass of new or newly consolidated settlements had no centers, no streets worthy of the name,
usually not even a church, and no masonry structures; while the relatively few villages of some administrative and commercial significance,
and comprising perhaps 100 to 150 households, were architecturally
little better off.

In August 1722 Peter I decreed that to control the spread of fire and
"for the sake of better construction" villages were to be built (or rebuilt,
after a fire) in accordance with a prescribed plan. The plan specified
that houses and yards were to be standard in size and to maintain a set
distance between them, and that the houses themselves were to face
forward, in a straight line, flush with a would-be street. *Reguliarnost*
("regularity") had come to the countryside. Compliance with Peter's
decree was not widespread until, once again, the time of Catherine II,
whose government converted the largest villages into towns, as mentioned, and vigorously enforced the planning and rebuilding of the rest.
By the end of the eighteenth century the linear village plan prevailed
throughout Russia, with houses — or cottages — and sheds positioned
flush with the street, in straight rows, and with the church and any
other public buildings grouped in and around a central square. Only in
a few villages, situated far from the main roads and regional centers, did
the random "circular plan" survive. . . .

The Petrine revolution in Russian architecture had proved irreversible. From St. Petersburg to the village the "new" style or the "modern"
in building (in Russian the word is the same, *novyi*) increasingly held
sway. Beginning with the revolutionary transitions of the turn of the
eighteenth century and culminating in Catherine II's grand *pereplan-
irovka* near its end, the Russian built world had been radically transformed. Moreover, by 1800 or so, if not earlier, Russians possessed
individual buildings and ensembles of buildings, parks and gardens,
squares and other public spaces, whole townscapes and landscapes that
could stand comparison with the best of architecture anywhere in the
European world. Indeed, the success of the revolution was such that by
1800 or so Russia had become, at least in architecture, an integral part
of that world.

At the most important level of building the Neoclassicism of
Catherine II, having succeeded the Baroque of Peter I and his daughter,
Empress Elizabeth, was succeeded in turn by the Empire style of
Catherine's grandson, Alexander I (reigned 1801–1825), a style that

represented yet another enactment of the European Classical heritage. Again measures were taken by the central government to impose architectural uniformity throughout the Russian Empire; and the reign of Alexander, especially after the victorious conclusion of the Napoleonic wars, witnessed another great boom in building. Then, following a phase of Romantic or Muscovite revivalist architecture in the middle and later decades of the nineteenth century, and of uncontrolled industrial expansion at its end, both classicism and rigorous town planning made a comeback in the early twentieth — to be given widespread application in the Soviet Union by the Stalin regime after the defeat of the local avant-garde. But the larger historical point to be registered is that at every stage advances in European architecture were more or less immediately reflected in Russia, where fully formed variants of the successive international styles were produced and major technical innovations more or less readily absorbed.

We have traced this momentous development to the reign of Peter I. Yet even then, it deserves stressing, it was perceived by contemporaries as having begun. In the words of Feofan Prokopovich, the leading bishop of the day, thanks to Peter the defenses of the state had been greatly strengthened, Russians were much better protected than formerly against the elements, and they now had buildings of which they could justly be proud: buildings of a "most commodious convenience, shining forth in beauty and splendor." In this as in other respects, Prokopovich proclaimed to the grieving Russian elite, assembled for their monarch's funeral, Russia under "Peter the Great" had been reborn.

N. I. Pavlenko

St. Petersburg

The second of these readings, by N. I. Pavlenko, who may be considered the current dean of Soviet historians of the Petrine era, concentrates on St.

From N. Pavlenko, *Petr Pervyi* [Peter the First], 1975, pp. 338–50, 354–55, 358–60. Published by Molodaia Gvardiia, Moscow. Trans. by Reef Altoma.

Petersburg as the new commercial and cultural center of Russia. Pavlenko extols Peter's role in the creation of the city and the speed with which it was built, and sees the new capital as the enduring symbol of an era of great reform. The note of patriotic pride is unmistakable.

St. Petersburg was not only Peter's pride and joy but also the symbol of his reign, a reign expressive of an age of reform. Of course, the new capital did not represent all of Russia. On the contrary, it was a unique city not only architecturally but also with regard to its way of life. Nonetheless, St. Petersburg can rightfully be considered an example of that new character which Peter strove to give Russia — and which had only begun to emerge. Decades more would be needed for the sprouts of the new to be strengthened and to spread over the whole country. But the foundations had been laid, and the process had become irreversible. . . .

How did this new city appear to the tsar, and how did it differ from the old capital of Moscow? It differed, first of all, by reason of its straight streets, spacious parks and boulevards, and system of canals, which were the basic means of communication. The building of the city was carried out according to a plan worked out by the government. The plan envisioned all the details of the city's construction: the distribution of its streets and squares, types of building, etc.

The construction of the city, unprecedented in its intensity, began in earnest in 1717. Several hundred new houses were erected yearly, so that by the end of Peter's life the capital had been transformed into a large city with a population of 40,000. The rise of a major center on a vacant site and in such a short time was a sensation, an event without precedent in Europe.

In 1716 Peter commissioned the well-known French architect Le Blond to draw up a general plan of the city. Le Blond's designs and plans of model buildings were sent to Peter for approval the following year. The tsar postponed approval until his return, and made the following interesting remark: the windows in residential buildings must be made smaller, he said, "since we do not have the French climate." Le Blond acted according to contemporary notions of urban planning, with their concentration on the so-called regular city. Everything was to be planned by the government, and for their own well-being residents had only to execute its instructions conscientiously. The city in Le Blond's plan was elliptical in form, cut by straight streets on the Admiralty Side and by canals on Vasilevskii Island. In the middle of the island a huge palace square was planned, to be surrounded by the palaces of dignitaries and government buildings. Le Blond indicated where churches should be built and markets, squares, and places for public celebrations and punishments established. Buildings were to be the same height along the whole length of a street. . . . But Peter rejected Le Blond's plan as too expensive.

By 1725 St. Petersburg had acquired a high level of amenities. In 1710–1711, a foreigner who left a description of the city had noted: "When it rains for just one day there are no pathways, and with every step you sink into mud." Now all the streets of the capital were paved with stone. The duty of paving the streets was assigned to the residents themselves. Every cart arriving in St. Petersburg had to bring three stones weighing no less than five pounds, and every vessel, ten to thirty stones. The stones were used not in the middle of the street but in strips one and a half to two meters wide in front of the houses. These we would now call sidewalks.

Nevskii Prospekt [avenue], which ran from the Admiralty out to the Alexander-Nevskii monastery, already astonished contemporaries. In the eyes [of a German visitor in 1721]: "The Nevskii Prospekt is a long and wide avenue, paved with stone." Along either side stood three or four rows of trees. Distinguished by its unusual beauty and cleanliness, the Prospekt left a most favorable impression on [this visitor]; as he said, it presented "a marvelous view [prospect], the likes of which I have nowhere encountered."

On May 27, 1718, the Senate received an edict from the tsar: "For the best order of this city we have assigned the duties of police chief [politseimeister] to our Adjutant-General Devier, and have given him instructions in the matter." . . .[1] The instructions were composed by Peter himself. The police chief was to supervise the proper construction of the city, the reinforcement of its river banks, the cleaning of its streets

---

[1] Anthony Devier, a Portuguese soldier of fortune who had risen high in Peter's service. — Ed.

and lanes, the maintenance of order in the markets, and the quality of the products being sold. He was also obliged to cut short deliberate price increases, to eradicate gambling, to enforce fire prevention measures strictly, and to set up night patrols "with sentries who should walk with alarms, as is the custom in other lands." . . .

In 1721 the inhabitants of the capital witnessed a novelty introduced for the first time in Russia: the streets of St. Petersburg began to be lit with lamps. Five hundred and ninety-five of them were installed. The lamplighters were to pour hempseed oil into the lamps, light the wicks, and after five hours extinguish them. . . .

How did the city look at the end of the tsar's life [1725]? Few buildings remain from that time, but one can judge the external appearance of the capital from plans that have been preserved. In the city, single-story houses in wattle and daub, painted on the outside in imitation of brick, still predominated. There were no completely built-up areas; only the area between the Neva and the Fontanka rivers had been developed. But even then several structures drew attention, some because of their grandiose dimensions, others because of their splendid decoration. Among the former the Admiralty stood out. Its courtyard was an enormous quadrangle bordered on three sides by buildings in which materials for rigging and equipping ships were stored. . . . At the Admiralty shipyard they could make everything from keel to mast, from anchor chains to sails. Ships stood in building stocks. The keels of some had only recently been laid, while others were being readied for launching. At first they built small and medium ships at the shipyard. The first ship, armed with only eighteen guns, was launched at the end of April 1706. After the battle of Poltava, Peter ordered that the fleet be expanded to include powerful warships. At the end of 1709 he laid the keel of a fifty-four-gun ship named *Poltava* in honor of the victory over the Swedes, and it was launched almost three years later — in June 1712. In the 1720s the shipyard successfully mastered the building of one-hundred-gun warships. The design of the first such ship was worked up by Peter, and he directed its construction. The shipyard was enclosed by an earthen rampart, and its bastions on the river side were armed with cannon. Beyond the rampart was a moat filled with water. The Admiralty shipyard was not only the most important industrial enterprise in the country; it was also a fortress ready to rise to the defense

Facade of the first Winter Palace, St. Petersburg, built 1711; Dominico Trezzini, architect. Etching by A. Zubov, 1717. (State Hermitage Museum, Leningrad)

of the recently founded city against attack by land or sea. . . . Up to 10,000 men worked full-time at the Admiralty in these years.

In 1725, on the site of the present Winter Palace, stood the just finished three-story house of Admiral Apraksin. According to contemporaries, this was the most magnificent and luxurious structure in the city. Beyond it stood the houses of other dignitaries as well as Peter's Winter Palace. The palace was not notable among the adjacent buildings. The interior decoration of its living rooms reflected Peter's tastes and love of small chambers with low ceilings. The Winter Palace was built so that its height was consistent with that of the surrounding buildings, Peter having resigned himself to the demands of the architect. But he saw to it that secondary, lower ceilings were built within.

Not one of these buildings from Peter's time has been preserved. But Peter's Summer Palace remains. It is a regular two-story house built according to [architect Dominico Trezzini's] standard design for people of means and furnished without luxury or finery, although, as a contemporary noted, it was "very beautifully decorated with Chinese wallpapers." Rooms with marble floors were hung with many mirrors. Yet contemporary visitors were attracted less by the Summer Palace than by the park adjoining it. It always enjoyed the special care of the tsar. Wherever he was, in his "paradise," as he called St. Petersburg, or out of town, he remembered the Summer Garden and gave instructions for its improvement. He would summon fountain masters from Moscow to St. Petersburg and order flowers delivered from the old royal park [near Moscow] of Izmailovo.[2] He would send for a description of the park at Versailles. In 1706 he dispatched the roots of white lilies from Kiev and ordered his gardener to "cover [them] carefully." He commissioned his ambassador in Holland to buy up two thousand lime trees. While in Poland [in 1716] the tsar was keenly interested in the condition of his garden, complaining at one point that he had received no reports about it. Peter remained true to his habit of getting to the heart of every matter. When he was in France [1717] he would study the layout of the park at Versailles and then give quite professional instructions, just as he did in connection with the construction of ships or fortifications. He nursed the Summer Garden to the end of his life, and in the end achieved what he had striven for: his park with its artfully aligned paths, its trees and shrubs clipped in the shape of cubes, its pyramids and globes, its flowerbeds, numerous statues, vases, busts, fountains, and ponds, yielded nothing to the best European models. . . .

The Summer Garden was indebted to Peter for the arrival of a guest from the ancient world: a statue of Aphrodite, or "Venus" as she was called in Russia, sculpted in the second century of our era. The sculpture, found in Rome with her head broken off and without arms, was bought [1718] by Iury Kologrivov, who had been sent to Italy by Peter to supervise Russian architectural students. The statue was safely delivered

---

[2]The designers of fountains in St. Petersburg and its environs, mainly Italians and Germans, all came, in fact, from Europe. — Ed.

to St. Petersburg and erected in a gallery of twelve pairs of columns that stood at the entrance to the Summer Garden. Peter greatly valued the Venus and established a twenty-four-hour watch over her. Later, the statue was transferred to the Hermitage. . . .[3]

Beyond the Summer Garden were located two more buildings which enjoyed great popularity in the new capital. One of them — the Kikin Palace — attained fame because it contained two culturally significant institutions: the first museum in Russia [the *Kunstkamera*] and the first public library. The Kikin Palace, a two-story structure, had been confiscated by the treasury in 1718 after the execution of its owner, Alexander Kikin, who was implicated in the Tsarevich Aleksei affair.[4] Peter ordered this house to be fitted to accommodate the *Kunstkamera* and the library. The tsar knew the exhibits of the *Kunstkamera* well; either he had himself acquired them abroad or they had been sent on his orders from various corners of Russia. Thus Peter was considered the best guide. He loved to show foreign ambassadors as well as Russian dignitaries around the premises and to talk to them about the exhibits [which consisted mainly of anatomical, zoological, and geological collections]. Owing to the wealth and diversity of these exhibits, the *Kunstkamera* was already famous by the end of Peter's life. . . . On the second floor of the Kikin Palace stood shelves crammed with books. The library was formed from various sources with Peter's active participation. In 1725 it was, by the standards of the time, enormous. Its collections included about 11,000 volumes, and a contemporary described it as "second to none in its variety and wealth of first-class books."

Located near the Kikin Palace, on the bank of the Neva, was the second most important industrial enterprise in the new capital, the Foundry. In size it was greatly inferior to the Admiralty but, like the Admiralty, it was an industrial complex: cannon barrels were cast in

---

[3]Reference is to the so-called Venus of Taurida, since identified as a Roman copy from the first century AD of a Greek original of the third century BC. From 1790 the Venus resided in the Taurida Palace of Prince Potemkin, Catherine II's great favorite; in 1850 it was moved to what is now the State Hermitage Museum, Leningrad, where it may be seen with other classical sculptures acquired by Peter I. — Ed.

[4]For the trial of Peter's son, Tsarevich Aleksei, see Part VI. — Ed.

"East Front of the Imperial Library and *Kunstkamera*," St. Petersburg, built 1718–1734; G. J. Mattarnowy, architect. Engraving by G. Kachalov, 1741. By permission of the Houghton Library, Harvard University.

the main workshop, which was serviced by various auxiliary shops. . . . The Foundry could attend to everything needed to produce artillery: here barrels were drilled and gun carriages, fuses, and even harnesses were manufactured.

On the opposite bank of the Neva stood the Peter-Paul fortress. By the end of Peter's life it had already acquired its present contours: the walls and casements had been built, and the decoration of the massive Petrovskie gates completed. Inside the fortress, visible from all points of the city, was the church of Sts. Peter and Paul. This was the most important monumental building of the capital, its architectural center. In 1725 its construction was still not complete, but the expressive silhouette of the belltower with its clock and huge spire, covered with copper-gilt plates, already gleamed in the sun. The tsar had wanted the height of the spire to exceed that of the highest structure in Moscow, the belltower of Ivan the Great. The spire thus symbolized the status in his realm of the new city.

In 1725, the Neva embankment on Vasilevskii Island had only just begun to be built. The spit of the island was supposed to become the administrative and commercial center of the capital. Here the renowned building of the Twelve Colleges was being constructed. Originally intended to house the Senate and Synod as well as the colleges, its simple, economic composition was achieved by repetition of individual three-story buildings of the same style united under one long roof. . . . The equal size of the individual buildings and the uniformity of their external appearance emphasized the equality of the colleges in the system of central state institutions founded by Peter.[5]

A new *Kunstkamera* became one of the most prominent structures of the capital. Its two wings were joined in the middle by a multitiered tower, the top floor of which was intended to accommodate a giant globe made in Germany. Although Peter hurried the builders along, the collections of the *Kunstkamera* and his library were moved from the Kikin Palace to the new building only after his death. An especially large number of complications was caused by the globe. More than one hundred people participated in its transfer, including 25 carpenters who made the packing crate. Loaded onto a special barge, the globe was transported to the *Kunstkamera*, where it was raised by blocks to the third floor and placed in the center of a round hall.

Yet one more sight within the new capital commanded attention: the port. Sailboats moved up and down the Neva as well as wooden barges and galleys. Giant sea-going vessels sat in their moorings flying English, Dutch, Danish, German, and French flags. Along the right bank of the Neva a huge number of wooden barges jostled one another, waiting to be unloaded, and other barges, also numbering in the hundreds, rode at anchor or approached the city. Naval ships, all brightly decked with flags and lamps, would enter the Neva to celebrate victories. The Baltic fleet, in the creation of which the tsar expended much personal labor, was his pride. In 1724 the fleet numbered 32 ships of the line and more than 100 lesser craft. A land power which three decades earlier had not possessed a single warship had been transformed into a mighty naval power, having at its disposal the most powerful fleet in the Baltic. The fleet defended the maritime borders of Russia and the new capital of the empire, St. Petersburg.

St. Petersburg had become the chief port of Russia. Its trade turnover exceeded by several times the turnover of the old port city in the north — Archangel — and those of the newly annexed port cities on

---

[5] Peter's new Senate, Synod, and administrative colleges are described in later sections of this book, particularly in Part III. — Ed.

the Baltic — Viborg, Reval, and Riga. In 1724, 180 foreign ships registered at St. Petersburg while at Archangel it was around 50. St. Petersburg was now Russia's window on Europe. Here goods were delivered from distant regions of the country for sale abroad; and from here goods brought from western Europe were dispatched in various directions. The life of the port reflected the economic life of Russia. . . .

Thus the significance of St. Petersburg was multifaceted. First and foremost it was the capital of the empire and the residence of the tsar. It was also the largest commercial port of the country, serving an enormous hinterland. The development of manufacturing gradually gave the city an industrial character as well.

St. Petersburg was a concentration of innovations in town planning and a city of monumental structures of secular purpose. Indeed, the first scientific and modern educational institutions in Russia were opened in the new capital. The first higher technical school, the Naval Academy, was founded here. The Academy of Sciences, another child of Peter, was also established in St. Petersburg. The documents show that he had thought about organizing an academy for quite some time. In those days, as now, the word "academy" bore two meanings: a higher educational institution, and a center of scientific research. Both Russians and foreigners had proposed in writing that the tsar organize such an academy in Russia, but its creation was delayed partly because Peter was busy with more urgent matters and partly because of the difficulties of attracting foreign scholars. The tsar insisted that scholars invited to the St. Petersburg academy should be the most prominent in Europe. . . . In the course of 1724 and the greater part of the next year, negotiations with foreign scholars were conducted, and the St. Petersburg Academy of Sciences opened for business in August 1725. . . .[6]

---

[6]For an account of the subsequent history of the St. Petersburg Academy of Sciences, see V. Boss, *Newton and Russia: The Early Influence, 1698–1796* (Cambridge, MA: Harvard University Press, 1972). — Ed.

Ian Grey

Creation of the Russian Navy

The third of Peter I's truly distinctive achievements, one closely related to his victory in the Northern War and to the founding of St. Petersburg, was his creation of the Russian navy — an achievement all the more remarkable in that neither Peter himself nor his people had had any prior naval experience whatever. In this article, Ian Grey, author of several books on Russian history, provides an account of how, in his words, "a nation of landsmen had, within the span of [Peter's] reign and following his indomitable will, become a naval power."

While watching English naval maneuvers in the Solent in March 1698, Peter the Great is reported to have told the officer accompanying him that he would rather be an admiral in the English navy than tsar of Russia. The incident reflects the love of ships and of the sea that early became an obsession with this extraordinary man and that fired his ambition to create a navy and make Russia a sea power. Of his many activities and achievements, none was more remarkable than his realization of this ambition, not only because of the immense difficulties he faced, but also because by his vision, dynamic energy and relentless persistence he carried his task through with such success.

Peter's delight in ships was born in a chance incident that happened shortly before his seventeenth birthday. Already, to the horror of his subjects, he was turning away from the Muscovy of his forebears and seeking knowledge among the Western craftsmen and soldiers who lived in the "German Suburb" (*Nemetskaia Sloboda*) beyond the eastern limits of Moscow. There he had found a Dutchman, named Franz

From Ian Gray, "Peter the Great and the Creation of the Russian Navy," first published in *History Today*, vol. 11, no. 9 (September 1961), pp. 625–31. Reprinted by permission of *History Today*.

Timmermann, who could teach him mathematics and the use of the astrolabe.

At this time Timmermann was his constant companion, and it was with him that Peter, visiting a village out of Moscow, came upon a derelict boat, quite unlike the flat-bottomed barges plying the Russian rivers.

"What kind of boat is that?" he asked Timmermann.

"An English boat," was the reply.

"What's it used for? Is it better than our Russian boats?"

"Yes. If it had a new mast and sails, it would move not only with the wind, but against the wind as well," Timmermann explained.

To Peter this was an astonishing revelation. He could not rest until the boat had been repaired and he had learned to sail her on the rivers and lakes.[1] His enthusiasm aroused, Peter carried all before him. He had boats built on Lake Pereiaslavl [north of Moscow], and then, dissatisfied with the boats and the restraints of a lake, he traveled to Archangel to satisfy his longing to see real ships and the sea.

The Dutch and English merchantmen that crowded the mouth of the Dvina to unload at Archangel, Russia's only port for trade with Europe, stirred new ideas in Peter's mind. He sailed for nearly two hundred miles in a small twelve-gun yacht as part of the escort of a convoy of merchantmen returning home. Already he was making plans for a visit to the White Sea in the following summer. He established a wharf near Archangel and, with his own hands, laid down the keel of a ship to be built during the winter. Then he sent instructions to Nicholas Witsen, Burgomaster of Amsterdam, who on occasion carried out commissions for the Russian government, to build him a forty-gun frigate in Holland to be delivered to Archangel in the coming summer. The safe arrival of this frigate, *The Holy Prophecy*, was to prove the highlight of his second visit to the White Sea and, after conducting maneuvers in her, he returned to Moscow with the idea in mind of building a galley fleet.

---

[1] This account, which Peter himself wrote 32 years later, of the birth of his love of ships and of his visions of sea power, is taken from his autobiographical introduction to the *Naval Statute* of 1720.

At this time, Russia was at war with both the Turks and the Crimean Tatars. It was not a state of active war, but the Russians suffered from incessant Tatar raids, and the Cossacks in the southern lands were also growing restless.[2] Distracted by ships and by exercises with the personal regiments that were soon to form the nucleus of his new army, Peter had ignored these troubles in the south. Now, however, he decided on a campaign, not against the Crimean Khanate, but against the mighty Ottoman port of Azov. It was a bold decision, and the factor that most influenced him in making it was that the capture of Azov would give him access to the Sea of Azov and to harbors where he could build a fleet to challenge Turkish naval power in the Black Sea.

Peter's first Azov campaign was a failure. Standing before this stronghold, he could only watch powerless as Turkish ships brought supplies and reinforcements by sea. He was compelled to retreat, but he at once devoted his furious energies to preparations for a second campaign in the following year [1696].

The chief feature of these preparations was the construction of a fleet, and it was a formidable undertaking. No shipbuilding facilities of any kind existed, and the Russians, acquainted only with the primitive barges on the Volga and the Don, lacked any experience with ships. But Peter seemed unaware of the magnitude of his task. He had to decide where the ships would be built, establish shipyards, assemble timber and other materials, find competent shipwrights and train crews. The fleet he planned was large, consisting of 25 armed galleys, 300 barges to transport troops and supplies, and 30 sea-going boats, as well as pinewood rafts and fireships. He required all these to be built in the five months of the winter of 1695–1696. And they were built.

Voronezh, with access to the Don and with forests nearby to provide timber, was the chief center for the construction of this fleet. Here, 27,828 unskilled laborers were mobilized from one province alone. The galleys were built at Preobrazhenskoe on the model of a Dutch galley, which Peter had ordered from Holland for the purpose.[3] Within three months, the 25 galleys had been finished and sent by land to Voronezh for launching.

---

[2] The Cossacks were irregular frontier forces. — Ed.
[3] Preobrazhenskoe was Peter's favorite country estate, near Moscow. — Ed.

Supported by this fleet, Peter's second Azov campaign was instantly successful. His armed galleys anchored off the mouth of the Don, effectively blockading Azov. A Turkish squadron approached and attempted to land troops, but made off as soon as the Russian galleys weighed anchor and prepared to attack. Peter's army, advised by Austrian siege engineers and gunnery experts, inflicted such damage on the fortress that on July 22, 1696, the Turks capitulated. While elated by this victory, and especially by the part his fleet had played, Peter was not carried away. He recognized that this hastily improvised collection of galleys, barges, and rafts, made of green timbers and manned for the most part by untrained peasants, was not the foundation of the navy he wanted. He returned from Azov working on the practical details for two great and, for Russia, revolutionary projects: the first was the creation of a real navy and the second the dispatch of young Russians to Europe to study seamanship, navigation, and shipbuilding. He determined to travel abroad himself for the same purpose.

Before departing, Peter gave explicit instructions through his Boyar Council for the navy he required. Twenty thousand men were to be assembled from Ukrainian towns within six months and, at Taganrog on the shores of the Sea of Azov, they were to build a town and harbor. He then allocated responsibility for building and maintaining ships on a basis of individual wealth. The church and its monasteries were to produce one ship fully rigged and armed for every 8000 serf households attached to the lands they owned, while civil landowners had to deliver one ship for every 10,000 households. Landowners with not less than 100 serf households were inscribed in companies for the construction of ships on the same scale as the great landowners; those having less than this number of serfs made a contribution in money.

The government provided timber, but the landowners had to find all other materials. Furthermore, they had to build their ships at Voronezh and have them ready for service not later than April 1698, a period of eighteen months. They were also responsible for maintaining their ships and, if lost, replacing them. Merchants as a class in the capital and provinces were to provide twelve ships and, when they petitioned to be relieved of this burden, Peter at once increased the number to fourteen.

This ukaz allowed no exceptions. The patriarch owned private estates containing 8,761 serf households. He was therefore directed to provide one ship in respect of 8,000 households, and to join in a company, adding his remaining 761 households to those of two metropolitans,[4] an archbishop, and twelve monasteries, to build another ship. Landowners who failed to deliver their ships on time faced heavy penalties, and most of them contracted with foreign shipwrights for the building.

Always planning ahead, Peter had foreseen that he would have to engage shipwrights from abroad, since he had none among his own subjects. While laying siege to Azov, he had, therefore, sent urgent requests to the Doge of Venice, and to the courts of England, Holland, and Sweden, for skilled shipwrights to help him in his war against the infidel Turk. During the first half of 1697, no fewer than 50 Western shipwrights reached Moscow and went on to work at Voronezh. At the same time, the first groups of young Russians were setting out for Europe to begin their naval training. Peter himself was to engage hundreds of engineers and craftsmen from abroad; yet, such was the scale of his undertakings, he never had enough skilled foreigners to meet his demands. On the other hand, he never lost sight of the need to train his own people and to win independence from Western tutelage.

In March 1697, traveling incognito, Peter set out with his Grand Embassy for Europe. The formal purpose of the Embassy was to negotiate a European alliance against the Ottoman Porte; Peter's real purpose, however, was to satisfy his curiosity about the West and, above all, to study shipbuilding and the means that would help him to create a navy. The countries he most wanted to visit were the naval powers — Holland, England, and Venice. It happened that he was unable to visit Venice, but in Holland, and especially in England, he completed his naval studies as well as enlisting the services of a large number of officers, seamen, and technicians. His three months in England, where William III presented him with a magnificent yacht, *The Royal Transport*, and ordered special naval maneuvers for him in the Solent, proved the highlight of his first European tour. . . .

On his return to Moscow, Peter embarked on a policy of Westernizing and reorganizing his tsardom. He managed, nevertheless, to keep an eye on the Voronezh fleet, which had been built, but was

---

[4] Senior bishops. — Ed.

doomed never to reach the Black Sea. Increasingly, however, his time and energies were absorbed by his numerous reforms and then by the Northern War.

Recognizing that the Ottoman Porte was too powerful to be defeated decisively without allies, Peter turned north to challenge Sweden, another of Russia's traditional enemies. Sweden at the end of the seventeenth century was a great power, supreme in the north, and the effective bar to Russian access to the Baltic. With the ascent of the boy-king, Charles XII, to the Swedish throne in 1697, the time seemed propitious for Russia to seize the Baltic province that had been one of the major objectives of Russian policy for over two centuries.

Peter, like his allies, could not have foreseen that the young Swedish king would prove one of the most brilliant generals of the age, nor that the Northern War would last for 21 years. At Narva, in 1700, Charles XII inflicted a crushing defeat on Peter's massive, but untrained, army. It seemed then that Russia was out of the war; but during the next five years, while Charles, contemptuously turning his back on his Russian enemy, pursued his vendetta against the king of Poland, Peter advanced towards the Baltic, conquered Ingria, and thus gained access to the sea. At the mouth of the Neva he at once founded a port and a fortress, named St. Petersburg after his patron saint. He ordered a fortress to be built on the small island of Kronstadt, guarding the approaches to his new port; and at Lodeinoe Pole, on the banks of the river Svir, work began on ships for his Baltic fleet.

News of the Russian conquest of Ingria spread quickly in Europe. Many governments were alarmed by the tsar's breakthrough to the Baltic, and reports sent out from Moscow disturbed them further. To the Russian ambassador in London Peter's chancellor wrote that the tsar would soon have in the Baltic a fleet of 20 warships and frigates, 78 galleys, and 100 brigantines, and that some of these ships were already in service. At this time the frigate, *Shtandart*, with three or four snows and ten galleys, represented the full strength of this fleet.[5] But shipbuilders were working furiously at Lodeinoe Pole and in November 1704, Peter moved the main shipyards to St. Petersburg, establishing the Admiralty on the banks of the Neva.

---

[5] Snows were small sailing vessels. — Ed.

At this time Peter could not devote his full attention to his growing navy. Charles, having dealt with his other enemies, had turned at last to march on Russia and, as Peter understood well, the fate of St. Petersburg and of his fleet depended on the outcome of this campaign. He had, however, during these years not only founded cities and built ships and industries; he had also forged a new army. At Poltava in June 1709, this army brilliantly proved itself by crushing the Swedes, who were led by their hitherto invincible king. It was a momentous victory, and it eliminated Sweden as a great power in the north; for Peter, its significance was summed up in his own comment: "Now, with the help of God, the final stone in the foundation of St. Petersburg has been laid."

The Northern War, however, was to drag on for twelve more years. Peter might have brought it to a close earlier, had he not involved himself in alliances against Sweden. An ill-considered and badly conducted campaign against the Turks, ending for him in an ignominious defeat on the river Pruth [1711] and the surrender of his foothold on the Sea of Azov, had, moreover, made him extremely cautious on all fronts. For many months he tried fruitlessly to negotiate a joint Russo-Danish landing on the Swedish coast. But his fleet was not inactive. In April 1713 this fleet, comprising 93 galleys, 60 brigantines, and 50 large boats, carrying in all 16,050 troops, sailed from St. Petersburg with Peter as rear-admiral in command of the vanguard. He defeated the Swedes in a series of actions and during the summer captured the whole of southern Finland.

In the following summer came the naval action that, crowning Peter's naval ambitions, made him master of the Baltic. The Russian fleet, commanded by General-Admiral Apraksin and Rear-Admiral Peter, had put to sea in May (1714) to cruise in the Baltic. It was a large fleet of some 20 ships of the line and nearly 200 galleys. Peter attached special importance to these galleys, which could get under way and maneuver easily in this sea where islands and sheer cliffs could immobilize ships depending on sail.

At the end of June, the Russian ships anchored at Tverminne, some six miles to the east of Cape Hango — or Gangut, as the Russians called it — where the Swedish fleet of sixteen ships of the line, five frigates, and other small vessels stood at anchor. In this position the Swedes barred the way to the Aland Islands and the Swedish mainland. Completely outmaneuvered on July 26, Admiral Watrang managed to escape to sea with part of his fleet, but the ships under command of Admiral Ehrenskjold took refuge in Rilaks Fjord. Peter led his ships into the fjord on the following morning. He first invited Ehrenskjold to surrender on honorable terms, and then, his offer having been rejected, he attacked. The Swedes had superiority in armaments and in the skilled seamen manning their ships, but the Russians outnumbered them by more than three to one. For Peter, therefore, victory depended on getting alongside and boarding the Swedish ships.

The fighting raged for three hours with heavy casualties on both sides. Gradually, ship by ship, the Swedes were beaten. Ehrenskjold in the frigate *Elephant*, seeing that he had no hope of victory, struck his flag. He himself tried to escape to the shore, but was taken captive by Captain Bredale, master of the thirty-gun *St. Paul*, one of the many Englishmen who helped to build and officer Peter's navy. The remaining Swedish captains were now prompt to surrender, and the victorious Russian fleet led back to St. Petersburg as prizes not only the *Elephant* and nine galleys, but also the crew and troops from each vessel.

Peter took tremendous pride in this victory, which he considered equal in importance to Poltava. Then he had destroyed Sweden's army; now he had decisively defeated her navy. But other powers, and especially England, did not share his pleasure.

The accession of George, Elector of Hanover, to the English throne had been warmly welcomed by Peter, who had been seeking without success to conclude a close alliance with England since the early years of his reign. George I was known to be anxious to expel the Swedes from northern Germany, and Peter was convinced that England would now join him in bringing the Northern War to an end. But England was alarmed by the emergence of this new power in the Baltic and deeply disturbed that the tsar might not only dominate Baltic trade, but also make his new capital the emporium of commerce between East and West. Jealous, suspicious, and watchful, England was in no mood to help Russia against Sweden.

The year 1715 opened with a third coalition in which George I joined against Sweden, but Peter was to be disappointed in his hopes of action by the English navy. From Copenhagen his ambassador wrote that "although the English King has declared war, it is only as Elector of Hanover, and the English fleet has sailed to protect its own merchants . . . ." This judgment of the position was to prove correct.

A squadron, commanded by Admiral Sir John Norris, escorted a convoy of merchantmen into the Baltic. Norris anchored his ships off Reval where Peter entertained him heartily, but Norris held strictly to his orders to take no part in operations against the Swedes. Soon, moreover, Peter's alliance with Mecklenburg and George I's suspicions were to have the effect of making England openly hostile to Russia. In St. Petersburg the English resident, Jefferyes, became obstructive, and proposed to deprive the tsar of his English shipwrights and naval officers. This would, he advised his government, maim the new Russian fleet, which was arousing so much uneasiness, the more so because experts had now conceded that Peter's ships were "as good as any in Europe." But Jefferyes had little success, because the majority of the Englishmen were reluctant to leave Russia, where they enjoyed privileges and the special favor of the tsar himself.

Britain and Russia, however, were coming near to war in the Baltic. The Russian ambassador reported from London on the widespread hostility towards Russia and the general agreement to defend Sweden so that the balance of power would be maintained in the north. At the beginning of 1720, however, he was assured that eight out of every ten members of Parliament, both Whig and Tory, were convinced that open war with Russia would be contrary to England's interests.

Meanwhile the Swedes, harried by Russian landings, agreed to cede Bremen and Verden to Hanover on the condition that the English squadron, then at Copenhagen, would defend Sweden against further Russian attacks. In 1719, and again in 1720, Admiral Norris sailed his squadron into the Baltic, but while the presence of English ships of war disturbed Peter, it did not prevent him from carrying out two further damaging raids on the Swedish mainland and defeating a Swedish squadron. To the Swedes it became clear that naval protection was insufficient without allied support also by land. George I, unable to organize land support and troubled by domestic problems, himself finally counseled the Swedes to come to terms with the tsar. At Nystad in the following year [1721], Peter won his peace by which the Swedes ceded in perpetuity the Baltic territories of Livonia, Estonia, and Ingria, and the Viborg district of Finland.

Peter's navy was now secure in the Baltic and his new capital was growing and expanding as a port under his urgent supervision; but he did not neglect the navy and continued to hold regular maneuvers. In the summer of 1723 he made these maneuvers a special occasion. The little boat, known now as the "Grandfather of the Russian Navy," which he had come upon as a boy of sixteen and which had first stirred his naval ambitions, was brought to St. Petersburg.[6] Peter, returning from sea to Kronstadt, stationed his fleet in the harbor. The little boat was then lowered from the deck of a galliot into the water. She was flying the imperial standard and, with Peter steering and four senior admirals rowing, she passed slowly by the 22 ships of the line, the galleys, and the innumerable small naval craft, all firing salvoes in her honor. The ceremony triumphantly proclaimed the fact that Russia, a nation of landsmen, had within the span of Peter's reign and following his indomitable will, become a naval power.

[6] Peter himself gave this name affectionately to the little boat, which is now preserved in the Central Naval Museum in Leningrad.

"Peter the First/Emperor of the Russians." Engraving by J. Houbraken (1717) after portrait in oil painted from life by Carel de Moor in Amsterdam, 1717. (Harvard College Library)

III Political Reform

M. M. Bogoslovsky

The Transformation of State Institutions

M. M. Bogoslovsky (1867–1929), a pupil of V. O. Kliuchevsky, was his successor in the chair of Russian history at Moscow University. A leading specialist on Petrine Russia, Bogoslovsky concentrated on Peter's various attempts to reform his state's administrative structure with a view to promoting efficiency and increasing revenue. In this excerpt, from a book intended for general readers, Bogoslovsky provides a brief survey of Peter's efforts in this field. It should be noted that of the new institutions described here, only the Senate survived into the nineteenth century. In fact, if Peter succeeded in engendering greater efficiency and accountability in the central government, his attempts to establish a form of municipal self-government and to separate justice (the court system) from administration (the state bureaucratic apparatus) unequivocally failed. In spite of renewed efforts by his successors to continue his work, real municipal self-

From M. Bogoslovsky, *Petr Velikii i Ego Reforma* [Peter the Great and His Reforms] (Moscow: Kooperativnoe Izdatelstvo, 1920), pp. 95–105. Translated by Reef Altoma.

government and an independent judiciary were established in Russia only in the later nineteenth century, some 150 years after Peter's death. On the other hand, his sweeping attempts at reform in this field, whether they succeeded or failed, demonstrate clearly the dynamic, experimental, didactic, and, in context, radical nature of his regime.

Time and again Peter reorganized state institutions, adapting them to new conditions of life. Over the course of his entire reign old institutions were broken up and new ones introduced; some of these institutions turned out to be lasting while others, having just arisen, were quickly dismantled and replaced. Nevertheless, by the end of his reign newly introduced institutions had taken shape in the system. We might begin a survey of this system with the highest central institutions of the state.

In place of the crowded Boyar Duma of the Muscovite sovereigns, whose members comprised the three highest service ranks (boyars, *okolnichy*, and the duma nobles), stood a Senate of nine members. Peter founded the Senate on February 22, 1711, when he was planning to embark on a lengthy campaign against the Turks. The Boyar Duma was a state council which acted in the presence of the sovereign, from whom it was almost never parted. If the sovereign left Moscow to go somewhere, for example, to one of his summer residences, the Duma gathered there for meetings under his chairmanship. The Duma offered its opinions to the sovereign; matters were decided by the sovereign himself. But the edict on the Senate's establishment said, "We have determined that there be a governing Senate during our absences for administration," and the Senate was instituted precisely in order to act without the sovereign and to rule over the state independently. The Senate was to replace the sovereign in his absence, and subjects were obliged to submit to it, wrote Peter, "as to Us Ourselves." If anyone noticed that the Senate violated its oath to the sovereign in some matter, he was to remain silent until the sovereign returned and then to lodge a complaint.

The composition of the Senate, its rights and procedures, were established by separate decrees issued one after the other, which is why these features constantly changed. Thus originally all matters were to be decided unanimously, but from 1714 it was instructed to decide matters by majority vote. An edict of 1718 changed the composition of the Senate: now it was to consist of the presidents of the new administrative colleges. But this entailed a major inconvenience, as the highest institution in the state, the Senate, was to have supervision over all the other institutions and consequently over the colleges as well. The presidents of the colleges were to supervise themselves. In 1722 Peter acknowledged the mistake and named new presidents for the colleges; only the presidents of three colleges — those of war, navy, and foreign relations — retained the right to sit in the Senate. Still, by the end of Peter's reign its jurisdiction had been established more precisely. Even though it was founded to replace the monarch in his absence and therefore to exercise complete authority, its right of legislation was taken away after the conclusion of the Northern War (1721). It could not issue laws, although it retained the right to participate broadly in the legislative process by composing and presenting draft laws to the sovereign. In practice the Senate had never made use of the full range of supreme power, even in the sovereign's absence. It never issued important decrees without Peter's approval, never conducted foreign policy, and never administered military affairs. In all its diverse activity the Senate invariably maintained the same chief characteristic: it was the primary executor of the sovereign's instructions. In the area of administration in the strict sense, it conveyed his instructions to the colleges and the regional governments and supervised their implementation.

In 1722 the office of procurator-general was established under the Senate. Two main responsibilities were entrusted to this official: first, he was made head of the Senate's chancellery, whose two chief secretaries were to act as his assistants; second, he was charged with supervising the activity of the Senate itself. The absence of such supervision had caused Peter much trouble. Manners were such that senators had had to be rebuked and reminded that they were to conduct themselves as state officals and not as fishwives. In 1715 a special inspector-general, V. I. Zotov, had been appointed to the Senate; he was to sit during its sessions at a special table and to keep order, take the minutes, and see to the execution of its decrees. But Zotov carried out his duties somewhat sluggishly, and the office of inspector-general was abolished after three years. His duties were then entrusted to the Senate's chief secretary, Anisim Shchukin. He was commissioned to ensure that "in the Senate all is done properly and [that] there be no idle conversations, shouting, and suchlike"; matters were to be decided according to a specified procedure and recorded in the register. Having reviewed a case, the chief secretary was to give the senators half an hour for reflection and discussion; and to measure the time he was given a special hourglass. If a case was very difficult and urgent as well, at the request of the senators he could give them an additional half hour; but in no case was it to be more than three hours, at the expiration of which he was obliged to bring paper and ink to each senator and require him to write down his opinion. And if this was rejected, he was to abandon everything and report to the sovereign or, in his absence, send a written message. But the chief secretary also did not satisfy Peter; indeed, he could not have, since his assignment placed him in a contradictory situation: at one and the same time he was to be subordinate to the Senate as head of its chancellery, which gave it the power to punish him, and he was to supervise it. Peter soon changed this arrangement and entrusted supervision of the Senate's activity to officers of his guards regiments, who were to rotate duty in the Senate each month. They were to see that the Senate acted in everything according to instructions, and in the event of any deviation, they were to remind the senators of their duty; if after three such reminders the Senate persisted, the officers were to bring the matter to the attention of the sovereign. "And if any of the senators," Peter's order vigorously adds, "begins to swear or behave impolitely, he will be arrested and taken to the fortress." But such a military regime was not consistent with the dignity of the supreme institution of the empire, and it too was soon replaced. Then the procurator-general, P. I. Iaguzhinsky, was appointed. He was to be independent of the Senate and accountable only to the emperor. The procurator-general was to summon the senators to sessions, monitor their proceedings, grant them leaves of absence, and keep order during their sessions. He was also the intermediary between the emperor and the Senate.

A third responsibility entrusted to the procurator-general was supervision of the activity of all governmental offices in the empire. In this respect he had two weapons. First, officials called "fiscals" (*fiskaly*), who were appointed in all the provinces, and their chief, were subordinate to him. These officials were to discover if anyone was conducting unjust legal proceedings or plundering the treasury, and so on; their reward was half the fine imposed on the guilty parties. Second, in every college and in all the higher courts, procurators subordinate to the procurator-general were established. The relationship of these procurators to the colleges recalls the relationship of the procurator-general to the Senate. They were to ensure that the colleges did not violate the law, and in case of any transgression, to inform the procurator-general. Using both of these weapons, the procurator-general was to be, as Peter said, "the tsar's eye and personal representative in state affairs."

Coming next after the Senate in the administration of the state were the colleges, which replaced the old *prikazy* [singular, *prikaz*]. In the second half of the seventeenth century there were as many as fifty *prikazy*, and business was distributed very irregularly among them. The new colleges numbered ten in all, and the distribution of responsibilities was clear and precise. Three colleges managed the external and military business of the state: the College of Foreign Affairs and the War and Navy (Admiralty) colleges. Three others managed state finances: one collected the revenues; another was in charge of state expenses; and a third inspected all financial matters. The next three were in charge of industry and trade: the College of Manufactures, the College of Mines, and the College of Commerce. Finally, the College of Justice oversaw judicial affairs.

The system of colleges was a novelty for Russia, too, and their composition and procedures were defined by a *General Regulation* [1720]. Every college was to consist of a president, vice president, and several councilors and assessors. All proceedings were to be recorded on paper, and thus a special chancellery was set up in each college comprised of a secretary, notary, actuary, archivist, clerks, subclerks, copyists, and subcopyists who were to operate the complex paper machine of registries, minutes, summaries, etc. According to the *Regulation*, meetings of the colleges were to take place in impressive surroundings. The meeting hall had to be well carpeted, and the table at which the college members sat was to be placed under a canopy. Every case being considered by the colleges was initially subjected to "voluntary" discussion, and then a decision was decreed by majority vote. The members would vote in order of seniority, beginning with the most junior, "without interrupting each other." In the case of a tie, the vote of the president would decide the issue. But the president was not the head of the college, and this was especially emphasized by the *Regulation*. Chapter 24, "On Complimenting the President," instructed the other members to salute him on his entrance and exit by standing up, but otherwise freed them from deferring to him. Every member was granted full freedom of opinion: if his opinion was not in agreement with the majority, he could demand that it be inserted in the minutes. . . .

In December 1708 [Peter decreed that the Russian state be divided into ten great provinces or *gubernii*]. Governors were placed in charge of each *guberniia*. At first, the governors ruled the provinces alone. But in 1713 Peter decided to introduce in the provinces a collegial form of administration, having persuaded the local nobility to participate. Under every governor a council selected by the nobility was formed, with the governor as chairman: "the governor is not to act as a potentate in the council, but as its president." He was forbidden to settle anything without the council's participation. The very name of the members of this elected council, "landrats" [*landraty*], as well as the moment Peter chose to inaugurate the new system, indicate the underlying influence at work. Precisely at this time the question of preserving the old landrat councils in the newly conquered Baltic territories was being discussed.

In practice, the office of landrat was never elective, and Peter's edict remained on paper. The first landrats were appointed by the Senate on the nomination of the governors, and no elections by the nobility took place anywhere. Soon the office ceased being elective by law as well. In 1716 Peter instructed the Senate to appoint as landrats officers who had been discharged from military service because of injury or age, especially those who did not possess estates. Such appointments took on the character of pensions in reward for military service. Thus, not only were landrats not elected by the local nobility, they might not even belong to the landowning class.

Moreover, the landrat councils themselves existed for a very short time. They had scarcely begun to operate, and not in all the provinces, when an edict of January 28, 1715, significantly changed the office of landrat. By this edict the old officials known as *voevody*, who were subordinate to the landrat council, were generally abolished and preserved only in cities that had garrisons, which they commanded. The old district, or *uezd*, ceased to be an administrative subdivision of the province and was replaced by a new, more regular and uniform unit, the *dolia*, in each of which were located 5,536 taxable homesteads. The landrats were appointed heads of these new districts: in effect, they were put in charge of the rural population in tax and legal matters. Two landrats by turns were to attend the governor; at the end of the year all landrats were to assemble in the provincial capital where, under the chairmanship of the governor, they were to draw up reports and dispatch the most important business of the province. In practice, such assemblies convened infrequently, and the governor continued to rule his province personally. The landrats became his subordinates, over whom he stood precisely "as a potentate" and not "as a president." This system endured from 1715 until 1719.

What aims was the new provincial organization supposed to serve? Constantly changing in structure, it constantly pursued one aim. The provincial reform was penetrated by the same spirit which in general characterized all governmental activity in the seventeenth century: it was intended chiefly to increase state revenues in order to meet the needs of the army. His provincial reorganization seemed to Peter more suitable for this purpose than the previous form of administration. The replenishment and upkeep of the army became the main task of the new system. The Petrine province did not concern itself with local welfare; all revenues went to the state treasury, not to meet local needs. The main duty of the governor was to collect from the *guberniia* entrusted to him all revenues due the treasury and to guard them, so that all state obligations were fulfilled. If he wanted to earn the tsar's special favor, he had to seek out new sources of revenue. But there would be trouble if the governor did not succeed in gathering the revenue prescribed for his province. The tsar's wrath did not discriminate between a deficiency in the governor's zeal and the exhaustion of the taxpaying capacity of the population. The governor was subject to severe accountability for any deficits; in his edicts Peter directed the most severe threats to the governors, even though they were prominent figures. For not delivering the prescribed number of conscripts, a governor was subject to a fine of a ruble per person, and in some cases his estates might be confiscated. Time and again Peter promised "cruelly to torture" governors who did not carry out an edict to the letter. One of his orders on levying conscripts ended with the injunction that governors were liable to punishment "as traitors and betrayers of the fatherland" if the required numbers were not delivered on time. On another occasion, having received news that the proper number was not delivered to the appointed place, the tsar decreed: "Gentlemen of the Senate, if the governors do not improve soon, designate such punishment for them as thieves deserve, lest you endure it yourselves." In fact, although governors were prominent figures of high rank, junior guards officers were often sent with orders "to pester them incessantly and spur them to collect more money." Once, when he was informed of the unpunctuality of a governor in supplying lists of revenues and expenses, Peter became especially angry and ordered that one Lieutenant Karabanov be sent "to fetter the legs and put a chain on the necks" of all officials in charge of taxes and to hold them in the chancellery until they fulfilled the requirements.

The institution of the colleges at the center brought in its train a new reform of the regional (*oblast*) administration. First, a new, uniform administrative division of the land was introduced. We saw that in 1708 vast new provinces replaced the old regions but remained subdivided into unequal districts. From 1715 the provinces were divided into more equal districts: the *doli*. In 1719 this division into *gubernii* and *doli* was abolished, and a new unit was introduced: the "province" (*provintsiia*). The territory previously divided into eight, later ten, *gubernii* now constituted fifty provinces. Every province was divided into "districts" (*distrikty*).[1] The new division was more even in comparison with the previous one, and in this respect it was a step forward in the development of the regional institutions of Russia. During Peter's time the province was a completely separate unit. Unlike the situation under the previous *gubernii*, the provincial administration was now subordinated directly to the colleges and the Senate.

The new administrative unit was furnished with a complex administrative mechanism, borrowed from a Swedish model, which replaced the landrats. The activities of the provincial institutions were administered following uniform regulations common to all the provinces. Provincial administration was also divided up according to the type of business at hand, for which a special organ was created. A *voevoda* was

---

[1] The liberal use of foreign terms, usually complete innovations in Russian, was an outstanding feature of the Petrine reforms. — Ed.

placed in charge of each of the new provinces (*voevody* of provinces which had been centers of *gubernii* continued to be called governors and governors-general, but their authority did not extend beyond the borders of their provinces). The task of the *voevoda* was to see to the "interest of the tsar's majesty and the state's benefit in all things." He was to ensure that good order prevailed in his province and to supervise the activities of the other administrative organs. The *voevoda* maintained his own "Land Chancellery," where he was obliged to receive petitioners at certain days and times. Under him, as head of the chancellery, was the "land secretary" (*land-sekretar*). The reform also established special organs for the financial administration of the province. . . .

One of the most remarkable characteristics of the new administrative structure was its attempt to separate judicial matters. The whole state was divided into ten judicial districts and in each an Aulic Court (*Nadvornyi sud*) of several members was set up and made subordinate directly to the College of Justice. Municipal courts, which were located in every city, were in turn subordinated to the local Aulic Court.

The administration of the cities — that is, of the *posad* or resident commercial and industrial population — was separated from the general administration into a special department (the other estates living in cities — the nobility and the clergy — were not included in the number of "citizens"). The *posad* people themselves were reorganized. Previously divided according to wealth into three classes (*stati*), under Peter they were separated into two orders or "guilds" (*gildy*). The leading capitalists — the wholesale traders and prominent merchants — were assigned to the first guild, while the petty tradesmen and craftsmen of various sorts were assigned to the second. At the same time, all *posad* craftsmen were assigned to corporations (*tsekhi*), which were unions of people working in the same craft. This division into guilds and corporations was borrowed from Europe by Peter the Great. Changes were also made in the structure of *posad* government. Previously, the *posad* assembly chose an elder (*starosta*) to manage *posad* affairs. Under Peter municipal councils (*magistraty*) were introduced in the cities. Each municipal council consisted of several elected townsmen, whose number varied depending on the size of the *posad*. Thus, in cities where there were 200 *posad* households or more, the municipal council consisted of a president, four burgomasters (*burgomistry*), and eight alder-men (*ratmany*). In towns with a smaller number of *posad* households, the councils had fewer members. The presidents and members of the councils were elected from the townsmen at *posad* assemblies and were in charge of collecting taxes from the *posad* and of the work of the *posad* court. All of the municipal councils were subordinated to the Main Municipal Council established [1720] in St. Petersburg, which was to concern itself with the welfare of the *posad* population in the cities.

Such was the structure of the administration introduced by Peter the Great. Heading it was a Governing Senate, the closest confidant of the sovereign, which concentrated in its hands all branches of the administrative and court system and supervised all other organs. From 1722 a procurator-general was appointed to the Senate as "the tsar's eye" and given charge of the procurators and "fiscals" who stood watch over the administration and courts. The colleges occupied the next level of the administration, dividing among themselves the various branches of government (war, foreign affairs, finance, justice, etc.). A new regional division of Russia into fifty provinces, and of the provinces into districts, was introduced. In charge of each province was a *voevoda*, who was responsible for the other local officials and obliged to look after the welfare of the province. . . . A judicial system headed by the College of Justice was separated from the rest of the government and divided into ten district Aulic courts and subordinate municipal courts. Separate municipal councils in charge of the *posad* population of the towns were also established under the Main Municipal Council (*Glavnyi Magistrat*). This new and complex governing machine was to serve the broad goals which Peter the Great projected for his state. His state was to stand on a level equal to the other European states and to lag behind them in nothing.

Claes Peterson

Swedish Antecedents

The Swedish influence on Peter I's governmental reforms was alluded to by M. M. Bogoslovsky in the previous reading. Claes Peterson, professor of law at the University of Stockholm, summarizes here his lengthy investigation — conducted in both Swedish and Russian archives — into the matter. Pointing out the reluctance of Soviet historians to admit any such thing, Peterson argues that the Swedish influence was extensive and that Peter himself played the key role in seeking Swedish models for his reforms (at the time, the kingdom of Sweden was generally considered one of the most advanced states in Europe). Peterson also points out that much of the Swedish "loan" proved ineffective particularly at the level of local government, primarily because the social preconditions for a successful transfer of Swedish institutions — especially a free peasantry — did not exist in Russia.

The aim of this study has been to investigate the preconditions for the administrative and judicial reforms of the last decade of Peter the Great's reign with special regard for the role of Swedish administrative institutions and Swedish law as models for these reforms. The question of the role of Swedish administrative law for Peter's reforms has a long tradition in Russian historiography, but it has never before been the subject of a monographic study of any length.

Contemporary Soviet historians do not by any means deny that the Swedish administrative system was studied in connection with the extensive reforms of the central and local administration carried out in Russia during the last decade of Peter the Great's reign, but it is a common perception among them that the Swedish influence was very limited. They argue that the Swedish administrative forms and legal concepts which were in fact borrowed first went through a "creative reworking," for which reason they find it incorrect to speak of any direct

From Claes Peterson, *Peter the Great's Administrative and Judicial Reforms: Swedish Antecedents and the Process of Reception*, trans. Michael F. Metcalf (Juridical Faculty, University of Stockholm), 1979, pp. 410–417. Published by Nordiska Bokhandelns Forlag.

Russian borrowing of Swedish prototypes. According to Soviet historians, Peter and his collaborators were aware that no foreign administrative system could be implemented in Russia without modifications and therefore chose to borrow only those elements they found applicable to Russian political and social conditions. In addition, the aspects of the Swedish state administration that Peter considered suitable for the Russian reforms were subjected to a thorough reworking. Since no comprehensive study of the Petrine reforms has ever been published in the Soviet Union, however, no one has ever demonstrated how this so-called "creative reworking" was actually carried out.

In view of the lack of any such comprehensive study, one aim here has been to include in this study all of the central and local administrative organs which began to be organized in 1718. Primary interest has been devoted to the initial stages of the reform, while the changes in the central administration carried out in 1722 — the reorganization of the Senate and the founding of the office of procurator-general — have not been touched upon. The presentations of the various administrative sectors have varied in scope as a result of the author's uneven access to Russian archival materials. For this reason, the study of the organization of the new fiscal administration has been the most thorough. . . .

This study has employed a method involving comparison of the Russian administrative organs with their Swedish counterparts in terms of organization and responsibilities. Here the goal has not been to trace verbal agreement between the Swedish and Russian legislative documents; such a goal would not have provided sufficient material for solving the task at hand, since the activities of some Swedish administrative organs were not completely regulated by, or described in, any legislative acts. In cases such as those of [Peter's new financial colleges], therefore, it has been necessary to reconstruct the operating procedures of the comparable Swedish colleges in order to obtain relevant comparative materials for the Russian collegial instructions. The working hypothesis in these cases has been that the Russian legislative documents involved, such as the instructions for [those colleges], were drawn up on the basis of descriptions of the actual operations of the comparable Swedish colleges provided by someone who had had an opportunity to study the activities of the Swedish administration at close hand.

The results of the present study can be summarized in the following manner. Plans for reorganizing the Russian state administration by means of a comprehensive reform first took form in 1714. It was clear from the very beginning that the Swedish administrative structure was viewed as a suitable model for such a reform. The man who took the initial steps and who later emerged as the driving force behind the reforms was Tsar Peter himself. He not only issued directives concerning the measures to be taken; he also participated in drawing up the legislative acts concerning the new administrative organs. Knowledge of the Swedish administration was provided by a German named Heinrich Fick, who had previously served the Swedish crown and whom Peter had sent to Stockholm in 1716 to study the Swedish colleges at first hand. On his return to St. Petersburg, Fick had with him printed or manuscript copies of a very large number of Swedish legislative acts, and his role in the planning and implementation of the Russian administrative reforms can hardly be exaggerated. Soviet historians have described Fick's part in the reforms as that of a passive instrument for the tsar and his collaborators. In sharp contrast to this portrayal, the present study has clearly demonstrated that Fick not only supplied the tsar and the Senate with correct information about the Swedish administrative system, but also took initiatives of his own, thereby influencing the development of the reforms in a direct manner. In recognition of his efforts in the planning of the collegial reform, the tsar gave Fick the estate of Oberpahlen in Estonia. That he enjoyed Peter's goodwill is also evidenced indirectly by Fick's application to the tsar in 1724 to accept him as his special advisor in economic matters.

The principal finding of this study is that the Russian administrative reforms were more dependent upon Swedish prototypes than has hitherto been assumed. Not only was the framework of the administrative structure borrowed from Sweden, but the internal organization and activities of the various administrative organs were also patterned on those of their Swedish counterparts. Thus, we have established that there were connecting links to the comparable Swedish organs within each sector of the Russian administrative system that began to take form in 1718. This study has shown that the Swedish influence was especially strong when it came to the new fiscal administration, while the military administration seems to have been organized independently of Swedish prototypes. It must be emphasized, however, that the Swedish administrative apparatus was a functional entity consisting of fiscal, legal, and military organs, and it was above all in this respect that it came to serve as a desirable model for Petrine Russia. Special interest seems to have been aroused by the military allotment system, which was used to finance Sweden's standing army during peacetime.

Peter's reforms also brought a large body of foreign legal and administrative terminology into the Russian language. Friedhelm Kaiser, who catalogued the foreign legal terms in the Petrine legislative acts, claimed that the administrative terminology was mostly of German origin. At the same time, he pointed out that it is impossible to determine whether these legal terms were borrowed directly from German or via other languages. The present study, however, has demonstrated that a large portion of the administrative terminology that entered the Russian language in connection with the collegial reform came directly from Swedish. This is not to say, of course, that the Swedish administrative terminology was a native Swedish product. To a great extent, the administrative terms used in Sweden had developed from German roots, as Kaiser correctly pointed out. . . .

Foreign administrators were recruited into Russian service to help set up the administrative system that had been borrowed from Sweden. Their task was twofold: they were to facilitate the implementation of the new administrative routines and to train their Russian colleagues. In spite of the fact that the tsar made it very attractive for foreigners to enter Russian service, the recruiting campaign did not achieve the expected results. As an alternative, then, Peter turned to the foreigners already inside Russia, that is, to the Swedish prisoners of war, in his search for foreigners with administrative expertise. As things turned out, however, it proved even more difficult to convince Swedish officers and other Swedish prisoners to enter Russian service. This negative attitude on the part of Swedish prisoners of war is explained by the fact that they were careful to avoid any commitments which might prevent their return home upon the conclusion of peace between Russia and Sweden. Once having entered Russian service, there was a very real risk that a prisoner of war would not be allowed to leave Russia, and even if he were allowed to leave, it was common knowledge that he could face severe punishment at home for serving the enemy in any capacity. According to reports dating from 1720, therefore, there were only ten Swedish prisoners of war in the service of the Russian colleges, and of them only three came from Sweden proper. At the same time, the quota of foreign officials in the colleges amounted to some ten percent of the total administrative personnel.

Many problems were encountered in implementing the reforms of 1718. Having foreigners introduce the new administrative routines proved to be ineffective, since these officials not only had a poor command of the Russian language, if they had any at all, but most of them knew very little about the Swedish administrative system they were charged with introducing in Russia. It soon became apparent that the newly established administrative organs would be unable to operate according to the Swedish methods. The lack of educated and experienced personnel was a difficult problem to remedy given the short period of preparation allowed for the reforms, but the most serious obstacle to a successful implementation of the administrative reforms lay in another area. The structure of the Swedish administration was strictly hierarchical, and each level of the structure could operate successfully only if the level immediately below it also functioned according to its instructions. The whole system was based on a specific social infrastructure that had emerged from a long historical development. Not only did the Swedish local administration require the cooperation of a free peasant class, but its smooth operation was entirely dependent upon a cameral system that was an integral and necessary part of the administrative method.[1] If the Swedish administrative experience were to be reproduced in another country, Swedish legal principles concerning real estate and its taxation would also have to be copied.

The link between the local administrative system and the cameral system would have to be maintained if a loan of the Swedish administrative system were to have the intended effect. But the legal status of the Russian peasantry, that of serfdom, was entirely different from that of the free Swedish peasantry, and this fact was reflected in the way the Swedish local administration was emulated in Russia. The Russians decided, for example, to eliminate the lowest, or parish level, of the

---

[1] As Peterson earlier states, "cameralism was a fiscal and administrative doctrine . . . directed above all toward developing methods to increase state revenues." Cameralist administrative theory and techniques, he argues, had to be learned before Russia could successfully adopt the "unified and regularly functioning" Swedish model of government. — Ed.

Swedish local administration, in which peasant representatives took an active part, and the Russian peasants were not allowed to participate in the administration of justice, as was the case in Sweden. On the contrary, when it came to judicial procedure, the Russian estate owners exercised complete and exclusive jurisdiction over their serfs.

One can see from the Russian collegial instructions, and especially from those for the financial colleges, that the Russian reformers were aware of the connection between the cameral system and the operation of the local administration. Nonetheless, nothing was done to change the Russian cameral system, since neither the political nor the social prerequisites existed for such a thorough restructuring of Russian society. As a result, the Russian local administration was unable to develop methods of operation corresponding to those of its Swedish prototype, and this in turn detracted from the ability of the colleges to carry out their various responsibilities. When the accounts to be submitted by the local administrative organs failed to materialize, the colleges, too, found it impossible to operate according to the manner prescribed in their instructions.

Against this background, it is impossible to agree fully with the thesis prevalent among Soviet historians that the use of the Swedish administrative system as a prototype for the Russian reforms was generally characterized by a "creative reworking." The Swedish prototypes were, of course, modified by the Russians in many ways, but if one considers the reform in its entirety, and especially the reform of the fiscal administration, it is clear that the Russian reformers attempted to introduce the Swedish system without considering the fact that the social preconditions necessary for such a loan did not exist in Russia. When it comes to the Russian administrative reforms, then, it is clear that Peter and his Senate were not as conscious of the important differences between the Swedish and Russian societies as Soviet historians have argued.

One question requiring closer treatment here is why it was that the Swedish administrative system and Swedish law were selected as the prototypes for the Russian reform. . . . It is necessary to comment on the explanations of this phenomenon that dominate Soviet historiography. Soviet historians have offered two basic explanations for Peter's special interest in the Swedish administrative system: (1) since Sweden's socio-economic development occupied an intermediate position between that of the backward and feudal Russia, on the one hand, and those of the more developed countries such as England and Holland, on the other, Peter and his aides did not find Sweden as foreign as they found the maritime powers; (2) Sweden's strictly centralized administrative structure reflected her absolutist form of government, and Peter thus chose it as a prototype for his reforms since it best answered the needs of the emerging Russian absolutist regime.

There is no doubt that Peter and his aides must have realized the differences in economic development between the countries mentioned above, but it is unlikely that this realization was decisive for Peter's choice of a prototype for his reforms. Once Peter decided upon a thorough reform of the Russian administration, his search for a prototype led him to look not so much for the country with the socio-economic structure most similar to that of Russia, but rather for the country with the most systematic and unitary administrative system. On the basis of this criterion, neither Holland nor England could be considered as prototypes for the Russian reforms. Holland's federal form of government was sufficient reason to eliminate it from consideration, and the Russians must have been dismayed at the decentralization of political power in the Dutch system. Nor did England provide a good model. While the tremendous expansion of the English military forces, and especially of the navy, since the Glorious Revolution [1688] had led to an expansion of the administration and to the development of more complicated and sophisticated administrative routines, English administrative developments were not characterized by any sort of systematization; the old institutions were retained at the same time that a series of new ones were founded. The English historian John H. Plumb, for example, has emphasized that "it is vital to remember that although the executive grew with great rapidity between 1689 and 1725, there was little or no reform: offices were created in abundance; next to none, except at Court, were abolished." Prerevolutionary Russian historians argued on these very same grounds that Peter could find nothing to borrow from either England or Holland. Pavlov-Silvanskii thus wrote that "the state institutions in England and Holland . . . were not very fit for adoption because of their close ties with the forms of government of these two countries and because they lacked the systematization which made it easier for Peter to borrow Sweden's administrative institutions."

It was in the Swedish administrative system that the Russians found a structure which suited their political aims and which, because of its apparently simple and rational organization, it seemed feasible to copy. As the Swedish central and local administrative systems emerged during the seventeenth century, they completely replaced all previous administrative organs. In its closed and unitary character, the Swedish state administration was unique in the Europe of the day and contrasted sharply with such administrative systems as that of France, where old feudal institutions continued to function alongside newly created administrative organs, thus producing constant disputes over jurisdiction and a considerable measure of administrative instability. The Swedish administration, all the way up from the lowest unit of the local administration to the nine central state colleges, presented a unitary pattern and a strictly hierarchical organization with clearly defined areas of responsibility and jurisdiction for each official and each administrative organ. Thus, the Swedish system had the prerequisites for a relatively effective central direction of society as a whole. In addition to this, Peter must have been influenced considerably by the broad integration of military and civil administration which had taken place in Sweden during the reign of Charles XI [1660–1697]. The Swedish fiscal administration was designed to create a stable economic base for the maintenance of the standing army during peacetime, and this was a problem that had become a pressing matter for Peter at the time of his reforms. Thus, it is especially important to note that the Russians used the Swedish administrative structure that had existed prior to the Northern War as the prototype for their collegial reform and ignored the extraordinary administrative organs created as a result of the war.

An interesting document in this context is the description of the Swedish government which Heinrich Fick wrote in 1718. In the section of this description entitled "Concerning the Swedish administration after the introduction of absolutism," Fick described what he considered to be the well-organized state apparatus that had emerged since Charles XI had become an absolute ruler. Among other things, he wrote that:

> it is known that there was great disorder in Sweden two hundred years ago and, although that state has since become a hereditary one, the Swedes were unable for many reasons to put it into good shape and good order until King Charles XI was given absolute power through public agreements in 1680 and 1682.

The legal and administrative development which took place during the reign of Charles XI is described here as the work of the monarch himself. The examples Fick cited of the king's contributions are very impressive, and one gets the impression that he was trying to portray Charles XI as a good model for Peter's own reign. Thus, one can read the following passage about Charles XI's accomplishments:

> *From that time good order has spread in Sweden to a great degree; naval regulations, military articles, the administration of the royal household, church regulations, academies, schools, the very best organization of the state colleges, instructions for governors and other officials, codes of law and the whole judicial system, including both high courts and low courts, an* indelning *(allotment) of the land and sea militia, revenues, commerce, customs and manufacturing affairs, the best order, and whatever else can be mentioned — all of this was brought to ultimate perfection during the king's reign, as many solid institutions demonstrate. And while that king was not taught much during his youth, he remedied that by his common sense and his interest.*

The parallels between Fick's description of Charles XI's measures to create an effective administration for the needs of the absolutist state and the administrative and judicial reforms carried out by Peter the Great are striking. Peter's goal seems to have been to create a state apparatus corresponding for all practical purposes to that of Charles XI's Sweden.

Richard Pipes

The New Service State

Motivated primarily by pressing military considerations, Peter I's transformation of the Russian state, as Professor Pipes makes clear, had two major social consequences: a fairly loose and diversified body of ordinary people

Reprinted by permission of Charles Scribner's Sons, an imprint of Macmillan Publishing Company, from *Russia Under the Old Regime* by Richard Pipes. Copyright © 1974 Richard Pipes.

— peasants, townsmen, slaves, destitute nobles, excess clergy — was consolidated into a single homogeneous class of taxpayers; and a largely hereditary landowning nobility was succeeded by a privileged elite whose wealth and status depended mainly on rank obtained in mandatory service to the state. The result, apart from intensifying social cleavages, was a new, or newly strengthened, "service state." Richard Pipes teaches Russian history at Harvard University.

For Peter the Great, the creator of modern Russia's military might, there were sound reasons for keen interest in military matters. Although he is remembered primarily as a reformer, Peter thought of himself first and foremost as a soldier. His inexhaustible energy directed itself from the earliest towards activity involving competition and physical danger. He began to walk when barely six months old and already as a teenager liked nothing better than to play with live soldiers. When grown to his full giant stature, he loved to share the life of ordinary soldiers on campaigns. When a son was born to him, Peter jubilantly announced to the nation that the Lord had blessed him with "another recruit." Peter firmly believed that military power was essential to every country's welfare. In letters to his very un-military son he emphasized the dominant role which war had played in history. Little wonder that during the thirty-six years of Peter's reign, Russia knew only one solid year of peace.

It took Peter no time to discover that with the hodge-podge of old and new regiments which he had inherited from his predecessors he could realize none of his military ambitions. This became painfully clear in 1700 when 8,500 Swedes, commanded by Charles XII, routed 45,000 Russians besieging Narva and then (to use Charles's own words) gunned them down like "wild geese." Nine years later, at Poltava, Peter exacted his revenge. But his triumph was really less impressive than it is usually made to appear because the Swedes, led by their erratic king deep into enemy territory, found themselves exhausted, outnumbered, and outgunned when the decisive battle took place. Two years after Poltava Peter suffered the ignominy of having the Turks surround his army on the Pruth — a predicament from which only the diplomatic skill of P. P. Shafirov, a converted Jew in his service, managed to extricate him.

The establishment of a large standing army, which Peter initiated, constitutes one of the critical events in the history of the Russian state. At Peter's death Russia had a powerful force of 210,000 regular and 110,000 supplementary troops (Cossacks, foreigners, etc.), as well as 24,000 sailors. Relative to the population of Russia at the time (12 or 13 million) a military establishment of this size exceeded by almost three times the proportion regarded in eighteenth-century western Europe as the norm of what a country could support, namely one soldier for each one hundred inhabitants. For a country as poor as Russia, the maintenance of such an armed force represented an immense burden. To enable it to carry the load, Peter had to revamp the country's fiscal, administrative, and social structures, and, to some extent, transform its economic and cultural life as well.

Peter's most pressing need was for money: his military expenditures regularly absorbed 80–85 percent of Russian revenues, and in one year (1705) as much as 96 percent. After experimenting with various fiscal methods, in 1724 he decided to sweep away the whole complicated system of payments in money, goods, and labor evolved over the centuries and substitute for it a single capitation or "soul" tax imposed on adult males. Before Peter's reform, the taxable unit in the village had been either a defined area of sown land or (after 1678) the household. The older methods of taxation permitted the taxpayer to practice evasion: to reduce the tax on land he curtailed the acreage, and to reduce the tax on households he crammed as many relatives under one roof as it would cover. The soul tax, being levied on every adult male subject to taxation, precluded such practices. This method had the added advantage of encouraging the peasant to increase his cultivated acreage since he was no longer penalized by higher taxes for doing so. Peter also increased the rolls of taxpayers by eliminating the various interstitial groups between the taxpaying and servicebearing estates which in the past had managed to escape all state obligations — such as slaves (*kholopy*), impoverished nobles who worked like ordinary peasants and yet were regarded as members of the service class, and clergymen without assigned parishes. All such groups were now integrated with the peasantry and reduced to the status of serfs. This reclassification alone increased the number of taxpayers by several hundred thousand. Characteristically, the amount of the soul tax was determined not by what the individual subjects could pay but by what the state needed to collect. The government estimated its military expenditures to be four million rubles, which sum it apportioned among the taxpaying groups. On this basis the soul tax was initially set at 74 kopeks a year for serfs of private owners, 114 kopeks for peasants on state and crown lands (who, unlike the former, owed no obligations to the landlord) and 120 kopeks for the *posad* [towns-]people. The money was payable in three annual installments and until its abolition in 1887 for most categories of peasants, it remained for the Russian monarchy a fundamental source of revenue.

The new taxes led to a threefold increase in state income. If after 1724 the government squeezed three times as much money out of peasants and traders as before, then obviously the financial burden of the taxpaying population tripled.[1] The money cost of supporting the standing army which Peter had created was henceforth borne primarily by the taxpaying groups which, it must be kept in mind, contributed also indirectly to the military effort by supporting with their rents and labor the service class.

And they bore this cost not only in money and services. In 1699 Peter ordered the induction into the army of 32,000 commoners. This measure was not an innovation, since the Muscovite government had claimed and exercised since the fifteenth century the right to call conscripts. But what previously had been a means of raising auxiliary manpower now became the principal method of complementing the armed forces. In 1705 Peter set a regular recruitment quota, requiring each twenty households, both rural and urban, to furnish annually one soldier — a ratio of approximately three recruits for each thousand inhabitants. Henceforth, the bulk of Russia's armed forces consisted of recruits drawn from the taxpaying classes. These measures represented an innovation of major historic significance. European armies in the seventeenth century were manned almost exclusively by volunteers, i.e. mercenaries; and although here and there men were pressed into service in a manner which came close to forceful induction, no country before Russia practiced systematic conscription. Spain introduced compulsory

---

[1] More recent research has shown this to be an exaggeration. Though the overall tax burden no doubt increased under Peter, it was unevenly distributed as well as vitiated by successive currency devaluations. — Ed.

levies in 1637, and so did Sweden during the Thirty Years' War; but these were emergency measures, and the same held true of the conscription adopted by France during the War of the Spanish Succession. In western Europe, compulsory draft became the norm only after the French Revolution [1789]. Russia anticipated this modern development by nearly one century. The system of annual drafts of peasants and *posad* people, introduced by Peter early in his reign, remained until the military reform of 1870 the normal way of providing manpower for Russia's armed forces. Russia therefore has every right to claim priority as the first country with compulsory military service. Although a recruit and his immediate family received automatic freedom from serfdom, the Russian peasant regarded induction as a virtual death sentence; required to shave his beard and to leave his family for the remainder of his life, the prospect he faced was either to be buried in some distant place or, at best, to return as an old, perhaps disabled man to a village where no one remembered him and where he had no claim to a share of the communal land. In Russian folklore there exists a whole category of "recruit laments" resembling funeral dirges. The farewell given a recruit upon induction into service by the family also resembled funeral rituals.

As far as Russia's social structure was concerned, the main consequence of the introduction of the soul tax and recruitment obligation was to consolidate what had traditionally been a fairly loose and diversified body of commoners, ranging from destitute nobles to ordinary slaves, into a single homogeneous class of taxpayers. The payment of the soul tax and (after nobles had been freed from state service) compulsory military service became hallmarks of the lower class. The contrast between it and the elite became sharper than ever.

Peter's successors made the landlords responsible for the collection of the soul tax from their serfs and formally liable for arrears. The state further charged them with the duty of supervising the delivery of recruits from their villages (the selection of the recruits was entrusted to the community, although this power, too, gradually passed into the hands of landlords). With these measures, the state transformed landlords into its fiscal and recruiting agents, a fact which could not help but enhance their authority over the population, more than half of which was then living on private, secular estates. The most onerous period of serfdom begins with Peter's reforms. The government now continues to abandon the proprietary serfs to their landlords' arbitrary authority. By the end of the eighteenth century, the peasant no longer has any civil rights left and in so far as his *legal* status is concerned (though not his social or economic condition), he can scarcely be distinguished from a slave.

The service estate also did not escape the reformer's heavy hand. Peter wanted to make absolutely certain that he extracted from this group the best performance possible; and with this aim in mind he introduced several innovations concerning education and service promotion which, as long as he was alive to see that they were enforced, made their lives more onerous as well.

Pre-Petrine Russia had no schools, and its service class was overwhelmingly illiterate. Apart from the higher echelons of the officialdom and the scribes, few servitors had more than a nodding acquaintance with the alphabet. Peter found this situation intolerable because his modernized army required men capable of assuming administrative and technical responsibilities of some sophistication (e.g., navigation and artillery plotting). Hence he had no choice but to create schools for his servitors and to make sure that they attended them. A series of decrees made it obligatory for nobles to present male preadolescents for a government inspection, following which they were sent either into the service or to school. Henceforth, hordes of young boys, torn out of their rural nests, were called for periodic inspections to towns to be looked over (sometimes by the emperor himself) and registered by officials of the Heroldmeister's office. A decree of 1714 forbade priests to issue nobles marriage certificates until they could present proof of competence in arithmetic and the essentials of geometry. Compulsory education lasted five years. At fifteen, the youths entered active service, often in the same guards regiment in which they had received their schooling. Peter's educational reform had the effect of pushing back the age of compulsory state service to the very threshold of childhood. Of his reforms, this was one of the most despised.

Another of Peter's reforms which deeply affected the life of the service class concerned the conditions of advancement. Traditionally in Russia, promotion in service rank depended less on merit than on ancestry. Although *mestnichestvo* had been abolished before Peter's accession, the aristocratic element remained well embedded in the service structure.[2] Members of clans enrolled in the Moscow nobility enjoyed distinct advantages over the provincial nobles in appointments to the choicer offices, while commoners were barred from the service altogether. Peter would have found discrimination of this kind distasteful even if it redounded to his advantage. Given his view of the Muscovite upper class as ignorant, irrationally conservative, and xenophobic, it was a foregone conclusion that sooner or later he would try to eliminate aristocratic privileges.

In 1722, after thorough study of foreign bureaucracies, Peter introduced one of the most important pieces of legislation in the history of Imperial Russia, the so-called Table of Ranks (*Tabel o rangakh*). The ukaz set aside the traditional Muscovite hierarchy of titles and ranks, replacing it with an entirely new one based on foreign models. The Table was a chart listing in parallel columns positions in the three branches of state service (armed services, civil service, and court), each arranged in fourteen categories, with one being the highest and fourteen the lowest. The military and civil services were formally separated for the first time, being assigned their own nomenclature and ladder of promotion. The holder of a position listed on the Table was entitled to a rank or *chin* corresponding to it — much as in a modern army, for example, the commander of a company normally holds the rank of captain. It was Peter's intention that every nobleman, regardless of social background, should begin service at the bottom and work his way up as high — and only as high — as his talents and accomplishments would carry him. In the army he was to start as an ordinary soldier. The richer and physically stronger nobles were permitted to begin in one of the two guards regiments (Preobrazhenskii or Semenovskii) where, after a few years of schooling, they were commissioned and either left to serve or else transferred to a regular field regiment. The others began as soldiers in regular regiments but promptly received their commissions. In the civil service, nobles began in the lowest position carrying *chin*. Common scribes, like soldiers and noncommissioned officers, had no ranking and therefore were not considered to belong to the nobility.

---

[2] *Mestnichestvo* was the Muscovite system of basing promotion on family connections. — Ed.

Peter was not content to establish a framework within which landowners were encouraged to better their performance. He also wished to give opportunities to commoners to join the service, and to this end he provided that soldiers, sailors, and clerks who had distinguished themselves in their duties and qualified to hold positions listed on the Table of Ranks were to receive the appropriate *chin*. Such commoners at once joined the ranks of the nobility because in Petrine Russia all who had *chin*, and they alone, enjoyed the status of nobles. Once on the list, they competed with nobles by birth. According to the Table, commoners who attained the lowest officer rank in the military were automatically elevated to hereditary nobility, i.e., gained for their sons the right to enter state service at the fourteenth rank and all the other privileges of this estate. Commoners who made a career in the civil or court services had to reach the eighth rank before acquiring hereditary status; until then they were considered "personal" nobles (the term came into existence later, under Catherine II) and as such could neither own serfs nor bequeath their status.[3] In this manner provisions were introduced for advancement by merit — an intention that ran contrary to other tendencies intensifying social cleavages, for which reason it was only partially realized.

Before long the Table of Ranks turned into a veritable charter of the service class. Since at that time power and wealth in Russia were attainable almost exclusively by working for or with the state, acquisition of *chin* bestowed on the holder uniquely privileged status. He was assured of a government job for himself and, in most cases, for his offspring as well. He also enjoyed the most valuable of all economic privileges, the right to own land worked by serf labor. In the words of Nicholas Turgenev, Russians lacking *chin* were *"en dehors de la nation officielle ou légale"* — outside the pale of the nation in the official or legal sense of the word.[4] Entry into the service and advancement in it became a national obsession for Russians, especially those from the lower middle class. Clergymen, shopkeepers, and scribes developed a consuming ambition for their sons to acquire the rank of a cornet in the army or

[3] In 1845 hereditary nobility was limited to the topmost five ranks, and in 1856 it was further restricted to the highest four. In the first half of the nineteenth century, personal, non-hereditary nobles constituted between a third and a half of all the nobility.

[4] Turgenev was a nobleman and leader of the "Decembrist" uprising in St. Petersburg in December 1825. — Ed.

commissar or registrar in the civil service, which carried the fourteenth *chin*, and in this way to gain access to the trough. The kind of drive that in commercial countries went into accumulation of capital in Imperial Russia tended to concentrate on the acquisition of *chin*. *Chin* now joined *chai* (tea) and *shchi* (cabbage soup) to form a triad around which revolved a great deal of Russian life.

In retrospect, Peter's attempt to change the character of the elite by an infusion of new blood seems to have been more successful in the lower echelons of the service class than at the top. Analysis of the composition of the highest four ranks reveals that in 1730 (five years after Peter's death) 93 percent of its members were drawn from families which had held high office and often analogous positions in Muscovite Russia. It was below these exalted heights, between the fourteenth and tenth ranks, that the greatest changes took place. The Table of Ranks accomplished a considerable broadening of the social base of the service class. The class as a whole grew impressively. The increase can be accounted for by the promotion of commoners to officer rank in the greatly expanded military establishment, the granting of *chin* to holders of lower administrative posts in the provinces, and the enrollment in the ranks of the nobility of landowning groups in such borderlands as the Ukraine, the Tatar regions on the Volga, and the newly conquered Baltic provinces.

New-style silver ruble depicting Peter I as emperor in classical Roman dress. Coin minted in Moscow, 1720. (editor's collection)

PART

IV Economic
Reform

M. E. *Falkus*

The Beginnings of Industrialization

To pursue successfully his wars against Sweden, principally, but also against Turkey and Persia, Peter I had to take steps to expand the Russian economy, particularly its infant industrial sector. M. E. Falkus, of the London School of Economics, surveys these steps and offers data suggesting impressive short-term results. At the same time, he indicates how different industrialization in Russia was from industrialization in western Europe, where it had begun much earlier. Industrialization was "forced" by Peter within a relatively "backward" Russian economy in order to "catch up."

In the economic sphere, as in so much else, the reign of Peter the Great marked a decisive break in Russian history. The last twenty-five years of Peter's life saw the growth of a substantial manufacturing sector which

From M. E. Falkus, *The Industrialisation of Russia 1700–1914*, 1972, pp. 20–26. Reprinted by permission of Macmillan, London and Basingstoke.

gave employment to several thousands of industrial workers. Old industries were expanded, and new ones introduced. Old centers of manufacturing were extended, new ones created. Foreign commerce grew and its main channel was shifted from the White Sea to the Baltic, from the ancient port of Archangel to Peter's newly-constructed capital at St. Petersburg.

Certainly, industrial growth during the first quarter of the eighteenth century was not without earlier foundations. Some large-scale undertakings had made their appearance in the previous century. Ironworks had been established, initially by foreigners, from the 1630s. Here and there "manorial factories," set up by estate owners and using the labor of their own serfs, existed. Self-sufficiency remained characteristic of the Russian village, but some regional specialization was developing, and small-scale village handicrafts and peasant cottage industries were sometimes producing for a wide market. Such specialization was found, for instance, in the iron products from the Tula and Moscow regions, in linens from Tver and Moscow, in leather from Nizhnii-Novgorod, and in salt from the Kama and Upper Volga regions.

The industrial structure that emerged during the first quarter of the eighteenth century was fashioned almost entirely to state requirements. Peter's frequent wars provided the principal driving force and, especially in the early years, the state itself set up and operated numerous enterprises geared to military needs. Cannon foundries and armaments works were constructed, iron and copper mining developed, and geological surveys were initiated to discover mineral resources. Woolen-cloth factories were set up to provide uniforms for the armies, while sailcloth, rope, and other manufactures were developed to provide equipment for the newly-formed navy.

The majority of these state enterprises were later sold or leased to private entrepreneurs, particularly after 1720, and the role of private enterprise in setting up new establishments increased as Peter's reign drew to a close. But the state played a dominant part even in the development of private works. Subsidies, tax exemptions, monopolies, and other concessions were employed to encourage Russians to found manufacturing enterprises. And the state was far and away the main customer for the products of the new factories.

From the second decade of the century, Peter's industrial policies were increasingly influenced by "mercantilism." With the object of lessening Russia's dependence on imported manufactures, Peter fostered a variety of industries such as glass, velvets, brocades, and silk, some of these products being manufactured in Russia for the first time. In addition to the usual subsidies, a strongly protectionist policy was adopted under the 1724 tariff, under which a wide range of goods were subjected to duties ranging from 50 to 75 percent *ad valorem.*

Industrial development under Peter thus bears the character of a "forced industrialization." The achievements were impressive, although there is controversy over the actual quantitative results of Peter's industrialization. At the beginning of the reign there probably existed some 21 "manufactories," of which four were run by the state. One estimate puts the number of new plants founded in Peter's reign at 233, but more recent research indicates lower figures. Another estimate puts the total at 178, of which 40 were for armaments and iron metallurgy and 15 for nonferrous metallurgy; there were also 23 sawmills, 15 woolen-cloth factories and 13 tanneries. Of these enterprises, nearly half were established by the state. The composition of Peter's industries reflected both the state's needs and the extreme backwardness of the country. Nearly all the new enterprises were founded to meet the state's demands, a few to serve the luxury demands of the nobility (a market itself influenced by Peter's Westernizing policies). A mass market did not exist, for as long as the country was tied to a regime of serfdom and as long as agricultural productivity remained low, a prosperous domestic demand could not grow.

Here, then, are some of the threads for an interpretation of Russian industrial history put forward by Gerschenkron.[1] In a very backward country substantial industrialization cannot take place on the basis of mass demand, private domestic capital, and available entrepreneurial resources. The state, if it desires industrialization, has to foster industries. At the same time, according to Gerschenkron, it was a characteristic of Russia that state measures to promote industry produced a further retarding force, a new dimension of backwardness. In Peter the Great's time came the strengthening of serfdom, the crushing taxation on the peasants (a poll tax was introduced in 1724), and various other adverse factors which increased the already powerful forces in the economy resistant to spontaneous industrial growth. In the latter part of the nineteenth century industrialization was again pursued at the cost of

[1] See the reading to follow by Alexander Gerschenkron. — Ed.

internal purchasing power, and at the cost, in consequence, of the spontaneous development of internal demand.

Among the positive results of Peter's "forced industrialization" were the foundation of important new centers of mining and metallurgy in the mountain regions of the Urals, the strengthening of various industries in the Moscow region, particularly textiles, and the creation of a wholly new center of manufacturing in St. Petersburg. By the end of Peter's reign a substantial proportion of cloth for army uniforms was produced by Russian factories, and dependence on imports over a wide range of manufactures had been lessened. St. Petersburg possessed not only factories supplying the needs of the army and navy but also those catering to the demands of Peter's court. In 1700 Russia had been an importer of iron; by 1716 she was a net exporter, and later in the century became the world's largest iron producer. In the Urals some 76 iron-works were in operation by 1725, and by the end of Peter's reign, the annual production of the Urals works amounted to some 800,000 poods of pig-iron.[2] By this time state enterprises were joined by private concerns, some of them, such as those belonging to the Demidov family, operating on a very large scale.

Nearly all the private entrepreneurs came from members of the merchant class, and a number of Marxist historians have taken this as evidence that Russia by the opening of the eighteenth century had reached the stage of "commercial capitalism." One must not exaggerate, however, either the availability of capital or the amounts required by Peter's industries. Some historians have drawn attention to the chronic shortage of capital in Russia at the time and have pointed out that the state played a major part in subsidizing even the private establishments. Moreover, the enterprises themselves were often exceedingly small, employing only a handful of workers and little fixed capital. Certain enterprises, it is true, were very large. Thus a sailcloth factory in Moscow employed 1,162 workers, and a state woolen-cloth factory employed 742, while a private cloth factory had a labor force of 730. The largest works were evidently to be found in the Urals iron industries, and the mining enterprises in the province of Perm employed some 25,000. But some of the big enterprises were in reality more like colonies of domestic handicraft workers, working for a single employer, than large-scale factories. . . .

---

[2] 1 pood = approximately 36 lb. (16.3 kg.).

In any event, the development of industries in the first quarter of the eighteenth century imposed severe problems for the backward Russian economy. The acute shortage of skilled labor was solved, to some extent, by the introduction of foreigners. Peter here, as in so many of his industrial policies, continued the policies of his predecessors but on a considerably enhanced scale. Returning from his first European visit in 1698, Peter brought back hundreds of foreign technicians and skilled artisans, and encouraged foreign entrepreneurs to set up establishments in Russia. Young Russians were sent to Europe to learn the secrets of Western industrial processes.

A further major problem was the recruiting of labor for the new enterprises. The grip of serfdom had increased in Russia during the seventeenth century, and there was no group in the stratified society that had emerged which could form the basis of an industrial labor force. Some free labor did exist, but on an inadequate scale for the new industries. Peter tackled the problem in part by drafting criminals and beggars to the factories. At the same time, state peasants were ascribed in large numbers to enterprises, both state and private. And — a new departure — merchants were allowed to purchase serfs for industrial labor. The latter concession was generalized in a law of 1721 which permitted merchants to buy whole villages for their enterprises. Such serfs did not become the property of the purchaser, however, but became the property of the industrial enterprise and would remain with the enterprise if ownership changed hands. These people became known as "possessional peasants," and their conditions and treatment were frequently far worse than those of agricultural serfs. Possessional factories were particularly important in the Urals industries, where the problems of recruiting a labor force were most acute.

Peter thus solved the problems of industrial labor by extending serfdom to industry. The growth of industry went hand in hand with the further depression of the status of Russian peasants and with further rigidities in the social composition of Russian society. The influence of the state in industrialization had consequences which were felt until the time of the Emancipation [1861] and beyond. Market forces could operate to only a limited extent in obtaining a supply of industrial labor. In numerous private manufacturing establishments the various government concessions and privileges, as well as the regulations that accompanied the establishment of possessional factories, involved the state bureaucracy in detailed administration and control. The financing of

Peter's industrial and military activities led to greater and greater burdens on the servile population, and the poll tax was to remain in force for more than thirty years after the Emancipation.

Peter the Great's industrialization policies have been discussed in some detail because they bring out important general factors in Russian economic history. It should be obvious that Russian society was very different from that in the West, and its problems were correspondingly distinct. Russia was more backward than her European neighbors, and only the state could mobilize the capital and entrepreneurship and provide a market sufficient for a major increase in the tempo of industrial development. Russia's political aspirations necessitated the establishment of certain industries; the realities of Russian backwardness dictated an institutional framework (such as the possessional factory and the strengthening of serfdom) which imposed further rigidities on the economy.

Arcadius Kahan

The Durability of Industrialization Under Peter

In an important revisionist essay, Arcadius Kahan, late professor of history and economics at the University of Chicago, is concerned to correct the negative view of earlier Russian historians regarding the durability of the industrialization in Russia begun under Peter I. Rejecting the notion of "years of slump," he characterizes the decades after Peter's death as a period of adjustments made within an essential continuity of governmental policy and economic activity, the latter as seen particularly in the development of manufacturing in Russia by a growing "entrepreneurial group." In so doing, he presents evidence of "impressive achievements" attributable to Peter's policies not only in industry, but in foreign trade and the mobilization

From Arcadius Kahan, "Continuity in Economic Activity and Policy during the Post-Petrine Period in Russia," *The Journal of Economic History*, vol. 25 (March 1965), pp. 61–85. Reprinted with the permission of Cambridge University Press.

of labor as well. Finally, Kahan makes valuable points about Peter's economic views and "command style" of leadership.

To discuss economic activity in Russia of the eighteenth century is to deal with an economic and social order that antedates the age of industrialization. Industrial activity in Russia during the eighteenth century was carried on within the political framework of an autocratic state, with ill-defined norms of legal behavior, and against the background of a serf agriculture which reached its apogee during this very period. The state of the industrial arts was low in comparison with western European standards, and the use of waterpower as a motive force in manufactories was introduced in Russia by foreign entrepreneurs only in the seventeenth century. Against this background, the efforts by Peter the Great to modernize Russia appear genuinely heroic. The demands of his policy forced the government to engage directly in a vast program of establishing new industries, of converting small handicraft workshops into large-scale manufactures, and of encouraging private entrepreneurs to follow the government's example.

The Petrine policy of what we would now describe as forced economic or industrial development was marked by a relentless race against time, dictated by political reasons. This haste and urgency led to major disproportions in the structure and production pattern of the "Petrine manufactories" and caused their mode of operation to differ from that of any other industrial complex built up elsewhere over a longer time span. It is the fate of the manufacturing sector in the Russian economy during the post-Petrine period that concerns us in the following discussion.

The early development of manufactures in eighteenth century Russia presents an interesting issue for the economic historian — namely, the problem of the continuity or discontinuity of the initial industrialization.

It will be argued that the economic process set in motion during the Petrine period continued during the post-Petrine period and that the policies that supported the early industrialization drive were not abandoned by Peter's successors. It will be assumed that the early development of a new branch of the economy is not necessarily marked by a smooth upward movement of its output curve. Such a development is in most instances a process by which the new branch asserts itself against various adverse social conditions, involving conflicts of economic interests and policies. However, when the general activity is being pursued and similar policies persist over a longer time span, the basic continuity is established.

The traditional concept of discontinuity in industrialization in Russia has given rise to two assertions voiced from diametrically opposed positions. The first concluded on the basis of this assumed experience that government intervention, so frequently undertaken during the period of early industrialization, is futile and unreliable as a factor in economic development. The second argued that this experience proves the dependence of continuing economic growth upon the continuity of an active governmental policy and hence that the government's direct involvement is the decisive element in the economic growth effort of a nation. Thus both the liberal school and the statist school of Russian historians have assumed the discontinuity in economic growth during the post-Petrine period of the eighteenth century to be a fact and have used it as an historical example to lend added credibility to their respective positions. . . .

In the following essay, three problems are singled out for investigation: (1) How durable was the industrial development in Russia that occurred during the Petrine period? (2) How serious and of what nature was the slump in economic activity during the immediate post-Petrine period, and what was its impact upon the industrial sector of the Russian economy? (3) Could the post-Petrine period be considered as one of major discontinuity in the economic growth of Russia?

The theses of P. N. Miliukov and V. O. Kliuchevsky about economic discontinuity may be summarized as follows: The growth of manufactories under Peter the Great cannot be attributed to the increase of demand in the domestic market and is therefore not a result of the organic development of the domestic industry; it was created by an extra-economic factor — the government — to serve its political ends. The existence of the manufactories depended upon government protection and special privileges, hence their instability. Periods of government inactivity in the economic sphere are therefore correlated with slumps or declines in industrial activity. Miliukov supports his argument about the lack of durability of the manufactories created during the Petrine period by the fact that by 1780 only 22 of them were in existence. Kliuchevsky reaches the sweeping but obviously erroneous conclusion for the whole period 1725–1762 that "industry after Peter did not make any noticeable progress."[1]

Although one might agree with some of these conclusions, I would question most of them as being irrelevant as explanatory factors and some of them as being simply erroneous. The general impression of a feeble state of manufactories in Russia and of a lack in indigenous entrepreneurship is largely built upon statements made by Peter the Great himself and upon the choice of methods used by him in his attempts to introduce and develop manufactories in Russia. Such a view ignores the historical experience of other countries at a similar stage in their economic development.

In discussing the nature of the post-Petrine period, one cannot ignore some features of the Petrine period that most impressed contemporaries and posterity (historians included). The features of Petrine economic policy that made the most lasting impression were: (1) the scope of public works and the creation of social overhead; and (2) the effort to supply the army and navy. Certainly in terms of employment (not in efficiency), the public works of the Petrine period remained unrivaled throughout the entire eighteenth century.

Thousands of forced laborers (drafted serfs) were employed in the construction of the Voronezh wharves and of the Black Sea navy during the turn of the century; many thousands were employed in the digging of a Volga-Don canal; thousands were mobilized yearly for the construction of the Taganrog harbor and for the erection of fortifications in Azov and Troitsk. All these projects were later discontinued and abandoned. For years, resources (human and capital) were squandered in the construction of the Vyshnevolotskii canal system, in harbor construction in Rogervik, etc. They all were monuments to the ability of the Petrine administration to mobilize the labor effort of the nation. Of course, the crown of Peter's domestic projects was the construction of the new capital, St. Petersburg. We now have some notion of the magnitude of its drain on labor resources (see Table 1).

The government's public works programs do not account for all of the redistribution of resources or forced savings that were channeled into construction. Government pressure forced both the nobility and the merchants to channel a part of their savings or wealth into housing construction in St. Petersburg, in addition to substantial government

---

[1] P. N. Miliukov is identified on p. 184, V. O. Kliuchevsky on p. 25. — Ed.

| TABLE 1 | Draft Quota and Actual Number of Landlord Serfs Employed in the Construction Works in St. Petersburg, for Selected Years |

Year	Draft Quota	Actually Employed
1706	40,000	20,000
1709	40,000	10,374
1710	43,928	n.a.
1711	30,448	24,381
1712	28,800	18,532
1713	33,779	n.a.
1714	32,253	20,322
1715	32,253	n.a.
1719	n.a.	6,232
1720	n.a.	4,853

expenditures. Such investments might have turned out to be profitable for the individuals in the long run, but within the time horizon of the people involved they were considered as an inferior alternative to the ones existing elsewhere as witnessed by the coercion applied by the government to enforce the investment in housing construction. Contemporaries regarded these involuntary investments as a form of additional taxation.

The channeling of labor and capital into construction and public works on such an unprecedented scale left its imprint both upon Peter's contemporaries and upon subsequent generations. No Russian historian has tried to find out what the real costs were, as though the mobilized labor force had zero opportunity costs. This is mentioned, not to question the economic rationale or political wisdom of the public works, but to call attention to the lack of elements of economic analysis in the works of historians. Obviously, the awe and admiration of posterity for the labor mobilization policies of Peter were strengthened in view of the fact that they coincided with army recruitment carried out on an almost yearly basis (see Table 2).

The volume of employment in manufactories is obviously dwarfed by the large numbers of the military draft and the forced labor mobiliza-

TABLE 2	Yearly Number of Draftees in the Army and Navy				
Year	*Number*	*Year*	*Number*	*Year*	*Number*
1701	33,234	1713–1714	16,342	1724	20,550
1705	44,539	1714	500	1726	22,795
1706	19,579	1715	10,895	1727	17,795
1707	12,450	1717	2,500	1729	15,662
1708	11,289	1718	15,389	1730	16,000
1709	15,072	1719	14,112	1732	18,654
1710	17,127	1720	4,000	1733	50,569
1712	51,912	1721	19,755	1734	35,100
1713	20,416	1722	25,483	1735	45,167

tion in the Petrine period. Any increase in industrial employment in the post-Petrine period could not compensate, in terms of sheer numbers, for the decline in employment in public works.

The effort to supply the needs of the army and navy during the Petrine period was most impressive. Within fifteen to twenty years the newly established ironworks and munition factories were able to supply the needs of an army of about 220,000 men. In 1715 the Russian artillery already had about 13,000 domestically produced cannons of various sizes; by 1720 the yearly output of military rifles exceeded 20,000; a navy on the Baltic and Caspian seas was constructed and well equipped. The textile industries supplied an increasing portion of army cloth, all of the sailcloth, etc. This was the work of one generation.

Miliukov assumed the survival rate of manufacturing enterprises to be *the* criterion of the durability of entrepreneurial effort of a particular period. Leaving aside for the moment the validity of this assumption, it is necessary to point out certain pitfalls involved in Miliukov's procedure. The computation of a survival rate of enterprises that ignores the distribution of enterprises by size or by industry branches is a biased measure. Moreover, to ignore the distinction between one-owner firms, partnerships, and joint-stock companies tends to obscure a great deal of what we know about the various elements that determine the life structure of firms in general. These criticisms may be made without even raising considerations of the peculiar characteristics of turnover in ownership of enterprises or of the survival rate of firms in most European countries during the eighteenth century in general and of the conditions of Russian manufactories in particular. But quite apart from all this, additional considerations make the survival rate a poor indicator of entrepreneurial activity. Available evidence indicates that industrial plant and equipment were not the largest item in the total investment expenditures of particular firms; hence, the continued existence of an industrial firm was only in part influenced by the desire to maintain the capital stock as a unit. We have evidence that skilled labor frequently constituted a greater asset than the physical capital stock. Therefore, transfers of capital stock and skilled labor from one firm to the other took place for entirely different reasons. Second, given the continuous engagement in domestic or foreign commerce, the occurrence of transfers, mergers, etc. might not necessarily reflect upon the viability of the manufacturing enterprises themselves. In addition, partnerships and joint-stock companies, organized to remedy the scarcity of capital, were frequently broken up, transformed, and replaced, thus distorting the purely numerical relationship between the number of firms and the stock of capital with which the firms were identified. By tracing the history of individual enterprises and the transfers of labor and equipment, it is possible to ascertain a much greater real continuity than Miliukov was able to observe. An additional fallacy of Miliukov's approach in making the survival rate of the firms *the* criterion of entrepreneurial efficiency lies in his total disregard of both general and specific conditions that affected the operations of enterprises during this period. He disregards such phenomena as the transition from war to peace and its impact upon the product mix — a transition that not all modern enterprises could survive; the relative insecurity of life and property; forced relocations; and the risks of fire and floods, to mention just some items of a rather extensive list.

The survival rate for private ironworks for the period 1725–1745 was 86 percent. A survival rate of 72 percent for the same period for enterprises in all branches of the textile industry further weakens the validity of Miliukov's assertion. A closer scrutiny of the older surviving enterprises reveals that they were of larger average size and of somewhat higher productivity than the ones that were liquidated or the ones established during the immediate post-Petrine period. Under conditions of an almost stable technology, the size of plant, output, and capital endowment was apparently among the most important factors determining the survival of the enterprises. Some advantage from an earlier start on a larger-than-average scale, from superior knowledge of the market, and from possible preferential or privileged treatment by the government should obviously not be dismissed. In result, the survival capacity of the Petrine manufactories was as great as that of any manufactories established during the later periods and certainly contradicts Miliukov's assertions.

The impressive achievements of Petrine policies were identified with the personality of Peter himself. His death could not but leave a mark upon the economic life of the country. From the many historical descriptions of the Petrine and immediate post-Petrine periods, the following general picture can be reconstructed about the immediate effect of Peter's death: Previously pushed and strained almost to the limit of endurance by the "Tsar-transformer," economic activity slowed down for a while. Entrepreneurs, hitherto conscious of a sense of direction, became uncertain whether the pressure in the same direction would be sustained by the new rulers before new directions were taken. The need for a reallocation of available resources, the accumulation and transfer of new resources, and the adjustment to a peace economy required time during which the pressures of the Petrine period had to abate. Consequently, some of the government projects were continued with diminished vigor (e.g., the Ladoga Canal, near St. Petersburg), new projects were not embarked upon, and the conspicuous and massive government activity diminished markedly. The decrease in the scale of government economic activity, however, did not decrease the total activity of the various branches of the economy to the same degree. Not only was there a different effect upon various branches, but the slackening of government economic activity was rapidly compensated for by increased activity in the private sector of the economy.

Let us consider the extent to which the contraction of government activity in the area of public works was accompanied by a general contraction of foreign and domestic trade. With respect to foreign trade, the only continuous data available pertain to trade with Britain, which was Russia's main trading partner (see Table 3).

A few comments are in order with respect to the degree to which the British data are indicative of the pattern of trade in general and for the years under consideration in particular. The chief characteristic of Russian foreign trade was its positive trade balance, the excess of exports over imports. Although the excess of total Russian exports over imports

TABLE 3	Trade of Russia with Great Britain (in £)		
Year	Russian Exports	Russian Imports	Excess of Exports
1715	241,876	105,153	136,723
1716	197,270	113,154	84,116
1717	209,898	105,835	104,064
1718	284,485	79,626	204,869
1719	140,550	55,295	85,255
1720	169,932	92,229	77,704
1721	156,258	95,179	61,079
1722	112,467	54,733	57,734
1723	151,769	56,697	95,072
1724	212,230	35,564	176,666
1725	250,315	24,848	225,468
1726	235,869	29,512	206,357
1727	144,451	21,883	122,568
1728	232,703	25,868	206,835
1729	156,381	35,092	121,289
1730	258,802	46,275	212,527
1731	174,013	44,464	129,549
1732	291,898	49,657	242,241
1733	314,134	42,356	271,778
1734	298,970	36,532	262,438
1735	252,068	54,336	197,732

was proportionately not as high as in the case of Russian-British trade, that excess can be estimated for the year 1726 as against the years 1717–1719 (including 1718, the peak year for Russian exports to Britain during Peter's reign). Exports amounted to 4,238,810 rubles and imports to 2,125,543 rubles in 1726, while for 1717–1719, exports of 2,613,000 rubles and imports of 816,000 rubles were recorded. Consequently, there was a substantial increase in exports for 1726 as against 1717–1719, which can be explained in part by a rise in exports of manufactured goods, both iron and textiles. Thus, the estimates for total trade as well as the British data testify to an unchanged pattern of Russian exports during the post-Petrine period.

The pattern of change of the imports of British goods into Russia during the immediate post-Petrine period can rather easily be explained in terms of the substitution of Prussian wool cloths for the British ones and is in general not typical for the growing tendency exhibited by Russian imports. To the extent that the foreign trade data for 1726 or for Russian exports to Britain can be used as indirect evidence of the state of the Russian economy after Peter's death, at least they indicate neither an interruption in Russia's economic development nor a decline in the industrial output.

The sources of information about changes in the value or the volume of internal trade are even scarcer than those about the changes in foreign trade. The only available series pertains to the volume of trade on the Makarievska Trade Fair, which was an important trading institution but probably not representative of the volume or composition of internal trade in general. But, since the Makarievska Trade Fair was the largest in Russia, it would be logical to expect that a serious economic disturbance would be reflected in the turnover at that fair. Although the figures suggest a general downward trend in the total taxes collected and show no evidence of growth in the custom-duty collections, which more directly reflect the turnover, on the whole the data do not point to a general stagnation in business after the death of Peter the Great (see Table 4).

Granted that there was a general slowdown in governmental economic activity, how strongly did it affect the industrial sector? Was there a slump in the output of Russian manufactories following Peter's death? The normal expectation would be that the cessation of war operations against Sweden (1721) and Persia (1724) should bring about a contraction of military output during the reign of Peter. The most affected branches of manufacturing would be iron and textiles, since their output level depended to a large extent upon the volume of governmental contracts. An examination of those industries ought to provide the clue to the nature of the post-Petrine slump in industrial output.

The change in the output pattern of the iron industry can be derived from the yearly data on total output and on the two sectors, state and private. The temporary decrease in output for 1726 and 1727 registered in the data can in part be explained by factors outside the general impact of postwar contraction. The decline in output was most clearly marked in the state sector of iron manufacturing. Documents

| TABLE 4 | Internal Taxes and Custom Duty Payments Collected on the Makarievska Trade Fair, 1718–1728 (in rubles) |

Year	Internal Custom Duties	Total Taxes Collected
1718	15,374	32,579
1719	14,074	30,957
1720	13,719	29,742
1721	13,735	26,845
1722	13,651	28,416
1723	16,525	28,619
1724	14,704	27,441
1725	15,121	27,340
1726	14,457	23,656
1727	15,803	24,278
1728	10,784	21,982

pertaining to this sector point to two causes: replacement of worn-out equipment, and labor unrest in the ironworks. The decrease of iron output is not explained by any inherent deficiencies of the industry. Of course, an adjustment period was involved during which some markets were expanded (notably foreign markets for state-produced iron) to compensate for the decreased military demand, and adjustments of the output mix had to be made. But there is ample evidence that even during the years of the "post-Petrine slump," there was net investment in the iron industry (see Table 5).

Further supporting evidence for the contention that the "post-Petrine slump" had little effect upon manufacturing may be found in the data of copper output. Not only had the output of copper almost doubled during 1725–1727, but by 1728 the rapid rise of private output had begun, a fact that indicates that private investments had been made during the preceding years, the "years of slump" (see Table 6).

The situation of the textile industry was not as clear-cut as that of the metal industry. A large part of the linen-hemp manufactories was geared to the production of sailcloth, and the sharp decrease in domes-

TABLE 5	Output of Pig Iron, 1718–1735 (in metric tons)		
Year	*State*	*Private*	*Total*
1718	3,636	5,635	9,271
1719	3,622	5,518	9,140
1720	2,539	7,435	9,992
1721	2,752	7,453	10,205
1722	3,125	9,831	12,957
1723	2,233	8,316	10,549
1724	5,012	7,699	12,711
1725	4,717	8,633	13,350
1726	3,586	8,634	12,220
1727	3,472	7.912	11,384
1728	5,025	9,390	14,415
1729	6,185	8,485	14,670
1730	5,307	10,369	15,676
1731	6,323	13,039	19,362
1732	6,387	10,780	17,167
1733	5,962	11,483	17,445
1734	6,421	13,530	19,951
1735	7,198	15,758	22,956

tic naval construction forced the manufacturers to seek foreign markets for their output and to change the output mix of the industry. This accounts for the lack of new investment in this area during 1725–1727.

The wool industry, in turn, had to overcome an internal misallocation of resources with respect to the proportion of wool cloth to coarse wool lining material, previously established as a result of the demands of Peter's army quartermasters. Nevertheless, new wool and silk manufactories were established during the years 1725–1728, indicating that these branches of industry were not paralyzed by what has been called the post-Petrine slump.

Available evidence pertaining to other branches of manufacturing (chemical, leather, etc.) points to a similar conclusion. The years immediately following the death of Peter were years of adjustment for the newly established branches of manufacturing and for the manufacturing enterprises. They were not years of slackening of total demand that,

TABLE 6	Copper Output, 1725–1735 (in tons)		
Year	State	Private	Total
1725	n.a.	n.a.	90.6
1726	155.2	3.2	158.4
1727	164.6	3.0	167.6
1728	150.7	15.8	166.5
1729	176.6	27.9	204.5
1730	166.3	51.2	217.5
1731	168.7	84.0	252.7
1732	143.9	68.8	212.7
1733	134.3	74.7	209.0
1734	179.8	100.3	280.1
1735	145.0	114.2	259.2

according to some historians, caused far-reaching decreases in output and in investment in the manufacturing sector.

Data on the total volume and rate of capital investment would throw light upon the existence of a hypothetical downward trend in manufacturing. Unfortunately, estimates of the total capital investment in manufacturing are not available. The closest approximations to such data are estimates of capital in the ironworks for certain years. Although a number of objections could be raised about the accuracy of the estimates, they can nevertheless be used in such conjectures.

The cumulative estimates supplied by S. G. Strumilin[2] for the period under consideration are the following:

Capital Investment in Ironworks (in 1,000 silver rubles)			
Year	Private	State	Total
1700	22	n.a.	22
1725	124	46	170
1735	288	83	371
1745	870	232	1,102

[2] Soviet economic historian. — Ed.

An approximate division of the total volume of capital investment in the private sector during the period 1725–1735 (1726–1729 and 1730-1735), using the number of furnaces and of forge-hammers installed as an approximate index of capital investment, would indicate about 40 percent for the earlier and 60 percent for the later period. An equal distribution of state investment between the two periods appears to be plausible on the basis of available evidence. Consequently, the distribution of the total 201,000 rubles of capital investment between the two periods yields 85,000 rubles for 1726–1729 and 116,000 rubles for 1730–1735. If we allocate the capital investment outlays for the period 1700–1725 not to the whole period but to about ten years of the most intensive capital construction of ironworks, we end with a yearly average of about 15,000 rubles, while the yearly average for the period 1726–1729 (excluding the outlays for capital repair) would reach the sum of over 20,000 rubles. In iron manufacturing, therefore, there is no apparent evidence of a decrease in the volume of capital investment during the years following the death of Peter the Great.

Among the basic elements of government policy with regard to industry that indicate continuity of the two periods, there can be no doubt that foreign-trade policy was of utmost importance. The need to obtain foreign markets for some raw materials and for industrial products led to a reexamination of the Petrine foreign-trade and tariff policies. This took place during 1727–1731 and resulted in a new tariff in 1731. Most Soviet historians have condemned the 1731 tariff as a betrayal of Russian industrial interests to those of foreign countries and as a major deviation from the Petrine tariff policy of 1724. A more careful analysis of the two tariffs does not substantiate the charge of major liberalization of tariff policies. While the 1724 tariff was unabashedly protectionist, that of 1731 was much more selective in its discriminatory features. It was protective with respect to products manufactured within Russia, both by the new manufactories and by the craft or domestic industries. It was protective with regard to the export of manufactured goods and set high duties upon the export of raw materials used by domestic manufacturers. True, it deviated from the 1724 tariff with regard to the level of duties in a number of cases but was much more effective in enforcing them, whereas previous widespread smuggling had rendered many prohibitive duties of the Petrine tariff ineffective. Built upon the reported market prices of Russian commodities, the new tariff resulted in continuous protection of the commodities produced for mass consumption and liberalized the import duties for so-called luxuries, the domestic production of which was clearly inadequate. The new tariff doubtless also resulted in more normal foreign-trade relations with other countries with which commercial treaties were subsequently concluded. While the desire to conclude long-run commercial treaties with some major partners was apparent, it must be realized that such an operation required concessions from both partners; therefore, commercial and tariff policies had to become more flexible. Although utterances were made about the desirability of Russian industries becoming more competitive in the domestic and world markets, the calculations upon which the tariff legislation rested tended to provide at least a 30 percent margin for the Russian manufacturers (based upon the assumption that the transportation and other costs came up to 30 percent of the price of the imports in the country of origin). Therefore, it seems safe to conclude that the tariff policy of Peter's successors was not less effective in its features protective of Russian industry. In fact, it introduced corrections into some of Peter's typical short-run measures which were designed to achieve high rates of growth in some chosen areas to the detriment of others. . . .

As far as fiscal policy is concerned, no additional burdens were put directly upon the manufacturers. It is difficult to assess the effect upon the demand for manufactured goods which resulted from an increased burden of direct and indirect taxation placed upon the agricultural producers.

There was, however, a turn in government policy that is of considerable significance for our problem. The policy change concerning the transfer of state-owned industrial enterprises to private ownership actually did not contradict the basic tenets of the Petrine period. However, prior to the change in policy it was necessary to test what could only be conjectured by some observers during Peter's reign — namely, the question of the relative efficiency of state-owned and private enterprises. The discussion pertaining to this subject was intensified during the period 1732–1736.

The policy accepted by the government may perhaps be summarized as follows: (1) The higher efficiency of the private enterprises was basically admitted. (2) The state's interest . . . ought to be safeguarded in any transaction involving the transfer of state-owned enterprises to private hands. (3) A major condition of such transfer remained the promise on the part of the entrepreneur to increase capital investment in, and the output of, the particular enterprises.

While the private share in total output increased as a result of the various transfers of previously state-owned enterprises to private ownership, this result was accompanied by an increase in the degree of state control and regulation of the private enterprises. The more refined aspects of the mercantilist system replaced the crude mercantilist policies of the Petrine period. The policymakers apparently decided that state control might serve in lieu of state ownership and that state ownership in the absence of profits was more expensive than the administration of state controls. We can, therefore, observe the simultaneous development of two interrelated phenomena. A more firm establishment of private property rights, accepted as a basic precondition of private entrepreneurial activity, went hand in hand with a more rigid definition of the conditions of exercising ownership rights in the area of manufacturing.

The major areas of government control over private enterprises (including information collection and interference) were defined as follows: (1) preservation of the system of licensing and control of entry into industry; (2) control of the size of operations and of some sources of raw materials and labor (principally when imports and serf labor were involved); (3) control to insure continuous operation of the enterprise; and (4) control and stimulation of capital investment. These policies or controls constituted a step forward in the direction of perfecting the mercantilist system in Russia and thereby could be considered as a continuation of the Petrine policies.

However, my main contention would be that the basic economic continuity between the Petrine and post-Petrine periods in the manufacturing sector was not so much provided by government policy as by the existence of a "natural" link of an emerging distinct group of Russian manufacturers.

It has already been pointed out that the prevailing notion (especially among Russian historians) about the lack of indigenous entrepreneurship and "entrepreneurial spirit" in Russia is based largely upon the views expressed by Peter the Great. In this connection four factors should be borne in mind. (1) Peter, in appraising the entrepreneurial capabilities of the industrialist and merchant group, made the comparison with contemporary western Europe. He underestimated the differences in property rights, risks, and investment returns in western

Europe and in Russia. Therefore, regardless of the many limitations imposed upon private enterprise previously (limitations among which Peter's fiscal policies were not inconspicuous), Peter's characterization of the Russian entrepreneur ought not to be taken as an unbiased observation. (2) Peter's view of Russian entrepreneurs was part and parcel of his political thought and of his ideas regarding his own calling and obligation. He considered himself the guardian of the welfare of his subjects who, because of their ignorance, had to be propelled into new conditions. Possessing superior awareness of new horizons and opportunities, he believed himself entitled to force his subjects to a rude awakening as a ruler who, by his own definition, placed the interest of the community above the interests of individuals. The rudeness of the treatment was justified, in his view, by the urgency of national interests as defined by him. (3) Command and outright coercion in social relations were not yet replaced in Russia by compromise and persuasion; therefore, imposing investment decisions upon entrepreneurs was almost perfectly consistent with methods generally employed in administering other areas of national activity. The impression given by Peter the Great is therefore a blend of "new" Western ideas and "old" Russian methods. (4) The Petrine period of development of manufactories was a period of almost uninterrupted war, with economic policies geared and tailored to the war effort. The largest investments were in the armament industries or those that supplied the army. The general pattern of resource use and the allocation of investment within industry differed from what would be considered optimal during a period of peace; the attitudes of entrepreneurs and the behavior of firms differed also. To understand the challenge and to evaluate the impact of a war lasting a quarter century upon a newly emerging entrepreneurial group were above even the very substantial analytical abilities and intellectual faculties of Peter the Great.

During the Petrine as well as during the post-Petrine period, this newly emerging entrepreneurial group was open to both gentry and the lower strata of merchants and even peasants, within the limits of government licensing. Its structure was in large measure determined by the serf society in which it found itself, and very little effort was exerted by the entrepreneurial group to defy the norms of that society. The main problem for the manufacturers was to be able to perform their economic tasks within the limits prescribed by the social framework. It would, therefore, be a mistake to attribute to eighteenth-century Russian entrepreneurs and manufacturers attitudes and concepts of liberal capitalism. While struggling for broader rights (to consolidate their position and to make more independent business decisions) they were quite willing to operate under an umbrella of basically paternalistic and protectionist government policies. Under the prevailing institutional arrangement, freedom of choice and decision for the entrepreneurs was limited. It was only through negotiations and pressures that the extension of freedom and greater independence from the government could be won, and at that the government was not always willing or able to understand the manufacturers' point of view. Peter seldom got involved in dialogues; his was the style of command. During the post-Petrine period, dialogues between the entrepreneurs and the government became more frequent. It is possible, therefore, to reconstruct some of the opinions and attitudes of the entrepreneurs and representatives of the government and to delineate and distinguish meaningful differences between their respective positions.

While the state officials would elevate the principles of output maximization and growth of investment as the chief criteria of success of manufacturing enterprises, the entrepreneurs would have the profit motive as their chief criterion. Therefore, once established in a particular branch of manufacturing, the owners of the enterprises would favor greater restrictions upon entry than the government would allow (in view of the slow growth in demand, the possibility to benefit from quasi-monopoly profits would rapidly disappear with free entry). The demands for exclusive monopoly privileges were perhaps less frequent during the post-Petrine period than during the preceding one.

The manufacturers were against government attempts to determine the product mix and to set quality standards of production. In the latter case the manufacturers exhibited a more intimate knowledge of the potentialities of the domestic market and the consumer demand.

The manufacturers resisted government measures that would impose upon them the financial responsibility of providing both social overhead (school buildings, roads, churches) and welfare measures for their labor force (accident and unemployment compensation, education, etc.).

They also resisted government price setting, both because of the principle involved and because of their anticipation that the price would be below the market level. Another source of this resistance was the suspicion that price setting ultimately leads to wage setting, which they wanted to avoid. This attitude does not imply that the private manufacturers were necessarily paying lower wages than the state enterprises but only that they guarded their rights to set wage rates in a manner that would maximize profits for the enterprise and would establish wage scales more flexible and geared to the effectiveness of the labor performance.

Needless to say, one of the major aspirations of the manufacturers was to gain a share in the opportunity to employ serf labor wherever that was profitable. Therefore, the actual extent to which manufacturers were able to acquire serf labor for the manufactories might be used as a tentative test of their economic and political influence.

We ought to begin with the assumption that prior to the decrees of March 21, 1762, and August 8, 1762, resistance to purchases of serfs by manufacturers was widespread among the landed gentry: they had been urging for forty years that such purchases be prohibited or limited. Clearly, since it was not until 1762 that such pressures took the form of law, it might be assumed that the existence both of counter pressures on the part of the manufacturers and of some reasons of policy led the government during the reigns of Anna and Elizabeth to steer a middle course. That the government did in fact pursue such a middle course, even going back to Peter's reign, may be learned from an examination of relevant legislation and from the record of actual purchases of serfs by manufacturers. First, about the evidence in terms of legislation: the Petrine policy expressed by the decree of January 18, 1721, was a typical compromise policy. It allowed merchants to buy villages by permission of the Colleges of Mines and of Manufactures under the condition that they remain forever attached to the plants. A similar compromise policy prevailed under Peter's successors.

Second, about the record of purchases: although the data may be inaccurate and somewhat confusing, they point to permission given for purchases of more than 60,000 serfs.

Thus the policies of the state, prior to 1762, allowed the owners of the manufactories to invest in serf labor, thereby enabling them to continue the operations of their enterprises in the absence of free labor. This measure lessened the dependency of the manufactories' owners upon the gentry serf owners and resulted in greater stability for the activities of the industrial entrepreneurs.

The data and observations presented above would indicate two general conclusions: first, that the process of development of manufactures, started in the pre-Petrine period and gaining momentum under Peter, continued — at least in the private sector — into the post-Petrine period; second, that during the post-Petrine period the tendencies toward a strengthening of the entrepreneurial group were developing within a framework of government policy that was rather favorably inclined toward cooperation with this particular group. Thereby, continuity in policy and economic activity between the Petrine and post-Petrine periods was essentially maintained.

Alexander Gerschenkron

Russian Mercantilism: A Specific Pattern of Economic Development

Alexander Gerschenkron, late professor of economic history at Harvard University, provides in this excerpt from a famous work a wide-ranging, highly critical analysis of the motives, costs, and effects of Peter I's economic policies. He highlights Russian "economic backwardness" as the key to the seemingly paradoxical nature of economic development under Peter: paradoxical, ultimately, in that as Russia moved closer to Europe economically and politically, it moved away from Europe with respect to the higher values of civilization — a matter, in essence, of Peter's heavy reliance on coercion to achieve his ends. The argument is clearly polemical at some points but suggestive nonetheless, especially in view of later developments in Russia and the pursuit of "modernization" elsewhere.

Turning . . . to Russian mercantilist experience, I propose to deal exclusively with the reforms of Peter the Great. To confine the presentation in this fashion does not imply that Peter had no predecessors.

From *Europe in the Russian Mirror — Four Lectures in Economic History* by Alexander Gerschenkron, 1970, pp. 69–96. Reprinted with the permission of Cambridge University Press.

Some elements of his policies no doubt were visible during the successive reigns of his father, brother, and sister. In the more remote past certain similarities can be discerned in the second half of the sixteenth century. But those inchoate attempts rather pale into insignificance when compared with what followed them. I know that continuity is an "O.K. word" with historians. Continuity, however, is a term that has more meanings than its users are usually aware of, and so has its antonym of discontinuity. If we use the term in the sense of a sudden change in the rate of change — meaning a kink in the curve of investment and output — then there is no doubt that the first quarter of the eighteenth century in Russia was marked by a momentous discontinuity. It opened a new chapter in the economic history of the country.

Militarily, the period was marked by continual wars, even though the intensity of the conflicts varied. Overshadowing the wars against the Turks — one victory and one ignominious defeat in which the fruits of the earlier conquest were lost — and saying nothing of the Persian War — there was the Northern War which started with the Russian debacle at Narva (1700), lasted for most of the reign, and eventually put an end to Sweden's Age of Empire. Viewed from the shores of the Atlantic Ocean, Sweden may not have stood in the forefront of Western civilization, but for Russia this was the struggle against the West, against an enemy immensely superior in culture, both spiritual and material. In the process of Russian expansion this was the crucial drive to the open seas, that is to say, the push toward the west into Europe. The Black Sea proved unattainable, for the time being, but the Baltic, which Ivan the Terrible [reigned 1533–1584] had craved, but could not hold, was the object of the war and the prize of victory. But while the task facing the Russian government — or, more personally, the Russian autocrat — was modern in the contemporaneous sense of involving him in a conflict with a modern power, all the resources at his disposal were abysmally backward. The problem, therefore, was to lift the military and economic potential of the country to a level more consonant with the nature of the task. In principle, this was the standard mercantilistic situation. In dealing with the economic policies of the Petrine state, I have to point out first the standard ingredients of mercantilism and then touch on its specific Russian aspects.

There is first of all the unification policy. Administratively, pre-Petrine Russia had already been centralized to an astonishing degree.

Still, Peter's administrative reforms greatly tightened the grip of the government over the territory of the state. Weights and measures became more uniform; some old measures were abolished; others were adjusted, as were some measures of length in order to accommodate the foot and the inch which Peter brought to Russia from his trip to England. By contrast, no attempt was made to remove the internal duties. They were not abolished until nearly three decades after Peter's death (1753). This, however, is not surprising. The Renaissance monarchy in France at times even raised the internal tolls and tariffs, the fiscal needs seeming more important than the goal of unification. It is such conflicts and inconsistencies, including that between investment and military expenditures (see below), that bedevil simplistic views of mercantilism which are indeed vulnerable to criticism. Inconsistencies of this sort essentially reveal instability of time horizons of statesmen, and they need not detract from the validity of broad interpretations. But physical unification — the problem of communications — was given great attention [by Peter]. Roads, canals, and bridges were built. The Baltic Sea was linked with the Caspian by a system that hit the River Volga rather far upstream, but still provided an essential connection with the eastern tributaries of the Volga and, by the same token, with the mines and mills of the Ural Mountains. The project to connect the Baltic with the Azov and Black seas by a Volga-Don canal was begun, but remained unfinished. The canal around Lake Lagoda was started as the first step to other and more effective inland waterways between the Neva and the Volga basin, although its construction took longer than anticipated and its completion did not occur before 1732.

As in the West, there was the previously mentioned problem of choice between immediate war expenditures and investment outlays to provide the basis for larger military resources after some lapse of time. There are some indications in the papers of the tsar that he was aware of the problem. But it is precisely at this point that something peculiar becomes visible in the Russian experience. For the impression that one receives, particularly from actions during the first part of the reign, say until 1715, is that the answer to the problem was not a calculated allocative decision, but the demonic feeling that development was a function of willpower translated into pressure and compulsion. The result was the simultaneity of effort in all directions: constructing and equipping the navy; building harbors; creating a new capital in the swamps of the Neva estuary; prospecting for minerals; opening mines; erecting blast furnaces; building factories (even though when it comes to plants that really deserve the name, the numbers were much less than had been assumed by earlier historians); and at the same time reorganizing and re-arming the army and reshaping the administrative machinery of the government. The new civil service was designed to push, press, and squeeze, to overcome resistance, indolence, and dishonesty — except that the deeply ingrained habits of government graft and corruption ate their ways into the new machinery. This happened in spite of the readiness of the tsar's whip, or rather the heavy cudgel he favored, to fall on the shoulders of the guilty dignitaries — to say nothing of torture to which some of them were submitted, of prisons to which they were sent, and of gallows on which they ended.

The very magnitude of the effort — its vigor, amplitude, and persistence — endow the Petrine reign with unique features. Nowhere else in the mercantilistic world do we encounter a comparable case of a great spurt, compressed within such a short period. Nowhere else was the starting point so low; nowhere else were the obstacles that stood in the path of development so formidable. And along with differences in the vehemence of the process were the differences in its character. Nowhere else was the state to any comparable extent the demiurge of economic development. Nowhere else was the latter so strongly dominated by the interests of the state. Hence came the composition of the nascent industry with its concentration above all on production and working of metals as well as on plants producing uniforms for the army, sails, ropes, and timber for the ships, and powder for the guns. Hence it came that the large-scale plants were established and run — at least for some time — by the state; that for those plants the state supplied everything: land and entrepreneurship and management, capital and labor (about which something more will be said presently), and, finally, the demand. It is true that at times, in a sudden flight of fancy, Peter would order the establishment of a factory producing Venetian mirrors or of a workshop producing Gobelin tapestries, but those short-lived although costly escapades must be seen as aberrations from a goal that in general was pursued with unswerving constancy. The *manufactures royales* in France did cater to the court's demand for luxury, and that demand served an important social and political function: the splendor of the court was to reconcile the nobility to its loss of power to the monarchy. In Prussia, much poorer than France, the problem, during a certain period, was solved by granting the nobility increasing rights over the peasantry and by appeasing them in this fashion. But in Russia the problem did not exist at all. The Russian state was poor but strong.

The combination of poverty and the strong state resulted in pressures that were incomparably greater than those produced by mercantilistic policies in other countries. The budgetary revenues were but one of the forms these pressures took, but the fiscal policies reveal them with particular clarity. The bulk of the revenue came from direct taxes and internal tariffs, the latter partly being in the nature of a sales tax and even a turnover tax. But nothing indicates the desperate urge of the government to squeeze additional money out of the population than the crop of new indirect taxes. An immense amount of ingenuity went into designing them. A new office — that of *pribylshchiki*, literally "profiteers," people working for the profit of the state — was created. Those were men whose job it was to suggest new revenues. It was one of them who had the idea — speedily put into effect — that every petition to the authorities was to be written on a special paper with an eagle stamped upon it, the petitioner having to pay for the value of the stamp. The requirements of this "eagle paper," incidentally, remained on the statute book until the revolution of 1917. Everything imaginable was taxed: watering horses and beehives, peasants' private bathhouses and their beards as well as the "illegal," that is, "un-German," dress of people in the towns. It is doubtful whether all these flights of fiscal imagination actually produced results that were consonant with the effort involved in inventing and collecting these taxes. According to Miliukov, the "eagle paper" in 1724 brought about two per mille of total revenue and the proceeds of taxes on dress and beards amounted to about one-quarter of one per mille of the total.[1] But no source of revenue, however small, was disdained. The fiscal edifice was finally crowned in the penultimate year of the reign by the introduction of a poll tax or "soul tax" based on regular censuses of the population — this tax, too, remaining in force for nearly 160 years. The precise evolution of the tax burden over the period of the reign is still a matter of controversy. A well-known Soviet economist, S. G. Strumilin, even argued that it was lower per head in 1724 than it had been in 1680. But this extreme position is based on very questionable computations and the only thing that can be concluded from the debate is that the rise in the per capita tax burden,

---

[1] The historian P. N. Miliukov is identified on page 184. — Ed.

while perhaps somewhat less than that computed by Miliukov in his standard study of Peter's budget, was still disastrously large.

Strumilin, for rather obvious reasons, is at pains to show that Peter's reforms did not lead to a "ruination" [*razorenie*] of the Russian peasantry. It should be noted first that the tax burden of 1680 was already intolerably heavy, and Kliuchevsky said with reference to that year that "the paying forces of the population had been stressed beyond the point of exhaustion."[2] On the other hand, it is natural that after the end of the Northern War (1721) some relief of the tax burden — as compared with the previous years — could, and in fact had to, take place. But a comparison between 1680 and 1724, interesting as it may be for some reasons, is of limited importance when the problem is to measure the weight of the fiscal burden imposed upon the peasantry during the first two decades of the eighteenth century. Using, wherever possible, data contained in Strumilin's study and making most conservative assumptions, I have computed the tax burden at the beginning of the second decade of the century — that is, *after* the decisive victory at Poltava in 1709 — as amounting to 64 percent of the grains harvested from the peasant household's allotment of arable land. This is surely a most shocking result, and whatever admiration Strumilin felt for the great achievements of the "Transformer" on the throne, should not have prevented him from making a similar computation. I may be not wrong in assuming that this making light of the disastrous cost to the people was designed to suggest and justify the inference that Stalin's superindustrialization and collectivization policies were also altogether tolerable.

Yet, compulsion went far beyond confiscation of a huge portion of the population's income which even Strumilin — very implausibly in the light of his own data — believes to have been around 20 percent of total national income. Also, 20 percent would be quite excessive in a country where the standard of living was probably below anything that would have been considered a subsistence minimum in the West. Supplying manpower for the army and navy, for construction projects, for mines and factories, for forest work and for transportation was the area where brute force was most clearly displayed. The tsar's lack of concern for the cost of his projects in terms of human lives was absolute. It may be an exaggeration that hundreds of thousands of workers perished in

[2] The historian V. O. Kliuchevsky is identified on page 25.

the construction of the — subsequently lost — port of Taganrog on the Sea of Azov, but the figure was plausible enough for a qualified acceptance by Kliuchevsky. And similar statements were made of the Baltic ports. It is probably natural that horrors of this sort appear to be of little weight to people of Strumilin's ilk who have lived through the contemporary experience of the Soviet industrialization.

As in the West, there were the stern measures against vagrants and beggars. Even in this respect, the Petrine state went one better on the West by attempting to punish not only the receiver, but also the giver of alms — a step that was bound to remain ineffective in a country where a beggar was considered to be a representative of Christ and possibly Christ himself. But the impressment of beggars represented only one aspect of the labor policy — even though in the factories in Moscow and two other cities (Iaroslavl and Kazan) in the 1730s more than 21 percent of the labor force apparently had been beggars before being brought to the factory. Year by year, orders went out to local authorities all over the newly established provinces of the huge country to send men — state peasants — to places many hundreds of miles from their native villages. Mines and factories received whole villages assigned to them; many of those villages were located far away from the place of employment. In the later part of the reign the government began to transfer mines and factories into private hands; individuals had to take them over whether they wanted to do so or not — or as Peter put it, "be it willingly or unwillingly." Thus even the private entrepreneur could be, and at times was, created by appointment — by a fiat of the state, just as Molière's Sganarelle was made a *médecin malgré lui* [a "doctor in spite of himself"] by having been beaten with a big stick. It was in this later period (1721) that the private entrepreneurs were given the right to purchase villages of serfs, who were to be tied permanently to the factories.

There has been a debate going on among Soviet historians as to whether the enterprises established under Peter were capitalistic or feudal. The faith in the usefulness of such ambiguous labels is more remarkable for its childlike quality than for its explanatory power. There is no doubt that skilled labor — masters and foremen — imported from abroad were contractual workers who earned very high wages and were extremely well-treated. Many of them proved ignorant and inept, quite unworthy of their hire. Some of those who came were just the jetsam and flotsam of foreign shores. But Peter did not follow the angry advice he received to send such men away in disgrace. Foreigners were needed, and there should be no tales told abroad about their ill treatment in Russia. . . .

By contrast, native workers were exposed to an entirely different treatment, both with regard to income and personal freedom. Even to the extent that so-called *free* labor was used, the adjective must be taken with the greatest possible caution. There is a regrettable tendency of some Soviet historians to speak of free labor as soon as a wage was paid. Apprentices were tied to the factory for seven years plus three more years after the completion of their apprenticeship. More importantly, delinquent debtors were sent to the mines, if they were able-bodied males (old people and minors, who as heirs also could be delinquent debtors, were to be put to less strenuous jobs); if they were females, they were dispatched to the weaving sheds. Criminals of both sexes naturally were used as heavy laborers. Prostitutes were sentenced to labor "without limit of time and if necessary until death." What mattered more was that time and again large numbers of artisans were forcibly collected in Moscow and other towns and sent to the Urals. A salter could ask the government for delivery of 9,000 laborers and, after some bargaining, receive 5,000. Year in, year out, decrees were issued ordering mobilization of 40,000 workers to be sent under guard to St. Petersburg from all over the country, including Siberia; while the home villages and home towns of the laborers were held to pay for their sustenance. Thousands of artisans were forcibly brought to St. Petersburg for permanent settlement. At times promises were made designed to attract contractually hired labor to factories and other projects, but when, later on, the census for the poll tax caught the so-called free workers in factories, they were subsequently tied to the factories for good, that is to say, enserfed. Children of soldiers as well as older soldiers were forcibly used as laborers, the service of a soldier in the Petrine army and afterwards being for lifetime and ending only with incapacity by illness or old age. Strumilin must admit that "after 1726 in state factories also recruits conscripted beyond the military needs of the army were added to the labor force." "But," he goes on to say, "they received wages just as other workers and fulfilled the same functions as the others." By this line of reasoning also a peasant serf put into a gentry factory and given money to keep body and soul together would be regarded as a freely hired laborer and the enterprise would become a "capitalist" enterprise. This is a fairly foolish position, stubbornly maintained in order to make a rather irrelevant point. What matters, of course, are not terminological quibbles, but the historical fact that it was the power of the state that was used in the historical process of creating the industrial labor force. Wage or no wage, the labor was essentially a coerced, forced labor, created as an industrial labor force by the fiat of the state. It is not surprising, therefore, that most of the mines and factories looked like fortresses and were guarded by detachments of soldiers in order to prevent escapes.

Nor is it surprising that industrial labor should be essentially unfree labor in a state that was a "service state," or as the Russian phrase runs, a "serfdom state." For it was not only the peasantry that was enserfed to the gentry.[3] The gentry, created by the state, was under the obligation to serve the state, and the serfdom of the peasantry had a clear social function — that is, to pay for the services of the gentry, both military and civil. By serving the gentry the peasant was serving the state. Therefore, the never-ending cogitations of Marxian historians in Russia about the class nature of the Petrine state — was it a gentry state or was it a merchants' state? — miss the essential fact that the state was not the state of this or that class. It was the state's state.

The Marxian approach which has yielded extremely useful insights in appropriate periods and circumstances — say England of the nineteenth century or Austria in the interwar period, to illustrate at random — becomes altogether sterile when applied to Petrine Russia. Marxism at all times had difficulty with explaining dictatorial power. Even when, as in the case of Napoleon III,[4] the state that was not dominated by a certain class could be presented as *originating* from an equilibrium of class power, the problem still remained that once the dictatorial state was established, it was able to pursue an independent policy of its own because it had become a power in its own right. Engels, who created the "theory" of equilibrium of class forces, was at pains to present such equilibria as "exceptional" situations arising from the special conditions of a moment.[5] Even Engels's own examples, which include two centuries of absolute monarchy, do not fit his definition too well. But when it comes to Russia, it is not only that the use of terms such as "exception" or "moment" is patently unsuitable to characterize the course of Russian history and the role of the state in it. The

---

[3] The term "nobility," rather than "gentry," is used in most of these readings. — Ed.
[4] French emperor, reigned 1852–1870. — Ed.
[5] Friedrich Engels (1820–1895), collaborator of Karl Marx. — Ed.

overriding consideration is that it would make little sense to regard the autocratic state as emerging from equilibrium of class power. It was not class power relations that created the state. The obverse was true: it was the state that was creating the classes: labor, and even the entrepreneurs, although soon more and more men became ready to make use voluntarily of the great benefits that were held out to them by the state. And even though the state did not create the peasantry, it was the policy of the state — through its methods of repression, its passport system, introduced by Peter, as well as its fiscal arrangements — which kept the peasantry put and tended to reduce, though not to stop, its escape from oppression into the wide open spaces of the East. But without classes as independent forces, the materialistic conception of history becomes sterile because the phenomenon of the independent state involves the primacy of the political rather than of the economic factor, the latter playing an instrumental role in the service of the former. Marxism in general found it difficult to place the mercantilistic state within its conceptual framework, but the degree of the difficulty varied from country to country, reaching its maximum in Russian mercantilism.

Before I proceed to summarize the comparison of Russian mercantilism with that of the West, I must refer to an aspect of Russian mercantilism that was less in evidence in Russia than elsewhere. I am referring to the fact that the Russians, among their manifold borrowings from the West, did not include the Western preoccupation with foreign trade and precious metals. To some extent, this is reflected in the lexical changes in the Russian language and a word thereon may be in order. As a result of the intensive borrowing from abroad, things never seen before and often even never heard of before made their appearance in Russia. New things — and concepts — required new words, and the language was therefore flooded with foreign words which were very frequently quite imperfectly Russified. It is interesting to note then that of some 3,500 foreign words that entered the language during Peter's reign, about one quarter of them were shipping terms; another quarter were connected with government administration; the third quarter were military terms; and the balance was taken up by miscellaneous words with a preponderance of luxury terms imported from France, either directly or by way of Germany and Poland. But what is striking is the absence of both economic terms and business terminology. There were perhaps two dozen borrowed words which could be stretched to suit the concept. In particular, accounting terms were missing altogether. This is as it should be. The economic enterprises created during the Petrine spurt were not oriented toward any careful calculus of costs and revenues. The state, that is, the Russian people, were to foot the bill, and profitability or its absence aroused little interest. The ingenuity of the previously mentioned "profiteers" that went into invention of new minute taxes — each of them requiring a special collecting apparatus — was not matched by a comparable endeavor in the sphere of industry, except, of course, for the perennial struggle against deceit and corruption. Incidentally, the "profiteers" themselves often showed excessive interest in their private profits. One of them died on the wheel for taking bribes, and the inventor of "eagle's paper," the king of the profiteers, died in prison before his trial for the same offense.

Very similarly, no terms were allowed to enter the Russian language from the mercantilist literature of the time. And indeed the interest in foreign trade and the balance of payments, as well as in precious metals, was clearly subordinated to the problem of economic development and foreign policies. An active balance of trade was indeed a matter of considerable importance. The export surplus was to finance the subsidies and bribes given to allies in the war against Sweden. It was needed to pay the foreign technicians. Foreign trade in a number of basic commodities (the so-called forbidden goods, such as potash, caviar, rhubarb, ship timber, furs, and others) was maintained as a government export monopoly, although most of those commodities were released to private trade in 1719. There were some import prohibitions, mostly directed against luxury goods, and there were some very loosely enforced measures of control of movement of precious metals. At one point Peter tried to find out how foreign prohibitions against exports of precious metals could be evaded. In addition, there was continual concern for the terms of trade, and particularly for the low prices offered for Russian goods by foreign traders in Russia. Peter tried to order the establishment of merchant companies in Russia precisely in order to raise export prices; but he did not pursue the matter and the project bore no fruit. Indeed, at no time did Peter in this field exhibit the boundless energy which was so characteristic of his actions elsewhere. Essentially, it was only in the last years of Peter's life, particularly after his visit to France [1717], that foreign trade began to attract more serious attention, resulting in the first protectionist tariff in which the degree of protection varied directly with the ratio of domestic output to total consumption — the duty rising up to 75 percent *ad valorem*.

This was the very opposite of an infant industry tariff and probably reflected the high cost of output in those branches of industry on the development of which greatest emphasis had been placed in the preceding years. It is reasonable to assume that those industries were subject to increasing rather than decreasing cost, and in some way the tariff, crude as it was, may have been broadly adjusted to such patterns of quantitative restrictions of imports as existed prior to its introduction. The main point, however, is the one previously made. Something that seemed to stand in the very focus of Western mercantilist thought appears to have played a very subordinate role in Russia.

A distinctive feature of Russian mercantilism was the almost complete absence in it of general theorizing. . . . But one of a couple of exceptions to this proposition may be mentioned here, because it tends to confirm the conclusion just reached. The reference is to the curious literary document of the period, composed by Ivan Pososhkov: *The Book of Poverty and Wealth* (1724).[6] Soviet and also some pre-Soviet enthusiasts liked to describe Pososhkov as one of the great economists of all times. This is fairly ludicrous. But the book of this autodidact of peasant origin (1652–1726) is remarkable in many respects and may be considered the only contemporaneous comprehensive mercantilistic tract on Russian economic policies. . . . It is, therefore, instructive to observe Pososhkov's distribution of emphasis.

Pososhkov does indeed deal with foreign trade. He is interested in improving the country's terms of trade by exerting pressures on foreign merchants. In the process, he incidentally assumes a very low price-elasticity of foreign demand for Russian goods, and obversely, a very high price-elasticity of Russian demand for foreign commodities. He is interested in expanding the volume of Russian exports and applies an infant-industry argument of sorts to them by suggesting that exporting at a loss for some time will be profitable in the long run. On the import side he calls for drastic steps against luxury goods and at one point even objects to purchases of foreign cloth for soldiers' uniforms, despite the existing price differentials, arguing in this and in a couple of other cases the advantage of keeping money at home. But all this is far from playing a central part in his argument. The balance of trade is never mentioned

---

[6] Since published in an English edition by L. R. Lewitter and A. P. Vlasto, *Ivan Pososhkov: The Book of Poverty and Wealth* (Stanford, CA: Stanford University Press, 1987). — Ed.

explicitly, and there is never the remotest hint that the export surplus as such is the source of the country's increase in wealth. For Pososhkov's main interest is directed to problems of economic development. Here the range of subjects he treats is very wide: the training of workers; improvement in the quality of products and the introduction of severe penalties for shoddy goods; technical innovations and the protection of inventors; the location of industries, with regard to which he, curiously enough, considers cheapness of food as exercising the strongest pull in determining the place of production; the development of a chemical industry; suggestions for efficient prospecting for minerals; criticism of inefficiency in collecting indirect taxes and proposals for reforming of Peter's direct taxation of peasants so as to increase the state's revenues. It was in the latter connection that he issued to the gentry a stern warning not to exploit the peasantry excessively, having a clear understanding of the existing competition for the product of peasant labor — and for that labor itself — between the state and the gentry. What in fact was intimated was a threat of "reversion" [*reduktionen*] of gentry lands to the crown upon the then recent Swedish model. Pososhkov said: "The landlords [*pomeshchiki*] are not permanent owners of the peasants. Their direct owner is the autocrat of all Russia, and the landlords' possession is a temporary one. . . ." And Pososhkov went on to say that peasants must be protected by Imperial edicts because "the wealth of the peasantry is the wealth of the tsar." Pososhkov made a number of suggestions designed to improve the lot of the peasants so as to prevent their flight "southward and to the border regions, and even beyond the frontiers, populating foreign territories and leaving their own land empty."

There is more, however, to Pososhkov's book than the important priority assigned in it to economic development. The book was finished in 1724, a short time before Peter's death. By that time, Russia's position as a great power had been assured, but at the cost of an effort that — very visibly to the eyes of contemporaries — had led to the impoverishment of the country. Hence came Pososhkov's insistence that continuation of economic development must be accompanied by increases in popular well-being.

A specific Russian pattern of economic development was reaching completion. And in this sense Pososhkov's book, while characteristic of Russian mercantilism, bears the mark of a precise historical moment in its evolution. We have, of course, no proper statistics to measure the speed of industrial growth during Peter's reign, let alone what happened to national income over the period. Even the estimates of the growth [in the production] of pig iron are quite uncertain. Still, it may be assumed that [such production] had grown at about eight percent per year between 1700 and 1725. It is most unlikely that any other industrial commodity could boast a similarly high rate of growth. But even if we assume the whole industrial establishment to have grown at the same rate, such an increase in what after all still was a tiny portion of the total economy was compatible with great reductions in national income — with the disposable incomes of the population decreasing even more. What certainly increased was the wealth of the state that was designed to support the power of the state. As Kliuchevsky put it: the state grew fatter and fatter, and the people grew leaner and leaner. The great historian was referring to the seventeenth century, but his pithy conclusion fits the Petrine period with particular force.

In attempting to draw conclusions from the preceding discussion of Russian mercantilism, the following points appear to stand out:

1. If we wish to conceive of mercantilism as a common European phenomenon, it is power policies and subordination of economic policies to the exigencies of power that provide the common denominator. Economic policies centered on economic development in general, and industrial development in particular.

2. For the rest we observe deviations from the basic pattern. The role of vested interests in co-determining the policies of the state varied from country to country. In viewing the Petrine experience no one possibly could claim, with Adam Smith, that "the sneaking arts of underling tradesmen have been erected into political maxims" or that "the merchants and manufacturers have been by far the principal architects . . . of this whole mercantile system."[7] They were the objects rather than the agents of Petrine policies. Even so, the emphasis on foreign trade, on an active balance of trade and the resulting influx of precious metals, and, finally, on protectionism was enormously strong in some countries and tended to be fairly insignificant in others.

---

[7]Quoting the famous Scottish economist, author of *An Inquiry into the Nature and Causes of the Wealth of Nations* (1776). — Ed.

3. In dealing with deviations of this kind, it is possible simply to register them as such and let it go at that. Then the economic history of Europe appears in a rather fragmentized fashion. . . . Yet something more can be said on the subject. As one reviews once more in one's mind the history of the Petrine era in Russia and looks for reasons for the overwhelming role of the state — with the ubiquitousness of compulsion, the weakness of vested interests, and the single-minded concentration on power — the economic backwardness of the country surely suggests itself as the main, if not the sole, explanatory factor. But if this is true, then the Russian experience does provide a clue to the understanding of mercantilism westward beyond the borders of Russia. The deviations from the basic pattern, beginning from the greater role of vested interests and the consideration of wealth as an independent goal of policies, are then to be regarded as a function of the decreasing backwardness of the countries concerned. If this proposition holds, as I believe it does, then it becomes possible to arraign mercantilistic countries according to the degree of their economic backwardness — starting probably with the Low Countries and continuing over England and France to Prussia, and finally, Russia. If the resulting picture should be one of a fair degree of continuity in the sense of gradual increase in the significance of the basic pattern until the naked power point is reached in the east of the continent, then indeed European economic history in the mercantilist period may be conceived as a unity — not a uniform, homogeneous unity, but a diversified, graduated unity, which, however, is comprehensible as such because of its relation to the degree of economic backwardness which serves not only as an organizing but also as an explanatory principle.

Assuming that this view of European development in the mercantilist period is at all defensible, it would seem to accomplish two things: it conceives of Russia as a part of Europe and by the same token it uses Russian history to add to our understanding of the economic history of Europe. . . .

Leaving aside the field of intellectual history, the field of doctrines and ideology, and riveting our sight to economic processes, it may indeed be said that in the West in some respects mercantilist policies prepared the soil for modern industrial development while in others they had created obstacles that had to be removed, at times requiring a considerable effort. Incidentally, some of those obstacles may have originally been in the nature of factors promoting rather than retarding economic development. . . .

I am not in a position to demonstrate here how the problem of obstacles created by mercantilist policies actually presented itself in the individual countries of Europe. But I should like to volunteer a general hypothesis and then say a few words on the conditions in Russia in this respect. The general proposition, or rather a surmise, I can offer is this: the less backward, economically speaking, that a country was when it went through its mercantilist experience, the less formidable were the obstacles to subsequent development that resulted from that experience and the more easily they were overcome.

Let me try to illustrate: the Austrian monarchy undoubtedly occupied an intermediate position with regard to its economic backwardness between Russia and the West. In Austria, Joseph II (reigned 1780–1790) was the great mercantilist on the throne, the man who liked to say that every single thread of the clothes he wore on his back came from indigenous material and labor. One of the outstanding features of Josephine policies, greatly intensifying those pursued by [his mother, Empress] Maria Theresa, was unification. "The whole Monarchy will become one mass of people ruled in the same fashion," he wrote to his brother. But unification meant, first and foremost, the creation of a strong centralized state. In the process the power of the bureaucratic machinery was greatly increased, most notably at the expense of the gentry diets and the local apparatus in the individual provinces, both German and non-German. There is little doubt that these policies under Joseph II favored the economic development of the country and facilitated the introduction and enforcement of economic reforms. But when in the nineteenth century the enlightened despotism of Joseph was replaced (in the period of reaction between 1815 and 1848) by the unenlightened despotism of Metternich, and economic progress began to be viewed with great suspicion and the railroads came to be regarded not as the welcome carriers of goods and persons, but as the carriers of the dreaded revolution: then the centralized state, the outgrowth of mercantilistic policies, clearly became an obstacle to the economic development of the country. If the same sequence was reproduced in

France by the absurd tariff policies of the Napoleonic bureaucracy after the demise of the Continental System, the intensity of the phenomenon and its negative effects were undoubtedly a good deal weaker and less damaging than was the case in Austria.

But a comparison of Austria with Russia is also illuminating, although in different respects. The effort of economic development and general reform produced by Joseph II, strong as it was, cannot be compared in magnitude and intensity to that of Peter the Great. This is as it should be, as the vehemence of the spurt, the magnitude of the change, can be expected to vary with the backwardness of the country. But, in particular, the problem in Austria was not to establish a general service state, one subjugating the gentry and forcing the peasantry to serve both the gentry and the state. Quite the contrary was true. The burdens of the peasantry were not increased but reduced. By Joseph's edict of 1781 personal subjection of the Austrian peasantry was abolished. . . . But abolition of personal subjection also meant, in addition to the right to marry without consent of the landlord and the discontinuation of the hated house services by the members of the peasant's family, the right to leave the land and choose a trade freely. This was surely an approach to the problem of forming a modern labor force that was radically different from that followed in Russia. It is true that peasant obligations to the lord which were attached to the land rather than to the person remained. But also in this respect, Joseph II tried a rather radical reform of compulsory commutation on a national scale. Under the terms of his edict of February 10, 1789 — significantly, five months before the start of the French Revolution — labor services to the landlords were to be abolished and instead the peasant was to pay in money a fixed proportion of his gross income to the lord and another fixed proportion to the state. This reform was never carried out for a number of weighty political and economic reasons. But the effect of the reform was perhaps not entirely nil. It left the gentry with the feeling that eventual emancipation was inevitable and, as a result, encouraged some of the landlords to conclude private redemption agreements with the peasants and to replace bonded labor with freely hired labor. Thus, at least in this respect the mercantilistic policies left no obstacles for the future.

The effect of the Petrine policies was very different. Peter, of course, was in no way the creator of serfdom in Russia. The last legal measures sealing the condition of enserfment were administered by

Peter's father in the code of 1649. And yet, it is fair to say that it was Peter's policies that in a very real sense greatly increased the effectiveness of the system of serfdom. The great improvement in the efficiency of the administration, the introduction of the passport system, and last but not least, the reform of the fiscal system by the establishment of the poll tax with its regular censuses as a form of registration of the peasantry: these measures for the first time rendered it extremely difficult for the peasants to escape from the yoke of serfdom. In the longer run, once the crisis of the last years of Peter's reign and of the few following years was overcome, the chances of a successful flight were very greatly reduced — unless indeed it was a flight from a poorer lord to a high and mighty one who often was in a position to use his influence in order to prevent the return of the refugee to his rightful owner. In addition, as a result of Peter's policies the burdens imposed on the peasantry increased very greatly — and this not only by extending peasant services far beyond the sphere of agriculture to industry, construction, and transportation, but also within the area of agriculture. As never before, the burdens the peasants bore were regarded as work for the state.

When the great experiment was over; when, after some stagnation, the country's growth was resumed at very moderate rates; when, finally, the Industrial Revolution in England ushered in a new era in industrial history: then it was precisely the institution of serfdom, so greatly reinforced by Peter and one of the carrying pillars of his edifice of economic development, that became the major block in the path of Russia's participation in the new industrial progress. For in the interval the nature of serfdom had profoundly changed. The reform work of the Petrine period, combined with the size of the country in area and population, effectively and long-lastingly liberated the rulers of the country from the necessity to undertake extraordinary efforts in order to maintain the military power of the country on a level sufficiently high for the purposes of expansion. For a full century after Peter's death, Russian arms and Russian power basked in the sun of continual successes. . . .

My usual way of looking at the Petrine experience (and applying the same idea to some earlier periods of Russian history) was to discern in it a series of sequences which I regarded as a specifically Russian pattern of economic development. To summarize the sequences briefly: (1) economic development was placed in the service of the country's military needs and was a function thereof; (2) as a result the development assumed an uneven, jerky, spurt-like character and was compressed within a relatively short period; involving (3) the imposition of high, if not intolerable, burdens on the population who had the misfortune of living in those particular periods and (4) the introduction of special repressive measures designed to force the population to bear those burdens; (5) the continuation of the spurt until the decrease in military pressures and/or the exhaustion of the population led to the termination of the spurt, which was followed either by stagnation or, at any rate, by a considerable decline in the rate of growth.

I do feel that this summarizes correctly the course of the Petrine experience. The crucial problem in the preceding sequences, from the point of view of this presentation, relates to point (4): the introduction of special measures of enforcement, that is to say, the enserfment of the peasantry. It is really this point that made me feel that quantitative differences apart, here lay the peculiar *qualitative* specificity of the Russian pattern. While the main purpose of the Russian development was to modernize the economy, and, in fact, much of its social and political framework, that is, to bring it closer to Europe in some of its most significant respects, it was by the force of the selfsame development that Russia was being forced in other, no less significant respects away from Europe, towards the despotisms of the Orient with their service states, which involved enslavement of the population by the state.

I do not feel that there is anything wrong per se with this presentation. It is a significant fact that as serfdom was on the wane in the rest of Europe it was greatly increasing in Russia. If human freedom is one criterion of civilization, then Russia was becoming less civilized as — *and because* — it was aspiring to move closer to Europe, to enter the community of European civilization.

Allegory of Peter the Great endowing a grateful Russia (woman in traditional dress) with "Truth, Religion, and the Arts." Engraving by F. Ottens, 1725. (editor's collection)

Ecclesiastical and Cultural Reform

James Cracraft

The Church Reform of Peter the Great

The achievements of the Petrine regime in Russia were not confined to the fields of war and diplomacy, nor to those of taxation and state administration, economics and public works. Various reforms were also undertaken, with varying results, in the ecclesiastical and cultural spheres (Peter's revolution in Russian architecture, embodied in the building of St. Petersburg, was highlighted in an earlier reading). In the first of these selections, Peter's church reform, the single most radical of all his administrative reforms, is discussed.

The institution of a regime of administrative colleges was discussed by Peter with the Senate as early as March 23, 1715, as can be seen from a

Reprinted from *The Church Reform of Peter the Great* by James Cracraft, with the permission of the publishers, Stanford University Press. © 1971 by James Cracraft.

memorandum on the subject in Peter's own hand preserved in the Senate's archives. And in an anonymous memoir submitted to Peter early in 1715 the institution of nine colleges was proposed, one of which was to be a "College of Religion [*Kalegium Very*]." An ecclesiastical college is not referred to again in the documents until November 1718. But meanwhile, in September 1715 Peter had ordered his general in Pomerania to obtain copies of Danish civil and military statutes and to find out about the colleges established there; "how many [there were], the number of members in each, their functions and duties, salaries, ranks, and everything else, from the most important [detail] to the least . . . ." By 1717 the institution of a regime of administrative colleges in Russia was considered a foregone conclusion. A report promulgated by the Senate on August 9 of that year announced that "Whereas His Majesty the Tsar most graciously intends to establish state colleges in his Russian Realm, he has therefore been pleased to order that suitable assessors [for the colleges] should be found." In December 1717 the presidents of the nine new colleges — including those of Foreign Affairs, Finance, Justice, War, Commerce, Mines, and Manufactures — were named. The presidents, it was also announced, were to form their colleges "in the new year [1718]," but were not to "interfere with things" until 1719 (a date later deferred to 1720), when "they shall begin to govern."[1]

Thus, by the end of 1717 provision for the establishment of a regime of colleges in Russia had been made. It remained to draw up their governing statutes. Heinrich Fick, one of the tsar's German advisers, was given overall charge of the task. Peter's instructions were that "all the Colleges are to be based on the Swedish Statute [*Ustav*]; but those points in the Swedish Regulation [*Reglament*] which are not suitable or are inapplicable to the situation of this Realm, are in my judgement to be set aside." The lesson was not lost on Herr Fick. At the conclusion of a report submitted to Peter at this time Fick suggested, with reference to the drafting of the collegial statutes, that "one could combine foreign models and regulations with local [ones]." Indeed, the resultant *Regulations*, promulgated over the next few years, can have had no exact equivalents in contemporary European legislation.

With regard to the institution of the collegial regime, therefore, it is perhaps safest to conclude that while the idea no doubt originated in

---

[1] For the larger administrative context of Peter's church reform, see Part III, particularly readings by Bogoslovsky and Peterson. — Ed.

Peter's acquaintance with foreign (especially Swedish) governmental practices, the actual implementation of the scheme in Russia contained only some distinctly foreign elements, most notably the new official jargon. At the same time, it must be stressed that the establishment of the colleges constituted a radical break with the traditional Muscovite system of government. But then that was the purpose of the whole operation. An official proclamation of December 1718 explained to the people that, "wishing to neglect nothing that might promote just government," it was now the tsar's intention to endow civil affairs with the same "good order" that had already transformed the military establishment, "with fruits that are known to all"; that therefore "colleges" had been created — "Colleges, that is, bodies composed of many persons (in place of the *Prikazy*) in which the Presidents or Presiding-officers [*Prezidenty ili Predsedateli*] do not, like the old judges [*sudi*: heads of *prikazy*] have the power to do as they please." The further advantages of the collegial system would be apparent, the proclamation concluded, when their "Regulations (or Statutes) are published." And it was at this time (late 1718) that Peter divulged to Iavorsky his intention of founding an Ecclesiastical College.[2]

Allowing for the other factors that came into play, Peter's decision to found an Ecclesiastical College must have been influenced by his contemporaneous provisions for overhauling the civil administration. It was there that the specific idea of creating an "Ecclesiastical College" must have originated. Yet neither the Ecclesiastical College that came to be, nor its governing statute, resembled their civil counterparts (or prototypes) in other than outward form. The Russian patriarchate, which the Ecclesiastical College was meant to replace, was not, for one thing, merely another governmental *prikaz* — a fact of which the first eleven members of the Ecclesiastical College were fully aware. As we shall see, their first order of business was to dispense with the name "College" in favor of the more distinctive and dignified "Most Holy Governing Synod."

Impatience with Iavorsky's conduct and intermittent opposition; a predisposition towards radical change; a belief that his power was absolute and that it extended equally to the "ecclesiastical order"; a distrust of

---

[2] Stefan Iavorsky (1650–1722), Ukrainian in origin, was metropolitan (bishop) of Riazan and Murom (from 1700) and acting head of the Russian church (1700–1721). — Ed.

the clergy; an awareness of the need to resolve, after eighteen years, the question of the patriarchal succession[3]; and a realization that the example of the civil colleges was relevant to the problem: all these factors certainly influenced Peter late in 1718, though the relative weight he gave to each is impossible to determine exactly. But having decided to found an Ecclesiastical College, Peter felt that his decision needed to be justified. And judging from the justification set forth in Part I of the *Ecclesiastical Regulation*, it was a distrust of the patriarchate as such, a belief in its potential for disrupting the tranquility of the state, that was the major factor which decided Peter to apply to the administration of the church the principle of collegial government.

By far the longest of the nine "weighty reasons" adduced in Part I to prove that an Ecclesiastical College was the "most perfect" form of government, "better than one-man rule" and particularly suited to a "Monarchical State, such as our Russia," is the one set forth under point 7. No single passage of the *Regulation* is more suggestive of the nature and flavor of Peter's church reform, and it may therefore be quoted at length:

> *The fatherland need not fear from an administrative council [the Ecclesiastical College] the sedition and disorders that proceed from the personal rule of a single church ruler. For the common folk do not perceive how different is the ecclesiastical power from that of the Autocrat, but dazzled by the great honor and glory of the Supreme Pastor [the patriarch], they think him a kind of second Sovereign, equal to or even greater than the Autocrat himself, and imagine that the ecclesiastical order is another and better State.*

The author of the *Regulation* thus makes somewhat tendentious use of the traditional Byzantine-Muscovite theory of the parallel powers (tsar and patriarch), and perhaps alludes to the fact that during the middle years of the seventeenth century the patriarchs of Moscow did in fact assume the title "Sovereign [*Gosudar*]." But the title had not been used by the patriarchs since 1658, when its last bearer, Patriarch Nikon, retired from public life. The passage continues:

> *Thus the people are accustomed to reason among themselves, a situation in which the tares of the seditious talk of ambitious clerics multiply*

---

[3] In 1700, following the death of Patriarch Adrian, Peter had declined to permit the election of a successor. — Ed.

and act as sparks which set dry twigs ablaze. Simple hearts are perverted by these ideas, so that in some matters they look not so much to their Autocrat as to the Supreme Pastor. And when they hear of a dispute between the two, they blindly and stupidly take sides with the ecclesiastical ruler, rather than with the secular ruler, and dare to conspire and rebel against the latter. The accursed ones deceive themselves into thinking that they are fighting for God Himself, that they do not defile but hallow their hands even when they resort to bloodshed. Criminal and dishonest persons are pleased to discover such ideas among the people: when they learn of a quarrel between their Sovereign and the Pastor, because of their animosity towards the former they seize on the chance to make good their malice, and under pretence of religious zeal do not hesitate to take up arms against the Lord's Anointed; and to this iniquity they incite the common folk as if to the work of God. And what if the Pastor himself, inflated by such lofty opinions of his office, will not keep quiet? It is difficult to relate how great are the calamities that thereby ensue.

These are not our inventions: would to God that they were. But in fact this has more than once occurred in many states. Let us investigate the history of Constantinople since Justinian's time, and we shall discover much of this. Indeed the Pope by this very means achieved so great a pre-eminence, and not only completely disrupted the Roman Empire, while usurping a great part of it for himself, but more than once has profoundly shaken other states and almost completely destroyed them. Let us not recall similar threats which have occurred among us.

In an ecclesiastical administrative council there is no room for such mischief. For here the president himself enjoys neither the great glory which amazes the people, nor excessive lustre; there can be no lofty opinions of him; nor can flatterers exalt him with inordinate praises, because what is done well by such an administrative council cannot possibly be ascribed to the president alone. . . . Moreover, when the people see that this administrative council has been established by decree of the Monarch with the concurrence of the Senate, they will remain meek, and put away any hope of receiving aid in their rebellions from the ecclesiastical order.

Behind the author's characteristic references to papal pretensions (quite irrelevant in a Russian context) plainly lay Peter's apprehension that a new patriarch should become a focus of opposition to his regime. However, the accuracy of these prognostications is not in question, but rather the evidence the whole passage provides of the motives underlying Peter's reorganization of the administration of the church. And compared with this passage, the eight other "weighty reasons" adduced in Part 1 of the *Ecclesiastical Regulation* appear more or less incidental, or merely rhetorical.

Thus: "1. In the first place, truth is more certainly discovered by a council than by a single person. . . . 2. And so far as there is more certain knowledge, there is greater power to act. For men are more inclined to accept and obey the decision of a council than the decree of a single person. The power of monarchs is autocratic, which God himself commands us to obey in good conscience: yet monarchs have their advisers, not only for the sake of better ascertaining the truth, but in order that disobedient subjects should not slander them by saying that they rule by force and caprice rather than by justice and truth. How much more so, then, should this be the case in church government, where the power is not monarchical and the ruler is forbidden to lord it over the clergy. . . . 3. . . . it should be noted that a college is not some faction secretly joined to promote its own interest, but rather is composed of persons gathered together for the common good by order of the Autocrat after consultation with his advisers."

Points 4, 5, 6, and 8 refer in the same vein to the practical and moral improvements that were supposed to derive from collegial, as opposed to patriarchal, government. (Again, the accuracy or fairness of the implied criticisms of previous patriarchal administrations is not at issue here.) Thus: "4. . . . when one man rules, procrastinations and interruptions in business often occur because of the overwhelming demands made on the ruler or because of his sickness or infirmity; and when he dies business stops altogether. It is otherwise with an administrative council; if one member is absent . . . business continues its uninterrupted course. 5. . . . in a College there is no room for partiality, intrigue, or bribery: . . . should one member be prejudiced for or against a person on trial, the second, third, and so on will be free of any such prejudice. How could bribery prevail when matters are decided not arbitrarily but only after regular and serious consideration? For any individual member will be wary lest he be unable to show good cause for his opinion and so be suspected of having taken a bribe. This would be particularly true if the College were composed of persons who could not possibly conspire in secret, that is, of persons of different rank and station: bishops, archimandrites, igumens, and leading members of the secular clergy. . . . 6. Similarly, a College enjoys greater freedom of mind to administer justice, for unlike a single ruler it need not fear the wrath of the mighty: to put pressure on many persons . . . it is not so easy as on one man. . . . 8. Church and State will further profit from such an administrative council because not only each of its members, but the president himself, is liable to the judgment of his brothers, that is of the College itself, in case of notable transgression. This is not what happens when one Supreme Pastor rules, for he is unwilling to be tried by his subordinate bishops. . . . Hence it would be necessary to summon a general council to try him, which can only be managed at great trouble and expense for the entire country; and at the present time (when the Eastern patriarchs live under the Turkish yoke, and the Turks are more than ever wary of our State) it would seem impossible."

The last of the nine reasons set forth in Part 1 states that "such an administrative council will become a kind of school of church government" from which "the most suitable members will deservedly advance to the episcopal rank." This "reason" is clearly rather a declaration of policy, a policy which was in fact partially observed by Peter's government in subsequent years when filling episcopal vacancies. Reason 9, and Part 1 as a whole, conclude with the sentence: "Thus in Russia, with God's help, grossness will soon disappear from the ecclesiastical order, and the best results may be hoped for." We are reminded that a simple, disinterested desire to reform the church cannot be discounted in any analysis of Peter's measures.

It will have been noticed that various passages of Part 1 of the *Ecclesiastical Regulation* gave further expression to the view that the sovereign's power is unique, absolute, and universally obligating. Yet it will also have been noticed that, ironically, this "autocratic monarch who need not account for his actions to anyone on earth" found it necessary to provide his subjects with a lengthy justification of his decision to establish an Ecclesiastical College and to abolish the patriarchate. It was perhaps an indication of Peter's awareness of the magnitude of the changes he proposed to make. . . .

The Ecclesiastical College was formally opened on February 14, 1721. It is one of the few events not directly connected with either military or naval affairs that is described in the official history of Peter's reign: "In the morning [of February 14] His Majesty and the Ministers, as well as the bishops and other church dignitaries, attended the Liturgy in the Trinity cathedral [in St. Petersburg], at the conclusion of which a sermon was preached by the Archbishop of Pskov, Feofan Prokopovich, concerning the inauguration of the Ecclesiastical College. Thereafter everyone left the church and went to the Ecclesiastical College, where His Majesty ordained that this College was to be equal in dignity to the Senate and in church services was to be styled the Most Holy Governing Synod." Similarly, the Synod's own journal opens with a brief account of how "After services in the Trinity cathedral . . . His Most Illustrious Majesty the Tsar was pleased to attend in the Synod together with all the Ministers, at which time [seven] points were submitted to His Majesty by all the members of this Ecclesiastical Administration and to which His Majesty subscribed resolutions in His own hand." The first of the points submitted to Peter, as the official history indicates, concerned the correct formulation of the new body's title for use in church services, where it was to replace the traditional commemoration of the patriarch or — since the death of Patriarch Adrian in 1700 — of the "Eastern Patriarchs": in response to the members' query, and having been assured that the title was "not to be attributed to any one member in particular, but only to the body as a whole," Peter graciously conceded that the form "the Most Holy Synod, or the Most Holy Governing Synod," was henceforth to be used.

His choice of words is highly significant. The term "synod," widely used in both East and West to denote an assembly of clergy, was something of a neologism in Russian, and served to distinguish the new body both from the new civil colleges and from church councils (*sobory*) of the traditional kind. The title "Most Holy" had been formerly used only with reference to the patriarch, while "Governing" was a distinction conferred by Peter on the Senate, alone among governmental institutions, to denote its all-embracing jurisdiction. Thus Peter, by his resolution of the first of the points submitted to him on February 14, 1721, confirmed that the Synod was to succeed to the patriarchal dignity and was to be considered, as the official history puts it, "equal in dignity to the Senate." The degrading term "Ecclesiastical College" was, accordingly, dropped from official usage. . . .

It is not too much to say that Peter promoted to the Synod as enlightened a group of clerics as could be found in contemporary Russia. Prokopovich and Iavorsky, in particular, were churchmen of European stature. Yet despite their learning and records of distinguished service — as teachers and preachers, as ecclesiastical administrators, or even as diplomats — the members of Peter's Synod did not enjoy his full confidence. Probably he doubted the depth of their loyalty to him and to his policies, and with some justification: Iavorsky's implacable, if discreet opposition, for example, was a known fact. In any event, in 1722 Peter declined to name a successor to Iavorsky as president of the Synod, appointed a civil servant to be the Synod's chief secretary, and created the office of chief procurator of the Synod, entrusting it to one of his guards officers. In view of the notoriety that this office later achieved, its origins should be carefully considered.

On May 11, 1722, Peter decreed that "a good man, who shall be fearless and able to acquaint himself with the administration of Synodal affairs, is to be chosen from among the Officers and made Chief Procurator [*Ober-Prokuror*]." On June 15 the Senate informed the Synod that Colonel I. V. Boltin had been appointed to the post by the tsar, that an *Instruktsiia* had been drawn up for him in Peter's presence, and that the oath of office had been administered to him in the Senate. On receipt of this information, the Synod requested the Senate to send it a copy of Boltin's instructions, so that it should know what duties he was to perform and be able to communicate this news to the subordinate departments of the ecclesiastical administration.

According to Boltin's *Instruktsiia*, "the Chief Procurator is obliged to sit in the Synod and strictly observe that the Synod fulfils its duties, and that all matters submitted for the Synod's consideration and resolution are dispatched truthfully, zealously, promptly, and in an orderly way. . . ." The chief procurator was to keep a journal of the Synod's proceedings and was to see that the Synod's decisions were conscientiously carried out: "he must determine who has received what [Synodal] decree, whether it was implemented within the prescribed time, and if it was not, he must discover the reason — an insurmountable obstacle, fear, or laziness — and promptly inform the Synod." At the same time, the chief procurator was "strictly to observe that the Synod conducts its business justly and impartially. And should he discover anything contrary to this [injunction], that very hour he must lay it openly before the Synod with a full explanation of how they, or certain among them, have not acted as they ought to have acted, in order that they might make amends. But should they not comply, that very hour he must protest, suspend business, and promptly report to Us [the tsar], if the matter is urgent; if it is not urgent, he will do as We command upon Our weekly or monthly visit to the Synod." Yet regarding his duty promptly to inform the tsar of the Synod's misdemeanors, the chief procurator was enjoined to act "discreetly and carefully, lest someone is wrongfully dishonored"; and attached to the enjoinder is one of Peter's typical sanctions: "should he submit an unjust report through fear, he will himself be punished according to the gravity of the matter." "Above all," stated Boltin's *Instruktsiia*, "the Chief Procurator must observe that [the Synod] conducts its business truthfully and zealously. And should someone transgress in this, he is to be judged by the Synod; and all of the procurator's reports are to be laid before the Synod in evidence, so that the trial may proceed accordingly." The chief procurator was to be in charge of the Synod's chancellery. He was to be, concluded the tsar, "Our eye and personal representative for the affairs of the State."

It was suggested above that Peter created the office of the chief procurator because he doubted the depth of the Synod's loyalty to him. Judging from Boltin's *Instruktsiia*, it is clear that Peter also distrusted the Synod's readiness to discharge its duties properly. But it should be pointed out that similar officials, under the overall supervision of a "procurator-general," had been attached to the civil colleges and even to the Senate, and that all these procurators were given instructions similar to Boltin's. In fact, in the closing years of his reign Peter increasingly made use of officers and sometimes noncommissioned officers and even ordinary guardsmen in an attempt to enforce honest and efficient administration at every level of the government. In this respect, therefore, the Synod had not been subjected by Peter to any special form of control. . . .

Indeed, the history of the Synod's relations with the secular government during the first four years of its existence suggests that in securing a position of equality with the Senate and of superiority to the colleges, the Synod had won but a formal victory. It is not merely that the Synod's judicial and administrative authority over the secular affairs of the church remained subject to regulation and control by various agencies of the secular government, leaving the Synod with exclusive jurisdiction over only a relatively narrow range of "ecclesiastical matters." Nor is it merely that the Synod was obliged to wage a constant struggle with the secular authorities to secure in practice a recognition of even that limited authority to which, in theory, it was entitled. Rather, on a more fundamental level, it is that both the statutory controls and the continual interference of the secular government were the inevitable concomitants of that reform of the church which had brought the Synod itself into being. Nothing could conceal the fact that the Synod was in reality a government bureau charged with administering the church in the name of the tsar. The Synod's grandiose titles, its status in the administrative hierarchy, its broad jurisdictional claims — all these were formalities, formalities which the secular authorities were not always disposed to observe.

Evidently the Synod was pleased to think that for administrative purposes the state was divided into ecclesiastical and secular spheres which were headed, respectively, by itself and by the Senate, each supreme in its own sphere and "equal" to the other. It was a sort of modernized version of the traditional Byzantine theory of the parallel powers. But the conception, whether or not it is rightly ascribed to the Synod, was greatly at odds with reality. Time and again we encounter, in the Senate's communications with the Synod, the telling formulas: "The Most Illustrious, Most Potent Peter the Great, Emperor and All-Russian Autocrat, being present this day in the Senate, has decreed: . . . and the Most Holy Governing Synod is to do as His Imperial Majesty has commanded." If the "Supreme Judge" of the Synod chose to rule it through the Senate, the Synod, to be sure, could do nothing about it. Nor could it compel the tsar to honor his commitment to pay a "weekly or monthly visit to the Synod," and to rule it directly, and thus to confirm that equality with the Senate which the Synod so eagerly sought. To judge from the printed record of its proceedings, in the last four years of his reign Peter personally attended meetings of the Synod no more than half a dozen times. And so the Synod had no choice but to accept the government's directives concerning matters which normally lay within its own jurisdiction and duly to forward them, under the seal of its formal approval, to the relevant departments of the ecclesiastical administration. The Synod could only insist that such directives should be communicated to it in the proper bureaucratic form: "memoranda" from the Senate, "submissions" from the colleges and other organs of the civil government.

For the Synod, it must be stressed, could not deny that it was "established by decree of the Monarch with the concurrence of the Senate." Nor could it, for this very reason, rightfully claim to be the successor of the patriarchs in any but the strictly temporal sense of the word. Indeed, it was the Synod itself that assured the tsar, on the day of its official opening, that it had "sworn faithfully to serve His Majesty's interest no less than the other Colleges"; and it was the Synod who pointed out to the Senate, as we have also seen, that "this ecclesiastical administration founded by [Peter] is not like that of the patriarchs . . . it does not govern in its own name, but rather by decrees of His Majesty, who . . . has established Himself as Supreme Ruler and Judge of this Holy Synod." Everything, as the Synod well knew, depended on the will of the tsar, including the appointment and dismissal of the members of the Synod themselves.

Nothing illustrates more clearly its real position in relation to the secular government than the history of the Synod's unsuccessful attempt to gain exclusive control of its own bureaucracy. That the Synod should have reorganized the ecclesiastical administration on the model of the secular bureaucracy was not in itself a radical break with the past; the structure of the patriarchal administration of the seventeenth century was closely modeled on that of the tsar's government. Yet the patriarch himself, not unlike the tsar, had stood outside and above his administrative machine: he was, in the ecclesiastical sphere, the counterpart, indeed the "equal, of the tsar in the secular; and this independent position of the patriarch, who could be removed from office only at great trouble and expense, had been the ultimate guarantee of the independence of the church — of the autonomy, that is, of its administration. Peter changed all that. The creation of the Synod destroyed the independence of the ecclesiastical administration. And during the first four years of its existence the Synod itself more or less willingly cooperated in carrying out measures that completed the incorporation of the church within the framework of the newly absolute, secularized, bureaucratic state. By the time of Peter's death the ecclesiastical administration had become to all intents and purposes an integral part of the one, vast, centralized bureaucracy to which everyone, layman or cleric, was subject.

A rose by any other name is still a rose. The Synod's original name was more appropriate to its true nature: it remained, in reality, Peter's College of Ecclesiastical Affairs. And from this point of view the Synod's endeavor to assert a special position in relation to the secular government may be seen as an attempt to minimize, if not to conceal, the degradation which the church had suffered. . . .

On November 8, 1721, the Synod resolved that copies of the newly-printed *Ecclesiastical Regulation* should be sent to all the bishops, so that each would "know how to conduct himself and what he must guard himself against." . . .

The Synod desired, quite naturally, that the bishops should acknowledge its supreme authority, which was not only like that of a patriarch but was an emanation of the power of the tsar himself. Thus in March 1721 Metropolitan Ignatius of Krutitsy was told pointedly that the Synod was to be obeyed "absolutely in all things," in accordance with His Majesty's edict; for this Synod . . . possesses the patriarchal power, honor, and authority." In November 1721 Metropolitan Sylvester of Tver was required to "answer the Synod, in terms of the strictest truth, as to why he disregarded a decree sent to him by the most Holy Synod . . . and as to why he conducts himself as if he were not subordinate, but equal to the Synod": Sylvester had apparently ignored a recent decree concerning the maintenance of military hospitals in his diocese, and had sent his communications to the Synod in the form of "memoranda" rather than "submissions." In short, the Synod had assumed an unrestricted right to dictate to the bishops which they, in turn, were in no position to challenge. Especially after the recognition granted to the Synod in 1723 by the Eastern patriarchs, which dealt the last (if unintentional) blow to the traditional order of church government in Russia, the Russian bishops had no one to whom they could appeal. Patriarchs and church councils, hitherto the embodiments of supreme ecclesiastical authority, were things of the past. It is not surprising, therefore, that apart from the two cases just mentioned the printed record of the Synod's proceedings for the years 1721–1725 contains no other reference to a case of episcopal insubordination.

On the contrary, during these years the bishops dutifully submitted to the Synod a host of reports concerning a wide range of matters which were coupled with requests for the Synod's instructions. In most cases the Synod's response was simply to enjoin observance of the relevant provisions of the civil or ecclesiastical law. In some cases, however, its considered judgment was required. In the case of a licentious priest of the Smolensk diocese, for instance, the Synod ruled that pending further investigation by the colonel of the local garrison and by the Smolensk episcopal *prikaz* (which had referred the case to the Synod), the priest could celebrate matins and vespers but not the liturgy. In January 1722 the bishop of Suzdal submitted a list of some twenty "doubtful" cases for the Synod's resolution: what was to be done with the daughter of a certain landlord who had been molested by him and then incarcerated in a convent? what was to be done with the unmarried daughters of two prominent persons who were being held in a local convent for killing their children at birth? how was the law prohibiting the bringing of ikons from church to private houses to be applied in certain cases? — etc. The Synod granted to one bishop additional funds for his school, to another an increased annual stipend, to a third permission to rebuild two of his churches. It advised the bishops as to how to deal with schismatics, heretics, and other nonconformists. It delimited episcopal jurisdictions, forbade any bishop to leave his diocese without its permission, provided for the burial of deceased bishops and for the temporary administration of their dioceses. In all these ways the bishops acknowledged their subordination to the Synod while the Synod, in turn, exercised its right to rule them.

Perhaps the Synod's most effective means of controlling the bishops was its power, under the tsar, over episcopal appointments. This matter is not referred to in the *Ecclesiastical Regulation,* except for the statement that the Synod was to be "a kind of school of church government" from which the "most suitable members will deservedly advance to the episcopal rank." Thus, the fourth of the points submitted to Peter by the Synod on February 14, 1721, concerned the exact procedure to be followed in filling episcopal vacancies: "is the [Synod] to choose a bishop, and upon reporting [its choice] to His Most Sacred Majesty the Tsar, to consecrate him and dispatch him to his diocese?" In reply, Peter resolved that the Synod was to "choose two persons, and him whom we designate, consecrate and dispatch." Yet in the following years neither the *Regulation*'s provision nor the tsar's resolution of February 14 was strictly adhered to by Peter. Between 1721 and 1725 only two members of the Synod were promoted to episcopal rank. As for the ruling that the tsar would nominate one of two candidates presented to him by the Synod to fill a given episcopal vacancy, we have only to consider the case of Archbishop Antony of Chernigov, whose future was summarily decided by Peter on the very day — February 14, 1721 — that he issued the said ruling: to the question of whether Antony, who had fallen under a cloud for "protecting seditious agitators," was to be allowed to return to his diocese, Peter replied that he was to be disciplined by the Synod and then transferred to the see of Tobolsk to replace the aged incumbent. The Synod dutifully ratified Antony's new appointment. . . .

In other words, after 1721, as before, Peter continued to intervene directly in the matter of episcopal appointments. And if prior to 1721 this direct intervention was contrary to tradition, after 1721 it was contrary to his own laws. But what was more important for the fate of the church was the fact that with the creation of the Synod and the promulgation of the resolution of February 14, 1721, the tsar's absolute control of episcopal appointments was firmly established in law. After February 14, 1721, no bishop could be consecrated without the prior and explicit approval of the tsar; and after that date no one could hope to become a bishop without having first attracted the tsar's attention or that of his agents or favorites. Indeed, the Synod's control under the tsar of episcopal appointments tended to reduce the bishops to the status of Synodal deputies in much the same way that the provincial governors had been reduced by Peter's administrative reforms of 1718–1722 to the status of deputies of the central government. . . .

The principal objectives of Peter's reform of the secular clergy were these: to eliminate "superfluous" clergy; to fix the number of "actually serving" clergy; to ensure that the "ecclesiastical order" should no longer serve as a haven for fugitives from state service; and to provide for the apprehension and punishment of vagrant or fraudulent clerics. At the same time, the reform legislation enacted in the years 1721 to 1725 manifests, once again, the propensity of Peter's government to make the clergy its agents in various, usually invidious ways. They were forced to cooperate in the campaign to suppress superstition and religious dissent; they were obliged to supply the government with the vital statistics of their parishioners (of, in fact, the Russian population); they were required, not only to take an oath of loyalty to the tsar and to his policies, but to administer in their churches the oath of loyalty required of all classes "except the peasants"; they were required, after 1721 as before, to read to their congregations on Sundays and feastdays the government's decrees on a wide range of political and economic matters; and, most significantly, they were required, in their capacity as confessors, to cooperate in suppressing opposition to the regime. This is not to deny, however, that the legislation under question also included an element of reform in the more purely beneficent or moral sense, in the sense of a disinterested attempt to eliminate petty corruption and clerical abuses and to improve the standards of clerical behavior. The key to this aspect of the reform was thought by Peter's government to lie in improved clerical education, and the attempt to implement this policy is discussed later. But the clergy were also enjoined to dress properly; to behave in public with dignity; to refrain from bargaining with their parishioners over the performance of religious rites; to impose penances prudently; to comfort sinners, the sick, the dying, and the condemned; and to desist from catering to the rich and powerful at the expense of their poorer parishioners. Regulations designed to prevent morally unfit persons from entering the priesthood were introduced. Yet somehow, in the mass of legislation subsequently enacted or implemented by the Synod, in the press of the politics of church reform under Peter, this moral aspect of clerical reform appears to have been largely neglected. During the remaining years of Peter's reign no serious effort to enforce a moral reform of the clergy, apart from improving their education, appears to have been made. It was perhaps beyond the power of Peter's government, or of any government anywhere at any time, to impose such a reform, to do anything more than publish numerous admonitions, exhortations, injunctions, and regulations. But whatever the reason, it must be recorded that a general reform of the clergy in the moral sense remained very much a secondary objective of Peter's government.

At the same time, it may be provisionally observed that elements of Peter's reform — the clergy's exemption from the soul tax and their duty to act in various ways as government agents — undoubtedly worked to identify them with the increasingly oppressive state and thus to divide them from the people they served. If, in general, Peter's legislation powerfully reinforced the division of Russian society into government and landlords on the one side, and everybody else on the other, there can be no doubt as to which side of the yawning social gap the ordinary parish clergy — the representatives of the church in the daily lives of the people — were being drawn.

On a more concrete level, there is evidence that at least in the short term one major aspect of Peter's church reform — his attempt to stabilize the number of secular clergy — failed miserably. If between 1722 and 1738 the number of churches in Russia remained relatively constant, during the same period the number of secular clergy more than doubled, an increase that was proportionately far in excess of the concurrent increase in the general population.[4] Perhaps there were far fewer "superfluous" parish clergy than Peter and his collaborators supposed. Or perhaps by exempting *all* sons of "actually serving" clergy from the soul tax, Peter's government had unwittingly ensured that

---

[4]From a total of 61,111 priests, deacons, and cantors in 1722 to a total of 124,923 in 1738.

places in the church would always be found for them. For the bureaucracy could not be indefinitely expanded to accommodate them; and their alternative was to be reduced to the status of tax-paying townsmen or peasants. In this situation, the sons of the clergy, like their fathers, were unlikely to surrender voluntarily their inherited and relatively privileged position in society.

The basic objectives of Peter's reform of the monastic clergy were similar to those of his reform of the secular clergy. With the promulgation of the *Ecclesiastical Regulation* and subsequent, related measures, a renewed effort was made both to reform the monasteries in the moral sense and to put them to various social uses. At the same time, an attempt was made not merely to stabilize the number of monastic clergy, but drastically to reduce it. The attempt appears to have succeeded. Between 1724 and 1738 the total number of monks, nuns, and novices in Russia was nearly halved,[5] a fact which contrasts sharply with the result of Peter's concurrent attempt to control the number of secular clergy. But then monks and nuns did not breed sons and daughters for whom places in the church would have to be found. And short of a wholesale dissolution of the monasteries and convents (which Peter seems never to have contemplated), their number of inmates could be greatly reduced by the simple device of restricting the entrance of newcomers. This, in essence, was Peter's policy. . . .

The Synod also took steps to implement the *Regulation's* provisions concerning the institution (or revival) of a system of episcopal schools for the training of clergy. In June 1721 it informed the Admiralty College that sons of clergy were no longer to be enrolled in the College's "cipher schools," since in accordance with the *Regulation's* provisions they were now to attend the episcopal schools. In November 1721 the Synod secured Peter's explicit consent to this ruling, which in effect abrogated his earlier order requiring the sons of clergy to attend the cipher schools and hence deprived the latter of a principal source of their students.[6] In January 1722 the Synod confirmed that "uneducated" priests were not to be appointed to the churches of Moscow. And in May it issued a lengthy declaration which was intended to clarify, once and for all, the educational obligations of the clergy.

---

[5] From a total of 25,207 in 1724 to a total of 14,282 in 1738.

[6] It has been estimated that sons of clergy accounted for 45 percent of the total enrollment of the cipher schools during the first ten years of their existence (1715–1725).

Citing the relevant provisions of the *Ecclesiastical Regulation* and various of the tsar's decrees, the Synod declared (in May 1722) that sons of clergy who were exempt from the soul tax were to attend the episcopal schools and only then (the bishops were reminded) were they to be ordained to vacancies in the church; that, accordingly, they were to be freed of the obligation to study "secular sciences" — arithmetic and geometry — in the cipher schools; but that, "since for training in grammar the teaching of arithmetic is indispensable, teachers appointed to the episcopal schools are to give instruction in both arithmetic and the most necessary parts of geometry, in order that both of these disciplines, needed by both church and state, should be learned"; and finally, that "because of the lack of adequate teachers for the most important subjects, that is theology and philosophy, as well as for the necessary languages," sons of clergy enrolled in the episcopal schools were to study only mathematics, grammar, and the contents of a new religious primer. In sum, the Synod declared that

> *having established the episcopal schools in accordance with the* Ecclesiastical Regulation, *the bishops are to inform the clergy of their dioceses that their sons are freed from the cipher schools . . . and that they shall be taught in the episcopal schools, whence a better and reformed clergy is to be hoped for. . . .*
>
> *And should any son of a cleric who has been exempted from the soul tax and is being trained for the priesthood in one of these schools prove to be lazy and negligent, for that very reason he is to be deprived of all hope of ordination and ecclesiastical service, and for his sloth joined to those sons of the clergy who, as superfluous and redundant . . . are obliged to pay the soul tax. This they are to be clearly shown, so that knowing it they should not become lazy but zealously apply themselves to their studies.*

The Synod's declaration represented yet another attempt to adjust the *Regulation*'s proposals to contemporary Russian realities: for lack of adequate teachers, theology, philosophy, and languages were to be dropped from the curriculum of the episcopal schools; for the sake of the needs of "both church and state," arithmetic and geometry were to be added to it. Still, all sons of the clergy were to possess at least an elementary education as a condition for ordination, a step that was itself a brave departure from previous practices. . . . And by 1727–1728 a total of some 3,100 students, the great majority of them sons of clergy, were enrolled in the episcopal schools of Russia and were thus receiving at least a rudimentary education. Even the distant diocese of Tobolsk in Siberia could boast of an episcopal school with 57 students and two teachers (though one of the latter, a foreigner who wrote in Latin letters, complained that his students were "extremely obtuse"). Indeed it was a hopeful beginning. Despite all the difficulties, only the most reactionary critics of Peter's reform could have regarded this beginning as an unwelcome development. And within ten years, it may be noted, the number of students in the episcopal schools had increased to 5,000 and seventeen seminaries, with a total enrollment of 2,589 students, had been founded. . . .

Only one of the educational books described in the *Regulation* was actually written and published during Peter's reign. It was an elementary catechism composed by Feofan Prokopovich with a view to fulfilling, presumably, the *Regulation*'s provision for a little book that would treat of the "most important dogmas of our faith as well as the commandments of God comprised in the decalogue." . . . The fourteen-page preface to this *Primer*, which is addressed to "pious parents, teachers, guardians, masters, and all others who exercise paternal authority over children," contains a concise statement of the basic philosophy of Peter's church reform in its specifically moral sense:

> *The whole moral life of man depends, pious Christians, on the education received in adolescence: as the boy is, so the man shall be. If sound schooling and the fear of God (which is the beginning of wisdom) are inculcated in youth, it may be hoped that in maturity a person will be good; equally, if in youth he is defiant and unrestrained, there can be little hope that he will lead another and better life; for such rarely happens.*
>
> *And we have seen this to be true not only with regard to individual persons, but with regard to whole nations. Where a people abide in goodness, there, it is to be noted, the children receive good instruction; and where there is much quarrelling, animosity, duplicity, thievery, violence, and other forms of immorality, it cannot be doubted that there the children do not receive good instruction. Childhood is as it were the root whence both good and evil grow throughout the whole of life. The reason for which is this: because of the sin of our first parents, we are inclined from birth to evil. . . . Thus what good can be expected where there is no good instruction for children?*

On the basis of these sentiments, Prokopovich proceeded to describe

> *how such education is lacking in Russia. There are many conscientious and apparently good people among us who, not knowing the power and law of God, do not know many of their sins, and remain without fear. They know, for example, the commandment: "Honor thy father and thy mother"; but how many know the force of this commandment, who is to be understood by the name of father, and what is commanded by the verb "honor" . . . ? And the same may be said concerning the other commandments.*
>
> *How can such people educate children? And what of the many others who remain in such darkness and ignorance that they have not heard of the law of God, and place all piety in external rites and physical exercises, never thinking that the foundation of true piety lies in believing in God the Saviour and in observing his law in fear and charity. . . .*

Moreover, it was a "false opinion" to hold that the education of youth consists only in teaching them to read and write, which some people regard as the highest wisdom; for they might not understand what they read, or take the trouble to understand it, or use it for their own improvement. Indeed, some such poorly-educated persons invented "evil doctrines, and create schism among the people: who could count the number of wicked little books produced by their pens!" And so,

> *Since many among us who exercise paternal authority themselves know little of the law of God, there has arisen a need for a little book explaining the ten commandments given by God. For although a few such books already exist in Russia, they are written in the high Slavonic dialect and not in the vernacular; and our youth have not been instructed by these books, wherefore until now they have been deprived of the education appropriate to them.*

Thus, finally,

> *Having perceived such a need in his people, and having been grieved at heart by the impiety of his subjects, the All-Russian Monarch . . . began diligently to consider how to establish in Russia an efficacious and indispensable rule for the education of youth. And God inspired him with this most wise counsel: to order that a little book clearly explaining the law of God, the creed, the Lord's Prayer, and the nine beatitudes should be written and printed together with a primer, so that*

*in learning their letters the children may learn not psalms and prayers
but these explanations; and having been thus instructed in religion and
the law of God, they could read with profit the psalms and prayers. And
in accordance with His Majesty's command this little book has been
written and printed.*

In addition to the section of literal and syllabic exercises, the *Primer*
contains, as promised in the preface, a lengthy exposition of the Ten
Commandments in the form of questions and answers, a phrase by
phrase devotional commentary on the Lord's Prayer, a brief "explanation" of each article of the Nicene Creed, and an essay on the
Beatitudes. The last is a pious and unremarkable exhortation to lead a
Christian life of humility, submissiveness, justice, and purity; it was
highly commended by Peter himself in a letter to the Synod in July
1722 and was subsequently published as a separate little book to aid the
faithful in their devotions and so to promote religious reform. The brief
"explanations" of the articles of the Nicene Creed seem, so far as they
go, not incompatible with traditional Orthodox teaching — although in
the political-ideological conflicts of the years after Tsar Peter's death,
Prokopovich's enemies were to charge that they contained "foreign" or
"heretical" or "Protestant" elements. As for the commentary on the
Lord's Prayer, the following passage is illustrative:

> *Give us this day our daily bread. Give us, merciful Father, all that is
> necessary to support our life: wholesome air, an abundance of the fruits
> of the earth, and thy blessing on our labors. Bless the government.
> Grant health and long life to our Most Blessed Sovereign Peter the
> Great, Emperor and All-Russian Autocrat, and to all his court and
> army. Grant that the chief lords may be utterly loyal. Preserve all the
> higher and lower officials in love and harmony. . . .*

And this tendency to subordinate piety to the interests of the state is
even more clearly evident in the detailed, practical, and highly didactic
exposition of the Ten Commandments which forms the longest and
most remarkable section of the *Primer*. For example:

> **Question:** *Are soldiers and judges to be considered transgressors of the
> commandment "Thou shalt not kill" when they put a man to death?*
> **Answer:** *No; for judges only execute the power entrusted to them by
> God. Nor do soldiers transgress this commandment when they slay
> the enemy; for they are only doing their duty when, in defense of their*

> country and in obedience to their Sovereign, they kill the enemy. It is
> the duty of kings to see that war is undertaken for just and substan-
> tial causes.

Or again:

> Question: What is ordained by God in the fifth commandment
> ["Honor thy father and thy mother"]?
> Answer: To honor all those who are as fathers and mothers to us. But it
> is not only parents who are referred to here, but others who exercise
> paternal authority over us.
> Question: Who are such persons?
> Answer: The first order of such persons are the supreme authorities
> instituted by God to rule the people, of whom the highest authority is
> the Tsar. It is the duty of kings to protect their subjects and to seek
> what is best for them, whether in religious matters or in the things of
> this world; and therefore they must watch over all the ecclesiastical,
> military, and civil authorities subject to them and conscientiously see
> that they discharge their respective duties. That is, under God, the
> highest paternal dignity; and subjects, like good sons, must honor the
> Tsar.

The second order of persons enjoying paternal authority, the *Primer*
explained, are the "supreme rulers of the people who are subordinate to
the Tsar, namely: the ecclesiastical pastors, the senators, the judges,
and all other civil and military authorities." The ecclesiastical authorities were to "guide the people along the path to salvation; the civil,
to dispense justice; the military, to teach sound military doctrine, to
lead skilfully, and to incite valiant deeds." The remaining orders of
persons vested with paternal authority included parents — "though first
in the natural order, the first two orders [mentioned above] have responsibility for the common good, and therefore greater dignity" — other
relations, teachers, lords, and masters, to all of whom children or
students or servants or the people generally owed love, honor, obedience, and loyal service. And the *Primer* provided certain maxims to
guide the faithful in the performance of these duties. "Aged persons
enjoy paternal authority, though civil authority takes precedence over
age; for a young king is a father to his aged subjects." Or:

> Question: What is to be done when one paternal authority commands
> one thing, and another forbids it?
> Answer: When neither of them has authority over the other, you must

look not to the persons who command, but to what is commanded. For instance: if your master commands you to do something with regard to the service you owe him, and your father forbids it, obey your master and not your father. But if one authority is superior to the other, obey the superior: thus if your master or father commands you to do something that is forbidden by the civil authorities obey neither your father nor your master. And if the civil authorities order you to do anything that the Tsar forbids, obey the Tsar.

Thus in the *Primer* of Feofan Prokopovich, which was intended to educate children in the "will of God" and to promote a "Christian reform," the idea of an absolute state is merged with the more traditional doctrine of paternal authority which Prokopovich had first publicly expounded in a sermon on Palm Sunday 1718. In the *Primer*, a hierarchy of power is erected which culminates, "under God," in the tsar, to whom the ecclesiastical, civil, and military authorities of the state were subject and to whom all the lesser "orders of paternal authority," and their subjects, owed ultimate obedience. To be sure, the *Primer* also attempted to enlighten the people and to improve their religious and moral standards: superstition, defined as the attributing of a "power to do good or evil to persons or things which in truth have no such power," and rebaptism (which was practiced by some schismatics), were explicitly condemned. So, too, were bribery, simony, the promotion of unqualified persons to positions of authority, dishonest business practices, all forms of slandering and backbiting, and the rendering of "true worship," instead of appropriate forms of "respect," to ikons. Overly scrupulous Orthodox Russians were assured that it was permissible to have sexual relations with their wives. But it is difficult to avoid the conclusion that the chief pedagogical purpose of the *Primer* was to instill a respect for all forms of authority, especially that of the tsar (or state). The things of God, the people were being taught by Prokopovich, were the things of Caesar, and vice-versa: the two could not be distinguished. . . .

Prokopovich's *Primer* was first printed in March 1720. It was reprinted in May 1721. It was reprinted again in June 1722. Indeed, in the space of four years it was printed and reprinted a total of no less than twelve times in St. Petersburg, once in Moscow, and once in Chernigov. The number of copies printed each time was large, and already by the end of Peter's reign there were perhaps 16,000 copies in circulation. Obviously the demand for the *Primer* was great, and not suprisingly. In 1722 the Synod ordered that in accordance with the relevant provisions of the *Ecclesiastical Regulation* copies of the *Primer* were to be sent to all the dioceses, where they were to be used in all the episcopal schools and studied — indeed "memorized" — by all the clergy, so that the "benefit to be derived from introducing this instruction should not be delayed" and so that the clergy should "not only know [the fundamentals of] the faith and the law of God, but be able to answer questions concerning them." Moreover, in February 1723 the Synod resolved that passages from the *Primer* were to be read in all the churches of Russia during the Great Lent, in order that "parishioners preparing for confession and communion may, on hearing the commandments of God and their explanations, examine their consciences, and be better disposed to a true repentance." It was not of course to be expected that the great mass of ordinary Russians could make use of the *Primer* to inform themselves or to instruct their children; that would have been to presume a degree of popular literacy that was achieved in Russia only in our century. And so it was prudently provided by the Synod that the people should hear the official explanation of "God's law," with its insistence on the duty of submission to the tsar and his officers, regularly read to them in the parish churches. . . .

Another of the Synod's functions, one which was closely related to its educational responsibilities and to its efforts to suppress religious dissent, was its power of censorship. In October 1720 the Senate decreed that because of the appearance in recent years of books containing certain irregularities — "prayerbooks have been clandestinely printed in Chernigov for some schismatics; in a theology book printed in 1710 there appears much Lutheran opposition" — that because of these "irregularities," the monastery presses of Kiev and Chernigov were to print only "church books" which had previously been published (and therefore approved by the central ecclesiastical authorities).

> *And prior to printing* [the Senate continued], *these old church books are to be corrected in accordance with the church books used in Great Russia, and made to agree with them perfectly, so that all differences and local idioms should be eliminated.*
>
> *And no other books, whether old or new publications, are to be printed in these monasteries without prior notification to the Ecclesiastical College and without its permission, in order that books adverse to the Eastern church and not in Great Russian print should not appear.*

The Senate's decree was confirmed by the Synod within a week of its taking office: the Moscow (former patriarchal) press and the new Alexander-Nevskii monastery press, the Kiev and Chernigov presses, "and the other presses of the All-Russian realm," were, by the tsar's decree, to be subject to its authority, "whence permission is to be requested for the printing of books; and without this permission no book is to be printed." And in fact a sentence of the *Ecclesiastical Regulation* provided that "should someone write a theological treatise on some subject, he is not to publish it, but first to present it to the [Synod]; and the [Synod] must consider whether there is anything in the treatise contrary to Orthodox doctrine."

The Synod took its power of censorship seriously. In July 1721 it set up a special office under the direction of one of its members "for a better supervision of the presses." The following month it confirmed once again the Senate's decree of October 1720 and also provided that two copies of all books printed at the presses should be sent "for inspection and consideration" to its special office, where one copy was to be permanently deposited. Nor could second impressions of any book be issued without the Synod's permission. And "now, everywhere, the title-page is to be printed thus: by the most gracious permission of the Great Sovereign Tsar and Great Prince Peter the First, All-Russian Emperor, and with the consent of the Most Holy Governing Synod, this book [title] is printed in the town of [name] at the [name] monastery. . . ."

Censorship in the service of an official ideology, one of the more characteristic features of the modern absolute state, was thus firmly established in Russia in the closing years of Peter's reign. And Peter's action in conferring this power on the Synod reminds us, once again, of what was at once the fundamental fact and the single most important result of his church reform: the transformation of the supreme administration of the Russian Orthodox church into an impersonal department of the Imperial government.

P. N. Miliukov

Schools Under
Peter the Great

The institution under Peter I of a system of episcopal schools for the training of clergy was discussed in the previous reading. Here, these schools are mentioned in a more wide-ranging survey of Peter's efforts to promote modern education in Russia. As Miliukov points out, Peter succeeded in laying the ground for the continuous development of secondary and technical education but not of primary education, which after Peter remained by and large in the hands of the church (mainly for church people), of the army (garrison schools), or of private tutors (for the upper classes); or it was left to the age-old apprentice system (for craftsmen, traders, and artisans). Miliukov further indicates that despite Peter's efforts the student body of the technical or professional schools soon came to be dominated by the nobility, and that general education either in preparation for state service or for its own sake was neglected altogether. In other words, impressive though it was in some respects, Peter's record of educational reform was on the whole quite mixed.

P. N. Miliukov (1859–1944), a pupil of V. O. Kliuchevsky at Moscow University, was a distinguished historian of Petrine Russia. He was also a leading statesman during the last years of the Russian Empire, for which reason he was driven into exile by the Bolshevik government in 1918 and eventually died in France.

While scholastic textbooks were being introduced into the academic curriculum by the brothers Likhud,[1] the sixteen-year-old Peter was hard at work on his mathematics notebooks. In a style that did little honor to his rhetorical and dialectical abilities and also grossly violated the rules of grammar and spelling, Peter worked out the rules of addition and subtraction and solved problems in artillery and astronomy. Everyone

From P. N. Miliukov, *Ocherki po Istorii Russkoi Kultury [Essays in the History of Russian Culture]*, Jubilee edition, vol. II, part 2, Paris, 1931 (izd. "Sovremenniia Zapiski"), pp. 732–743. Trans. Marc Raeff.

[1] Two Greek brothers who taught at the Slavonic-Greek-Latin Academy in Moscow in the later seventeenth century. — Ed.

knows the general results of these exercises: five years later, sporting a sailor's outfit, Peter was repeating in broken Dutch greetings and curses in Archangel, Russia's only port at the time. Still five years later, in the same sailor's outfit, but with a somewhat larger Dutch vocabulary, Peter was sawing and filing in Amsterdam. Upon his return home he demanded that all Russians who wanted to serve be as capable of sawing, filing, building, and navigating ships as he was himself.

The most direct way of acquiring this knowledge was to go abroad, as Peter himself had done, and as he compelled many of his contemporaries to do. But abroad the Russians proved too little-prepared and could not properly benefit from the trip. . . . For this reason, during his first trip abroad [1697–1698] Peter hired the Englishman Farquharson as teacher of mathematics and navigation. In 1701 a "school of mathematical sciences and navigation" was established in the Sukharev Tower in Moscow, and Farquharson began to teach navigation to Russian youth — "some voluntarily, some under compulsion."

In this fashion, alongside the Slavonic-Greek-Latin Academy, a professional school of theological studies, there arose in Moscow another professional school, that of navigation. The government's attitude with respect to the aims of education had not changed. As had been the case previously, science and schooling had to serve the practical needs of the state. It was only the nature of these needs that had changed: instead of correcting church books and protecting the faith, it was now a matter of transforming the army and navy. In establishing the first Russian secular school the young reformer was least interested in satisfying the needs of general education. But life itself corrected the omission. The sailors who returned from their study trips abroad and who graduated from the school of navigation had to be used not as specialists in their field, but as generally educated people. They became administrators, diplomats, teachers, builders, geodesists, engineers, etc. Peter soon had to realize "that not only for navigation was this school needed." In any case, the school of navigation had a military-naval character, and it preserved this character after moving to St. Petersburg in 1714, where it received the name of "Naval Academy."

The two academies, the Naval and the Slavonic-Greek-Latin, soon served as the foundation for a whole network of elementary schools that Peter set up in the provinces. It is this creation of a network of secular and ecclesiastical schools in Russia that marks Peter's reign as a completely new epoch in the history of Russian education. Without the two academies in the capitals the provincial schools could never have been established, for there would have been nowhere to obtain teachers. With respect to the provincial schools, the Naval and Slavonic-Greek-Latin academies played the role of teachers' colleges. In turn, the provincial schools were to serve as preparatory grades for the schools in the capitals: the lower secular school gave elementary mathematical knowledge, and the lower ecclesiastical school imparted philological knowledge.

The year the school of navigation moved to St. Petersburg, Peter ordered that there be sent to every province two of its students who had completed their work in geometry and geography, "for teaching in science young children of all classes." As a consequence of this decree, there were opened in the following year (1716) twelve schools in various Russian towns; between 1720 and 1722 thirty more schools were added. These new schools taught arithmetic and geometry and were called "cipher" schools. Fortunately, we are in a position to determine the results obtained by the cipher schools during the first period of their existence. According to information gathered in 1727 slightly over 2,000 pupils had been enrolled in these schools, voluntarily or under compulsion. With respect to their known class origin the pupils were distributed as follows:

1.	from the clergy	931	45.4%
2.	soldiers' children	402	19.6%
3.	children of clerks	374	18.2%
4.	children of artisans	93	4.5%
5.	children of noblemen and squires	53	2.5%

But this composition was not maintained for long. No sooner had these schools been established than various classes of the population began to protest against this novel school obligation. The artisans were the first to petition that they be exempted from sending their children to school, for the children should stay in the shops and learn their father's craft. In 1720 the government satisfied their request and the cipher schools lost part of their enrollment. But more significant still proved to be the competition between the ecclesiastical and the cipher schools.

Ecclesiastical schools made their appearance in the provinces in obedience to the rules of the *Ecclesiastical Regulation* that compelled bishops to set up diocesan schools attached to their sees (1721). In compliance with the rules, forty-six diocesan schools were opened in the course of the next five years. Thus, in the last years of Peter's reign, almost every provincial capital had two schools, a secular and an ecclesiastical. Students had to be driven into either school by force, and naturally competition developed between the two. The Synod demanded that all sons of clergy attending the cipher schools be returned to the diocesan schools. In this way a large number of pupils was withdrawn from the cipher schools. The magnitude of the loss can be gauged from the fact that after the withdrawal of the sons of clergy and artisians, fourteen cipher schools were left without any pupils. These schools had to be closed and their teachers returned to the Naval Academy. In the other twenty-eight cipher schools there remained almost exclusively the children of clerks. In 1727 there remained only 500 pupils out of the 2,000 enrolled at first. The known causes for this drop are graphically illustrated by the following table:

1.	sons of artisans and clergy withdrawn	572	37%
2.	fled, returned home, or did not appear	322	20.8%
3.	graduated after completion of course	302	19.9%
4.	illiterates, idiots, incapables	233	15%
5.	taken into various branches of state service before completion of course	93	6%

More than one-third of those who left school before completion had been withdrawn compulsorily; more than one-fifth left school voluntarily; one-seventh were dismissed by the schools themselves; one-seventh entered service without completing the course; and only for one-fifth of the cases did the school accomplish its purpose.

The question of the very existence of the secular school was raised immediately after Peter's death. Peter had put the administration of the cipher schools in the hands of the Admiralty College because their teachers were drawn from the Naval Academy. Now (1726) the Admiralty was trying to get rid of the responsibility and renewed Peter's earlier proposal (1723) of combining the cipher schools with the diocesan schools. But the Holy Synod objected to the merger, for in general it was not well-disposed to "secular maritime sciences." "To impart the knowledge of arthmetic and geometry without giving theological instruction is not the clergy's business. For this reason we request that the cipher and geometry schools remain under secular administration," declared the Synod in 1727. It was only because of this refusal that Peter's cipher schools lasted until 1744. At that time there were only eight schools left out of twenty-eight; and of these eight the three largest were combined with garrison schools. Garrison schools attached to regiments had been established in 1732; they were maintained at regimental cost and the teachers were officers and noncommissioned officers. Besides reading and writing, these schools also taught military drill, arithmetic, artillery, and engineering.

Peter's secular school did not prove very long-lasting. Its remnants were preserved as part of the military schools that took over portions of its curriculum. In this form it rendered an important service to Russian culture: even in the first years of the reign of Catherine II it was only in garrison schools that one could find individuals with an elementary knowledge of arithmetic.

Let us now look at the fate of the diocesan schools established, as we have noted, according to a provision of the *Ecclesiastical Regulation*. These schools were directly supervised by the local bishop, not by the lay authorities. State authorities did not interfere in their operation, as they did in the cipher schools. The government had no concern in providing a teaching staff for the diocesan schools. The teachers were recruited rather haphazardly; in the best of cases they were students of the Moscow academy and even of the Kiev academy; in other cases ordinary local clergy became teachers. In any event, the recruitment of teachers as well as the very existence of the diocesan schools depended on the good will of the diocesan authorities who had to maintain them at their own expense. Whenever a diocese changed hands schools might be set up or discontinued. Active prelates like Job of Novgorod, or Pitirim of Nizhnii Novgorod, Dmitry of Rostov, and Gabriel Buzhinsky of Riazan raised the level of the schools and filled them with hundreds of pupils. Other bishops allowed the pupils to return home, closed down the schools completely, or did not even open them at all under the pretext of lack of funds or teachers. The programs of instruction also depended on the means available and the zeal of local authorities. The best schools taught a program that approximated that of the Moscow academy and included all the liberal arts. In most cases, however, the curriculum was limited to grammar and rhetoric. In some cases, as for example in the school at Viatka, the pupils learned only how to read and write, as teachers of more advanced subjects were unavailable. Incidentally, it was necessary sometimes to rest content with imparting only reading and writing because of the great need for parish priests. In the school of Nizhnii Novgorod, for example, of 832 pupils, 427 (more than one-half) contented themselves with going through the primer only and immediately afterwards were ordained priests, deacons, etc.

As pupils were recruited in less harsh a way than the students of secular schools, the percentage of deserters was much lower in the diocesan schools. In 1727 there were forty-six diocesan schools in Russia; they had 3,056 pupils, and of these only 239 deserted. We should add, however, that of the remaining 2,827 almost one-half (1,331) belonged to ten schools in three Ukrainian dioceses (Kiev, Chernigov, Belgorod). Thus in Russia proper the number of pupils was slightly higher in the secular than in the diocesan schools. In some cases the secular schools were ahead of the diocesan in terms of the level of their instruction. But, as we have noted, Peter's secular schools had but a very brief flowering. The diocesan schools, on the other hand, proved more stable. Without any decrease, almost fifty diocesan schools survived until the time they were transformed into seminaries.

Their very transformation into seminaries was a consequence of their prosperity, while the transformation of cipher schools into garrison schools was the result of decline. The diocesan school was transformed into a seminary and its curriculum extended to the level of an academy by the introduction of intermediate and advanced grades in addition to the elementary. Besides reading and writing, the full curriculum included grammar, rhetoric, philosophy, and theology. . . . Such a program tended to transform the diocesan school from an elementary into a secondary educational institution, and in turn it became the focus for the lower type of schools that were arising within the confines of the diocese. . . . [With the exception of Novgorod, where the change took place in the first years of the eighteenth century], the diocesan schools began to be transformed into seminaries about 1737, when a general decree was issued to this effect. But the high cost of the transformation delayed the establishment of seminaries until the accession of Catherine II. After the first impulse given by Peter to the ecclesiastical schools, their further development proceeded slowly, as had been also the case of the secular schools. . . . In the reign of Catherine II the full program was introduced in only eight seminaries. (In 1738 there were seventeen seminaries with 2,589 students, and in 1764 twenty-six with 6,000 students.) . . .

With the fate of the cipher and diocesan schools we have almost exhausted the question of Russian school organization in the first half of the eighteenth century. The ground for a continuous development of Russian secondary education had been laid in this period, but not even this much can be said of the primary-school system. Peter's efforts in this latter respect remained completely fruitless. . . . But from the organization of the schools in the first half of the eighteenth century, let us turn to the goals they pursued.

As its first characteristic feature we should note that the Russian school of that time did not aim either at the moral upbringing of its pupils or at imparting general education; it aimed mainly at giving technical training for professional purposes. This was a point of view inherited in its entirety from the seventeenth century; the eighteenth century deduced from it only the necessity of a very comprehensive organization of the schools. This is the reason why some scholars have felt that the eighteenth century introduced something radically new into Russian pedagogy. In fact, however, a truly pedagogical point of view was as alien to the schools of the period we are considering as it had been to the schools of the seventeenth century. Both institutions saw the pupil merely as an object of pedagogical action. If he came on his own, the school treated him the way old-fashioned master craftsmen treated apprentices: on the basis of a voluntary contract.

If the pupil was sent by the government, learning became a form of [state] service. For the service he received a salary, and for nonfulfillment of his obligations he was subjected to the punishment specified by the service [regulations]. The responsibility of a pupil did not, therefore, differ from that of an adult person. A fault was equated with a regular violation of the law and punished like a crime. The task of "education" was limited to the setting up of external discipline. For absences, pupils were fined; for "impertinence" they were beaten with rods; for more serious misconduct they were given lashes in the schoolyard. Retired soldiers were in attendance in the classrooms, armed with a whip; "and if some student misbehaves, he [the soldier] ought to strike, regardless of his [pupil's] family origin."

Neither moral upbringing nor general education entered into the duties of the Petrine school. The new school of mathematics did not aim at the development of the mind but only at the acquisition of essential technical know-how. Only accidentally, to the extent that some preliminary general knowledge was a prerequisite for technical training, did the school acquire some functions of general education.

Following upon the acquisition of preliminary knowledge came the professional training: a general common preparation was given [the pupils] for the sake of this latter training. Peter's guiding idea was that the school had to prepare for various branches of the state service. In doing so, as we have said, he took over the seventeenth-century viewpoint. But to the single professional goal of the seventeenth-century Muscovite school — preparation of the clergy — he added a whole line of other state tasks.

Peter's first idea had been to entrust the execution of these tasks to the Slavonic-Greek-Latin Academy in Moscow. At any rate, upon his return from abroad [1698] Peter had the following interesting exchange with Patriarch Adrian: "Thanks to the Lord's mercy we have this school; and let persons who have studied in it with diligence be put to all kinds of uses: ecclesiastical service, civil service, military service, engineering and medical service." Soon, though, the tsar was bound to notice how far removed the clever rhetoric of medieval learning was from the real modern sciences he needed. As there were no special schools, at first his collaborators had to acquire the necessary learning directly in service, through practice: the naval officer learned his craft on a ship, the civil official in the office, the doctor in the hospital, the apothecary in the pharmacy — exactly in the same way as before Peter's time the priest had been trained in a church and the merchant behind the counter. Of course, this was not adequate. At the first opportunity professional training had to be given an educational framework.

Once such schools had been established, they became obligatory for those for whom service had been a compulsory obligation earlier. It is for this reason that attendance at Peter's military schools in itself became an obligation of the service class. At the same time, the schools became class-bound; and if the class-bound character did not become implanted immediately, it is only because at first the government valued the presence of anyone who was desirous to study, regardless of his origin. As a historian of the Naval Academy has noted, "not many noblemen entered this institution voluntarily; it was men from lower ranks [*raznochintsy*], not noblemen, who came willingly." This did not prevent a differentiation from taking place in the subsequent careers of members of these two groups. "Young men from the lower classes, *raznochintsy*, having completed the first two grades and learned how to write and count, terminated their studies and were assigned as clerks to various offices in the Admiralty or as assistant architects, pharmacists, etc. The sons of the nobility went on to higher grades for further study and for service in the army and navy. With the transfer of the academy to St. Petersburg it became an exclusively military school and gave preference in admission to noblemen, and wealthier noblemen at that. The school's lower grades were left open in Moscow for pupils from the lower classes. It is from among the latter that the teachers of the cipher schools were recruited." The same observation could be made in the case of another of Peter's military schools, that of engineering (founded 1712). It too had been destined exclusively for the nobility. In the absence of students from the nobility the school was filled with *raznochintsy*, and it became a strictly noble institution only at the time of its transfer to St. Petersburg (1719). The third school, for artillery (1712), continued to teach sons of gunners in its lower grades for a very long time; higher professional training was given only to the nobility and only the latter were admitted to higher military careers. . . . The class character of these schools became firmly established after Peter's death. . . .

Alongside the development of these schools' class character, there took place a definition of the particular range of knowledge that was to be characteristic of the nobleman's education. Included among the "noble" or "knightly" subjects were, above all, modern languages, fencing, and dancing. It was this curriculum that determined the program of the first school of general studies in Russia. Naturally, not all noblemen could attend the educational institutions in the capital. Those who did not attend them had to undergo schooling through "practice" in the guards regiments, and rise to the higher ranks through service.

Another branch, besides the military, that since Peter's time has required special training, was the civil service. For the performance of civil administrative duties it was increasingly necessary to be familiar with political, juridical, and economic subjects. The government endeavored to set up a professional school for this branch too. But it met with the nobility's old prejudice against "office" service. The school did not materialize, as there was no adequate social material for it. Peter insisted in vain on the necessity of preparing for the civil service, and in vain he entreated "not to hold this training against members of prominent and noble families, for without it no one can be promoted to higher and ministerial ranks. . . ." Not even the introduction of jurisprudence into the curriculum of schools for the nobility could force the noblemen to study this subject. Of 245 noblemen enrolled in the Noble Corps of Cadets in 1733 only eleven took jurisprudence.[2] Noblemen who had been sent to work in offices for a practical acquaintance with administration did not want to work together with clerks and had to be returned to military schools. . . .

All of this leads to the conclusion that under Peter and his immediate successors Russian society needed first of all *elementary* education and was looking for it wherever it could find it within the limited resources available. The government, on the other hand, needed men with *professional* training and made all possible efforts to drive the youth of all classes into the kind of professional schools that would prepare them for discharging their fathers' and grandfathers' duties. Lastly, *general education* was little valued for itself by either the government or society. This is the reason why the government first limited itself to the opening of a set of special schools to satisfy its own immediate requirements, leaving the remainder to time and society's own efforts.

John T. Alexander

Medical Developments in Petrine Russia

Peter I's efforts in the medical field, according to John T. Alexander, professor of history at the University of Kansas, merit for him the title of "the father of Russian medicine." In this special study of the subject Alexander shows how Peter, responding, as so often, to pressing military needs, multiplied by several times the number of medical personnel serving in Russia and personally shaped both a national medical administration and a native medical profession. Alexander concludes that these activities rank among Peter's "finest and most lasting achievements."

---

[2] Corps of Cadets (*Shliakhetnyi kadetskii korpus*) — a special school for sons of the nobility established in St. Petersburg in 1731. — Ed.

From John T. Alexander, "Medical Developments in Petrine Russia," in *Canadian-American Slavic Studies*, vol. 8, no. 2 (Summer 1974), pp. 199–217.

Peter's personal fascination with medical matters is generally known. Less appreciated, however, is his broader impact on medicine, for he may justly be termed "the father of Russian medicine." Although tsars since Ivan III had employed foreign physicians, Peter became the only Muscovite sovereign to learn the rudiments of medicine and surgery, to observe medical procedures firsthand, and to frequent medical institutions at home and abroad. Probably his early interest in medicine evolved from visits to Moscow's German Suburb, where several foreign-trained physicians lived. One of them, the surgeon Johann Termont — in Russian guise, Ivan Eremeev — proved just the sort of well-traveled adventurer, yarnspinner, and jolly drinker the youthful tsar welcomed into his entourage. Born in Friesland, Termont had entered Russian service under Tsar Aleksei. With three other foreign surgeons and two Russian apprentices, Termont accompanied Peter on the famous "Grand Embassy" to Europe in 1697–1698.

While in the Netherlands the tsar and his colleagues lightened their shipbuilding apprenticeship with visits to Dr. Fredrik Ruysch's anatomical museum, hospitals, botanical gardens, insane asylums, foundling homes, and medical lectures at the University of Leyden. Ruysch's artfully preserved and displayed exhibits amazed the visiting Muscovites, who rewarded him with a half-dozen sables. Peter preserved a lifelong affection for Ruysch, whom he dubbed "mein alter Lehrer [my old teacher]," and in 1717 purchased his collection for the first Russian museum — the *Kunstkamera* in St. Petersburg. Many specimens are still exhibited there today. Possibly Ruysch told Peter about the microscopic researches of his friend Antony van Leeuwenhoek,[1] who showed the tsar "among other remarkable discoveries, through his particular glasses, the marvellous circulation in the tail of an eel; which so delighted the Prince, that in these and other contemplations he spent no less than two hours. . . ." Even then the microscope's revolutionary implications for medicine were widely recognized, albeit only slowly realized.

Subsequent Russian medical development owed much to Dutch influence, which had begun well before Peter's trip abroad. The Russians were wise to emulate Dutch medicine; for by the late seventeenth century Dutch universities had surpassed Padua, the leader of Europe

---

[1] The famous Dutch naturalist and pioneer in the use of the microscope (1632–1723). — Ed.

in the previous century, to attain European preeminence in medical theory and practice. The clinical teaching of "the Batavian Hippocrates," Herman Boerhaave (1668–1738), brought students from all over Europe to the University of Leyden, whence they returned home to propagate a new, clinically-oriented "scientific" medicine. Boerhaave's fame early impressed the Russians. During Peter's second visit to Holland in 1717 he "did not repent lying all night in his pleasure barge against Boerhaave's house, in order to have two hours conversation with him on various points of learning the next morning before college time." Several Russian citizens studied under Boerhaave, and together with his foreign pupils in Russian service they introduced the latest Dutch achievements in medical practice.

In England in 1698 Peter and company marveled at Christopher Wren's Greenwich Hospital and visited other medical institutions. As in Holland they recruited surgeons and apothecaries; they purchased medicaments, surgical instruments, and an anatomy manual. Back in Moscow Peter sponsored anatomical demonstrations for a group of bewildered nobles. Thenceforth the tsar carried a valise of surgical instruments, performed some minor operations — especially pulling teeth — and often observed surgery and postmortem examinations. While in Paris in 1717, for example, he witnessed an eye operation.

Peter, like his forebears, hired foreign-trained medics to attend his person — at least one doctor or *leibmedik* (i.e., an internist) and one or more surgeons. . . .

The tsar and his physicians, especially the Scotsman Robert Erskine, believed in balneology. Peter visited Baden in 1698 and Carlsbad in 1711 and 1712 — in the latter cases because of his "great need" for treatment. Apparently his ailments involved the urinary tract and the gall bladder. He took the waters at Pyrmont for seventeen days in 1716 and the next year spent three weeks at Spa, where Erskine diagnosed his ailments as "lack of appetite, swollen legs, occasional gallic colics, loss of facial color." These visits to European spas stimulated Peter to seek mineral springs at home. Dr. Gottlob Schober, whom the tsar hired at Carlsbad in 1712, investigated springs in the northern Caucasus, where he honored his employer by naming one source "the Hot Springs of Saint Peter." Emperor Peter visited there in 1722 during the Persian expedition. He also stopped by the mineral springs near Voronezh and personally advertised the iron-rich springs of Olonets, which he sampled himself in 1719, 1720, and 1722. Indeed, Peter edited and partly wrote the officially issued "Announcement about the Martsial Waters" at Olonets [1719], perhaps the earliest example of a secular medical publication in Russian. During his last illness the tsar sought relief at Olonets in October, 1724, and drank both Olonets and Pyrmont mineral water — to no avail.

The condition that caused Peter's death on January 28, 1725, has spawned controversy. All agree the urinary tract was involved; but some speak of complications from syphilis, others of poison, still others of strangury — which might stem from either of the first two causes or from something else. In view of Peter's heavy drinking one can scarcely be surprised at renal difficulties, and inflammation of the prostate gland would also have been possible. Nevertheless, the issue remains unresolved in the absence of detailed, informed descriptions of Peter's symptoms. The allegation of syphilis, in particular, should be treated with caution.

If Peter's hiring of foreign physicians merely followed precedent, he did transform their quantity if not their quality. According to [one] index, which counts the number of doctors of medicine and each decade of their activity in Russia, the total doctor-decades for seventeenth-century Muscovy to 1690 was just 50. For the period 1690–1730, however, the index rose to 125. In other words, more than twice as many doctors were twice as active in less than half the preceding period. Since [another source] lists forty-three M.D.'s in Russia during Peter's personal reign, their average tenure approached three decades. This represented a substantial change from the past, when foreign physicians had been few, their tenure short, their sphere of activity restricted. The number of Russian-born, foreign-trained physicians increased sharply too. Dr. Laurentius Blumentrost, who treated three generations of the tsarist family from 1668 till his death in Moscow in 1705, had three sons who personify the trend. Two were born in Moscow. All three studied medicine abroad and returned to Russia to practice. Laurentius the Elder served as *leibmedik* to the grand princesses until his untimely death in the 1690s; Johann Deodatus directed the Medical Chancery, 1721–1730; Laurentius the Younger studied under Boerhaave at Leyden and became the first president of the Academy of Sciences. Of the many other foreign-born physicians in Petrine Russia, Nicolaas Bidloo and Robert Erskine spent the bulk of their careers there and enjoyed great influence with Peter personally. The nephew of a prominent

Dutch anatomist, Bidloo founded and directed the first permanent Russian hospital and surgical school. Erskine served fourteen years as Peter's *liebmedik*, accompanied him abroad in 1716–1717, headed the reorganized Russian medical administration as *arkhiater* (chief physician), and died a very wealthy man in 1718.

Peter's reign also claims the first native Muscovite to earn an M.D. degree. P. V. Postnikov (ca. 1670–ca. 1712), the son of a senior official in the Ambassadorial Bureau, attended the newly established Slavonic-Greek-Latin Academy in Moscow (1687–1691), where he learned Latin and Greek from the Likhud brothers, both of them graduates of the University of Padua. He became acquainted with two Greek physicians in Moscow, Jakob (or Giacomo) Pelarino and Johannes Komnin, likewise Padua alumni. Padua epitomized the achievements of Renaissance medicine. It had already trained many physicians from eastern Europe, Poland in particular. So in May 1692, with government support, Postnikov went to Padua, where he completed degrees in philosophy and medicine in 1694. He spent the next two years in advanced training at Paris and Leyden before joining the Grand Embassy at Amsterdam in 1697. In England Postnikov helped Peter recruit medical personnel, purchase instruments, medicaments, and books, and even received special permission to prolong his stay in order to inspect English academic (and presumably medical) institutions. Politics sidetracked his promising medical career in 1698, however, when the Russian delegation needed his linguistic talents as secretary and translator at the Congress of Karlowicz. Thence he revisited Amsterdam, London, and Paris to purchase medical instruments and to study further, returning to Moscow only in 1701. He left the next year to be unofficial envoy to Paris. Back in Moscow in 1710, he is last mentioned working on the translation of a French diplomatic handbook in 1712. Although Postnikov apparently never practiced medicine — in Russia, anyway — his career marked out the way for subsequent Russian M.D.'s. Grigorii Volkov, also the son of an Ambassadorial Bureau official, followed Postnikov to Padua in 1698, but his medical studies were quickly terminated in favor of language study in France to prepare him for a diplomatic career.

Of greater significance for broader segments of the population, especially the military, were increased numbers of lesser medical personnel — surgeons (*lekari*), surgeon's aides (*podlekari*), apprentices (*ucheniki*), and apothecaries (*aptekari*). One source lists a total of 124 foreign surgeons in Petrine Russia, but its data are not complete. If some of these medics stayed only briefly, others remained in Russia permanently. Thus Jan Hovy, one of the fifty-odd surgeons that Admiral Cruys recruited for the new Russian fleet in 1698, succeeded Termont as Peter's personal surgeon, accompanied him on the Persian expedition, became senior surgeon to the Admiralty, served Peter's three immediate successors, and died in Russia in 1743. The gulf in status between *doktor* and *lekar* loomed so large, however, that few if any surgeons of the Petrine era ever earned the M.D., which could only be obtained abroad. The most they could hope for was to become a staff surgeon (*shtab lekar*) after many years service. The same source counts thirty-two foreign apothecaries under Peter. The number of surgeon's aides and apprentices, most of whom were Russians, is less certain, but obviously increased substantially compared to the past. In numbers of medical personnel, then, Petrine Russia witnessed remarkable growth that formed the foundation for national medical institutions — first in the army, later in the rest of the country.

The practice of hiring medics abroad entailed many difficulties. It was expensive, the personnel of variable quality, their period of service limited. Since most foreign physicians knew no Russian, they could not easily instruct Russian students even if their duties had allowed. Furthermore, their effectiveness was diminished by the absence of auxiliary personnel and supporting services. A framework of medical institutions had to be created almost from scratch and, because of the imperatives of nearly continuous warfare, almost overnight. Indeed, it was the demands of war that first brought significant numbers of foreign medics to Muscovy. In 1692 the Apothecary Bureau, though greatly expanded in recent years, still concentrated on serving the tsar's family and the court, or, at the very most, the population of Moscow only. Under its jurisdiction were six doctors, five surgeons, seven apothecaries, two apothecary assistants, five apprentice apothecaries, and fourteen surgeon's aides and barbers — in all thirty-nine persons. Besides their state duties, many of these medics practiced privately. Even if all of them had been fully qualified, full-time military physicians, they could not have coped with the needs of Peter's reorganized, standing army and new navy.

Medical deficiencies had contributed to the collapse of Prince V. V. Golitsyn's campaigns against the Crimea in 1687–1689, and Peter himself had similar difficulties in his own first attempt against Azov in 1695. That same year, as a result, twelve field surgeons were hired in Riga. Of Swedish and German origin, these men do not appear to have epitomized medical skill and probity; three of them were injured enroute to the army when a drunken argument over medicines flared into swordplay. Probably they had only short-term contracts, too. In any event, one of Peter's instructions to the Grand Embassy of 1697–1698 urged the recruitment of surgeons and the purchase of medical stores for each ship of his projected Black Sea squadron. Hence Admiral Cruys in 1698 hired some fifty surgeons, mostly Dutchmen and Frenchmen — an unprecedented number in Russian medical and military annals. The Grand Embassy also employed five apothecaries in 1697 and bought large quantities of medicaments.

With the outbreak of the Northern War in 1700, the demand for military medics became acute. It has been estimated that over sixty Russian surgeons were in service in 1700 with "not a few" practicing privately. But even if these figures are accepted uncritically (one suspects they are generally inflated and lump together medics and paramedics), they fell far short of the number needed. As early as October 4, 1700, Peter spoke at the sickbed of Patriarch Adrian about the national necessity for educated clergy, military, civil servants, architects, and — not least — those who knew "the doctor's healing art." Recruitment of foreigners continued, but Russia proved too poor to hire all the medics required, while the extended duration of military action hindered both short-term contractual employment and the dispatch of Russians for medical training abroad. These were the circumstances that decreed the foundation of Russia's first permanent hospital and surgical school.

The Moscow *Goshpital* and surgical school had some native precursors. Like other Russian institutions, however, its legacy from the past was so ephemeral as to burnish, rather than tarnish, the brilliance of the Petrine achievement. Hospitals had existed in Muscovy, mainly in monasteries, but they were as much almshouses as centers of medical treatment. The same held true for the private institutions established by several benevolent magnates under Tsar Aleksei. Although state involvement was foreshadowed by Tsar Feodor's decree of 1682 establishing two *"shpitalni"* in Moscow, it is not certain these ever functioned. In any case, they had disappeared by Peter's time. In 1654 the Apothecary Bureau had recruited thirty youths to become military medics and instituted a short-lived school for their instruction. The training offered seems to have been barely rudimentary; indeed, the whole arrangement may have involved simply *ad hoc* courses. No matter how skillful and dutiful its trainees — one study lists thirty-two names — they were too few to redress the massive deficiencies of the still embryonic military medical science.

By contrast, the Moscow hospital and surgical school represented a higher level of institutional development. Planned, built, and administered by Dr. Nicolaas Bidloo, the Moscow medical complex reflected European architectural style as well as medical conceptions. Although several commentators maintain it was inspired by the Greenwich Hospital, scant evidence supports this surmise. After all, Peter's Grand Embassy had visited several hospitals in several countries, and Bidloo's origins and training would suggest Dutch models (as does his own, recently discovered, sketch of the Moscow hospital). Whatever its inspiration, the Moscow hospital and surgical school experienced many birth and growth pangs. The original building, of which no floorplan has been found, opened in 1707 near the Iauza River in Moscow's German Suburb. A wooden, two storied structure of several sections linked together in the Dutch style, with small windows and a church in the middle, it burned down in 1721 and was rebuilt only in 1727. It must have been a modest facility: in 1712 Bidloo told Peter that 100–200 patients were treated daily. Since 1708, he reported, 1,996 persons had received treatment, of whom 1,026 had been healed and 142 remained. Presumably the other 800 either died or were released as incurable. Although the Moscow hospital later became a military medical institution, it was not so at first. Throughout Peter's reign it remained under the Monastery Bureau, later the Holy Synod, for it was primarily a welfare and educational institution. Besides, it was too far from the front to treat large numbers of wounded soldiers; thus its patients were very mixed — beggars, monks, clerks, school children, the local garrison, the elderly, etc. The hospital staff comprised Dr. Bidloo, chief surgeon Heinrich Röpken (russified to Andrei Repkin), surgeon Laurenz Pochert, apothecary Christian Eichler, apothecary's aide Johann Schmidt, and surgeon's aide Iakov Bogdanov. Till his death in 1735, Bidloo ran everything singlehandedly.

If Bidloo had trouble obtaining staff, medicaments, instruments, and supplies for his hospital — not to mention rebuilding it after the fire of 1721 — the surgical school posed still tougher problems. Foremost was the shortage of qualified students — a legacy of Muscovy's poverty, illiteracy, and isolation. Peter ordered the school to enroll fifty students. Bidloo needed five years to recruit that number and reported in 1712 that only thirty-three remained. Eight had fled, six died, two left for other schools, and one had been drafted. The bulk of the students came from the Slavonic-Greek-Latin Academy, knowledge of Latin being essential since Bidloo and his associates scarcely knew Russian. Moreover, Russian was then poorly developed as a language of science, despite increasing borrowings and adaptations from Europe. One of the first students was a "sailor of Dutch knowledge," apparently sent because he knew Dutch. Evidently the students were all Russians or thoroughly russified. Many probably came from the Ukraine, where formal instruction in Latin was more widely available than in Russia proper. The conditions at the new surgical school and the humble status of *lekar* (or, even lowlier, *podlekar*) could not induce wealthy Russian or foreign families to enroll their sons; they preferred to seek higher status through medical education at European universities, Leyden and Halle especially.

Bidloo divided the students into three classes, based on knowledge. The term of instruction varied from five to ten years, summers included. Both medicine and surgery were taught, with the emphasis on practical application. Contrary to some Russian claims of priority for the Moscow school in the teaching of clinical medicine, the level of instruction there in the early years must have been quite low. Books were so rare the students had to rely on manuals of lecture notes, which their instructors rarely had time to correct. Predictably, the students' knowledge proved uneven. Bidloo praised his best graduates as equal to surgeons anywhere, but admitted that many could serve only as surgeon's aides because of their meager knowledge. The school faced constant demands from the military to provide medics, whatever their training. In 1708, for example, Peter ordered twenty "hospital surgeon's apprentices" sent to the army at Smolensk. Bidloo reluctantly selected six, but forthrightly informed the tsar they were "unskilled" because they had studied only anatomy their first year, not "treatment of wounds," and he implored that they be returned for further study. There was nobody else to send, he told his superior, "and even if some are sent anyway, there will be no good from them." Peter later tried to speed "production" by promising Bidloo 100 rubles for each surgeon and 50 for each surgeon's aide. Even so, the Dutchman's insistence on maintaining standards joined with the constant shortage of qualified entrants to limit the supply.

The first regular class graduated in 1712–1713, ten men in all. A year later a second, twelve-man contingent joined the service; ten were assigned to the Admiralty, two to the Apothecary Bureau. Ten more fledgling medics finished in 1719. In March 1723, when the War College demanded nine surgeons and twenty surgeon's aides for the army corps sent on the Persian expedition, the school could furnish only five surgeon's aides and four apprentices. Four years later the entire graduating class of sixteen were sent as surgeon's aides to the army in Astrakhan. Available data do not permit a complete tabulation of the medics Bidloo's school trained during Peter's reign, but at least seventy-one persons were enrolled up to 1723 — a significant increase in quantity, not to mention quality, over the short-lived "school" of the 1650's.

Just one of the early graduates attained any prominence. Sergei Evreinov, a soldier's son, studied at Bidloo's school from 1713 to 1721, continued as an apprentice at the Admiralty hospital in St. Petersburg from 1721 to 1724, went as a surgeon's aide in 1724 to the Astrakhan naval hospital where he was promoted to surgeon in 1728, and headed a field hospital at Azov in 1736 — the first Russian ever to occupy such a post. Whatever its early vicissitudes, Bidloo's creation survived to expand, mature, and deepen its influence on the evolution of Russian medicine, training about 800 medics in the course of the century. Its success facilitated the foundation of hospitals in St. Petersburg — the Admiralty hospital in 1715 and the "Land-hospital" in 1717 — in Reval (1715); Kronstadt (1716–1717); Kazan (1722); Tavrov, near Voronezh (1724); Astrakhan (1725); and Archangel (1733). Both hospitals in St. Petersburg and the one at Kronstadt formally added surgical schools of their own in 1733. Besides these primarily military institutions, the Chancellery of Construction in St. Petersburg had a hospital for the workers building the city, and Peter chartered eight private apothecary shops in Moscow. Wartime exigencies and Russia's slender scholarly resources rendered medical research dispensable until the establishment of the Academy of Sciences (1725), which developed a substantial research capability in the medical sciences.

Just as state intervention expanded in all spheres of Petrine society, so the government issued considerable legislation concerning medical matters. The principle of state responsibility for medical affairs and public health was clearly enunciated, even if the Leviathan failed to breathe life into many of its desires. Greatest attention went to the armed forces, of course, and resulted in significant achievements. In 1706 Peter reorganized the administration of military medicine, subordinating regimental surgeons to a surgeon-general responsible to the divisional commander. Each rank, from general to private, had to contribute a fraction of its pay for the purchase of medicaments. As a means of expanding paramedical service, regimental surgeons were ordered to select a soldier from each company, who, for double pay, would be taught to shave — doubtless as a sanitary measure — and to apply plasters. Meanwhile, the number of regular military medics grew steadily so that the Apothecary Bureau in 1713 reported 262 medics of all types in the service, not counting those in the fleet, yet noted they had not been paid for a year and had no medicine on hand. By 1720 the Baltic fleet employed 102 medics; seven years later their number had increased to 165. The *Military Statute* of 1716 further regulated the army's medical branch, assigning medics to each unit, providing field apothecaries, and organizing field hospitals and lazarets. The *Naval Statute* of 1720 did the same for the fleet. Peter proved ingenious in finding funds to finance these military hospitals; various fines (e.g., for using oared vessels on the Neva when the winds were favorable) were earmarked for hospitals, and each officer upon promotion had to contribute a month's pay.

Because war necessitated the mobilization of national resources throughout Peter's reign, the distinction between military and civil affairs — never very clear in Muscovy — tended to dissolve. Thus the improvements in military medicine brought some amelioration to portions of the general populace. Military medics often treated civilians, especially during epidemics, and after retirement many practiced privately. All available medical talent was used. In February 1714, for instance, the Senate approved a petition from the governor of Nizhnii-Novgorod to employ a captured Swedish surgeon, since "in Nizhnii and in the other towns of that province there are no doctors or surgeons."

Surgical practice in Peter's armed forces, especially in the war zone, must have been quite primitive. Doubtless the morbidity and mortality rates were appallingly high, and receiving treatment could be more dangerous than using folk remedies. Yet, on balance, the possibility of getting professional medical attention set the armed forces apart from the civilian population and probably improved the morale of servicemen. In addition to treating ailing servicemen, medics were often consulted by the Senate to determine whether individuals could continue to serve. . . . Old Petrine soldiers, if they did not die at the front from combat or disease, faded away in garrison service or poorhouses [or monasteries].

It was largely the problem of disabled servicemen and their dependents that led Peter to follow the example of Metropolitan Job of Novgorod in decreeing the establishment at monasteries of *"shpitali"* for the poor, the elderly, the infirm, and the sick. Apparently these institutions materialized mainly in Moscow and, despite their name, they were almshouses rather than hospitals, for few provided professional medical treatment. Aware of the high infantile mortality rate from personal experience — nine of Peter's eleven children by Catherine died early — the tsar also took the initiative in sponsoring foundling homes for the illegitimate and for orphans, but neither seems to have offered regular medical care. Even though legislation enjoined local authorities to support welfare and medical institutions, few had means to do so. Provincial localities could receive professional medical assistance only if a military unit happened to be stationed there or if an epidemic transpired.

Epidemic disease posed the principal medical problem of early modern Europe, Petrine Russia included. Warfare tended to foster epidemics because of the agglomerations of people and supplies in unsanitary conditions, as well as the disruption of normal residence and economic patterns. Petrine officials particularly feared epidemics in the army, hence their pains to bolster the military medical service. The long winters, in conjunction with the peasantry's pitiable (probably declining) living conditions, made Russia especially vulnerable to typhus and to diseases of dietary deficiency. Thus a contemporary British naval officer recoiled at the Russians' "mean, sordid way of living, being much addicted to salts and acids and extremely afflicted with the scurvy; and so accustomed to *bagnios* that unless they have recourse at least once a week to cleanse themselves, they are almost consumed with vermin." . . .

The medical nightmare of the era continued to be bubonic plague. "The Black Death" pandemic had wracked medieval Russia, and as recently as 1654 Moscow and central Russia had been scourged by the dread disease, at that time endemic in the Balkans, the Caucasus, and the Pontic steppes. Raiding expeditions and ordinary commerce, colonization and warfare among the contending local and imperial powers — Muscovy, Ottoman Turkey, Poland-Lithuania, the Crimean Khanate, the Turkic hordes, and the Cossack communities — provided preconditions for the development and transmission of plague. A widespread, albeit little-known, plague epidemic of 1690 illustrates the medical menace Muscovy met as it expanded southward.

The earliest noticeable mortality commenced in the spring of 1690 among the *streltsy* [musketeers] of Novobogoroditsk, a fortress established in 1688 on the southern Samara River upstream from its confluence with the lower Dnieper. There pestilence raged from February 22 to June 16 and wiped out 522 of the 762-man garrison. The local commander, A. I. Rzhevsky, died at his post; more than 100 soldiers fell ill but survived, while the townspeople fled en masse. The disease began slowly — seventy-one persons died in five weeks (from February 22 to March 31) — peaked in April with 325 deaths by May 2 (plus 76 in nearby Novosergievsk), and then subsided, claiming 126 more victims by mid-June. Cotton cloth and other wares from the Crimea were thought to be the vehicle of transmission — a likely supposition in the light of modern epidemiological knowledge. Although more than one malady might have been involved — louse-borne typhus generally occurs in the wintertime, whereas flea-borne bubonic plague requires moisture and warmer temperatures — its clinical picture and territorial expansion strongly suggest plague. Colonel Vasily Borkov, who later perished in the epidemic, reported on May 2 that his *streltsy* were dying "from the previous sickness; they suffer headache, and diarrhea, and swelling of the chest, and they go out of their minds during the sicknesses, and their loins ache, and from this the glands fall away." The last two phrases seem to describe buboes of the groin, the characteristic sign of plague. Another eyewitness spoke of high fever and observed: "with some the glands have fallen away from recurring sickness, and with others the glands have suppurated, and such people have recovered. . . ." These observations, too, concur with the known behavior of epidemic bubonic plague. . . .

The plague reached northward as far as Kursk, striking the *streltsy* settlements there in late June. Though it caused panic and massive flight, some local officials and clergymen denied its presence. Between June 21 and October 10, 1690, however, a total of 851 persons in Kursk were listed as plague victims, with isolated cases appearing until January

1691. The pestilence, in concert with the government's strenuous quarantine of Kursk — the cordon was only removed in October 1691 — brought the town to the edge of collapse. . . .

After these ravages, plague afflicted the Astrakhan area in 1692, supposedly with a mortality of 10,000, but then disappeared for nearly a decade. In the spring of 1701, however, it surfaced among troops in Tsarevo-Borisov, Izium, and nearby localities. Allegedly brought from Azov and points east, the disease began in Tsarevo-Borisov on February 13 and killed fifty persons in twenty houses. Precautions were taken at once, and the epidemic soon waned. That it occurred in February hints at typhus as the cause, though no description of symptoms has been found.

Minor outbreaks recurred in the south from 1702 to 1706, but they were droplets compared to the pestilential tide that swept over the Balkans, central and eastern Europe, and the Baltic from 1709 to 1712. Danzig, Stockholm, and Copenhagen suffered horribly. The pandemic impinged on warfare and politics, sapping the power of Sweden where the disease raged till 1713 and claimed about 100,000 victims. It obstructed Charles XII's attempts to return home from Turkey and facilitated the Russian conquest of Livonia, Estonia, and part of Finland. Some 100,000 persons died of plague in Poland, 200,000 in Courland. Hungary lost perhaps 500,000.

Reports of pestilence in Poland appeared in Russia's single newspaper as early as February 1705. Although in March 1709 Peter cautioned his commanders to watch for plague in the Ukraine, especially around Sumy, the armies advancing on Riga and Reval lost some men to the disease in the fall of 1709. Curtailed by winter, the contagion blew out afresh in the spring of 1710. On May 15 Field Marshal B. P. Sheremetev reported cases among his forces blockading Riga. Peter immediately ordered Sheremetev to pull his troops back across the Dvina, to set up a sanitary cordon, and to fumigate any dispatches sent into Russia. Unlike the Moscow plague of 1654 when no medical assistance had been provided, the tsar sent Dr. Christian Balthazar Wiel to supervise antiplague measures. Peter recommended Dr. Wiel, whom he had hired in Toruń, because he was "skillful for such malignant sicknesses and has been in those places where such sicknesses frequently occur." Simultaneously Peter dispatched medicaments to the army from the Apothecary Bureau in Moscow. To contain the epidemic, the tsar directed Sheremetev on June 3, 1710, to isolate sick soldiers "and order the doctors to use simple medicines for the [sick] soldiers and to give the healthy extra wine with camphor," as Dr. Dohnell prescribed. Doubtless more effective was Peter's order to keep healthy regiments far apart during the hot months, when plague was known to flourish. To prevent the pestilence spreading eastward, checkpoints were established around Narva and, when reports arrived of similar outbreaks in Kiev and Chernigov, the cordon was extended to the borders of Smolensk and Moscow provinces. On June 8, 1710, the Apothecary Bureau hurriedly dispatched a medical team to Kiev.

Riga, which capitulated to the Russians on June 3, 1710, bore the brunt of the epidemic. Sheremetev reported 60,000 died inside the city, while his forces lost 9,800 men from May 14 to the end of the year. In the first instance, the toll may be inflated — a diarist of the siege estimated only 22,000 victims — and of course starvation and other diseases swelled the total. Still, the losses on all sides were obviously considerable. Peter had to levy additional recruits to refurbish his plague-thinned soldiery. General A. I. Repnin sent Peter a report from Riga on June 27, 1710, which leaves little doubt that bubonic plague was the principal disease involved; the symptoms and seasonal incidence correspond to the disease produced by the bacterium *Pasteurella pestis*. As Repnin apprehended, the epidemic worsened in the summer and despite the sanitary cordon and the threat of death to anybody violating it, new localities became infected. Reval and its hinterland lost about 40,000 to the plague. To the south, Kiev, Nezhin, and Chernigov were hit. A surgeon sent to Chernigov reported on August 10, 1711, that thirty-one persons had fallen ill there, thirteen of them with "sores [e.g., buboes] and with blue spots and carbuncle[s]." The populace was evacuated to the field outside town and surrounded by troops. Further north the plague reached Narva, Pskov [and other towns]. So many died in Pskov, recorded a chronicler, that every church had to bury forty to sixty or more victims daily. Metropolitan Job of Novgorod instituted fasting and forbade marketing foodstuffs; the latter measure, if not the former, may have helped spare the city.

Peter followed the epidemic closely and anxiously. He sent special officers to investigate rumored violations of the sanitary cordon, for which the commandant of Narva, K. A. Naryshkin, was court-martialled. To General Repnin at Riga he relayed doctors' advice that the pestilence should abate with the advent of cold weather, and that smoldering fires of juniper or horse dung might cleanse the poisoned atmosphere — a reflection of the popularly held miasmatic theory of infection. The tsar constantly dispatched medics and medicaments to treat the army against the disease and, feeling these inadequate, ordered that every corporal daily inspect the troops under him — undressed — sending any with suspicious symptoms to designated places. Like Metropolitan Job, Peter also recommended the efficacy of prayer.

The plague gradually dissipated in Russia and the Ukraine by 1712, probably more from natural reasons — cold weather, population dispersion, extinction of the rat population — than from human action, although Peter's quarantine regulations may have interdicted the spread of the disease via infected merchandise (and from person to person if, as seems likely, pneumonic plague was also present). Lesser outbreaks recurred in the south in 1718–1719, but although locally severe the plague did not penetrate northward. As a precaution, however, a decree of December 13, 1718, ordered all householders in St. Petersburg to inform the police of any instance of death from fever on their premises. This order was extended to Moscow in 1722. In short, Peter and his government displayed greater initiative and sophistication than their Muscovite predecessors in fighting infectious disease. Although their police measures remained the same — cordons and quarantines — they also strove to provide medical assistance, if only to the army.

Medical developments in Petrine Russia, to sum up, display a broader, deeper, and more intensive government activity in contrast to their Muscovite legacy. The number of medical personnel multiplied several times. Peter personally shaped a national medical administration and native medical profession trained by the standards of contemporary European medicine. Compared to western European nations with their longer traditions of scientific activity, university medical training, and corporate organization of surgeons, midwives, and apothecaries, Petrine Russia lacked many of the prerequisites of public health institutions. Judicious borrowing and adaptation accomplished much in a short time, however, and Petrine medical progress compares favorably with similar developments in Prussia, for example, during the same period. Most important, Peter committed the state to further action in the field of medicine and public health. Considering his manifold activities in other spheres, Peter's advancement of medicine ranks among his finest and most lasting achievements.

Gary Marker

Printing and the Petrine Revolution

Historians have long been aware of the fact that the printing of books and other materials by modern methods enormously increased in Russia during the reign of Peter I. But did this relatively huge output signal a sweeping shift in Russian culture away from religion to secular concerns, from copying by hand to mechanical printing, and from an elite to a mass market? Gary Marker, who teaches at the State University of New York at Stony Brook, argues forcefully that it did not, and suggests reasons why this was so. We are reminded again of the extent to which Peter's policies were dominated by reasons of state; also, of how often his ambition for major change in Russia exceeded his people's grasp.

Modern Russian intellectual life, so the consensus has it, began with Peter the Great. As a corollary to that maxim, one might profitably suggest that Peter's accession also transformed printing into a significant aspect of life in Russia. During his reign, the number of printed titles burgeoned from about six a year in the second half of the seventeenth century to nearly fifty a year in the early 1720s, and the number of Russian or Church Slavonic presses grew from three in late Muscovite Russia to ten in operation at various times in Peter's reign.[1] All of the new presses, moreover, were placed under the direct control of the government rather than under that of the church. Not surprisingly, therefore, the topical composition of books shifted as well — and quite abruptly — away from works of faith and prayer and toward works with more secular concerns.

From Gary Marker, *Publishing, Printing, and the Origins of Intellectual Life in Russia, 1700–1800,* Copyright © 1985, Princeton University Press, pp. 17–25, 31–32, 39–40. Reprinted with permission of Princeton University Press.

[1]The word "press" here, and throughout the text, refers to a publishing operation or publishing house, rather than to the physical machine that prints books. When it is necessary to make the distinction, the latter will be referred to as a "printing press."

On the surface, these transitions seem to point to a precipitous decline in the status of the church and devotional publishing and a corresponding rise in the importance of the state and civic affairs. But before we can accept at face value what appears to be a sweeping cultural transformation, we need to examine the particular character of Petrine publishing more deeply. Changes of this magnitude required the active involvement of the tsar, the acquiescence of the church, the cooperation of the people who produced and distributed the new books, and to some degree, of those who read them. In addition, they cost a great deal of money to bring about. The questions, then, are: Why did such dramatic changes take place, and, secondly, what were their effects on Russian culture?

Most scholars, plausibly enough, have placed the primary responsibility squarely on the shoulders of Peter himself. In the most recent study of Petrine printing, for example, S. P. Luppov, the leading authority on the eighteenth-century Russian book, has suggested that the transformation of printing was one important feature of a more general modernization of society and politics which, although it began earlier, gained rapid momentum under Peter. Peter's insistence upon new schools, new technologies, curricular advances, greater foreign contacts, and the growth of enlightenment came together to give printing a greater role in Russian society. In particular, the creation of primary and secondary schools throughout the empire, although motivated by narrowly practical considerations, did increase literacy, expand the popular interest in both utilitarian and general knowledge, and thereby increase the demand for printed books.

One can discern in this pattern the emerging outline of some sort of structure that was initiated and largely controlled by Peter himself. Rather than being a one-sided reflection of the tsar's will, however, the publishing system, in Luppov's view, managed to establish a symbiosis in which the interests of the state as the producer of the printed word and those of society as the consumer somehow coalesced around a shared rejection of religious superstition and an interest in modernity and secular affairs. It was this symbiosis that prepared the ground for the subsequent flowering of Russian printing.

Luppov's thesis, if one may call it that, clearly succeeds in integrating printing into a broader context of political innovation, educational reform, and social change. And while it treats the emperor as the major domo of publishing, it eschews an overemphasis on Peter's role in favor of a more modulated picture of interaction between state and society. It achieves all this, moreover, with a wealth of newly uncovered and carefully studied evidence.

The image of a successful adaptation of secular printing to Russian society is not without its difficulties, however. It depends, first of all, on an overly optimistic characterization of reading in Russia, in that it presumes widespread literacy and a demand for secular books that cut across geographic and social boundaries. It fails to explain why, if the Petrine system was so successful and progressive, the secular printing network faced near-collapse and bankruptcy upon his death. Why, moreover, did those in charge of the presses subsequently choose to abandon the essential premises of Peter's printing system and, in essence, start over on a different institutional footing once Peter died? Why, finally, if secularization took such firm root in society, did the religious presses fare so much better financially than the state presses did?

All of these questions suggest a rather different experience for printing than the one which Luppov and most other contemporary scholars have described. In fact, a review of the entire publishing network from the seventeenth century onward reveals that the social, cultural, and institutional bases for such a dramatic rise in secular publishing were quite limited and, consequently, that the impact of Peter's reform was far more muted than Luppov and others generally assert.

When Peter came to power in 1689, he inherited a small church-controlled printing system which had had only an episodic impact on Russian culture. Between the late 1550s, when printing first came to Muscovy, and the end of the seventeenth century, Muscovite authorities had established only one major publishing house (*pechatnyi dvor*) in Moscow, and a handful of small presses in monasteries in the western borderlands. According to the most recent published estimates, these presses collectively printed fewer than 500 titles during the entire seventeenth century, most of which came out in moderate print runs of 1,200 or 2,400 copies. . . .

Peter, of course, set about to change all of this, and on the advice of such trusted correspondents as Gottfried von Leibniz, he embarked on an aggressive reorganization of printing in Russia.[2] During his travels in

---

[2] Leibniz (1646–1716) was a famous German philosopher and mathematician. — Ed.

western Europe during 1698, for example, he hired several Dutch printers and merchants, including Jan von Thessing, to establish Russian presses in Amsterdam for publishing maps, charts, and books on technical subjects. Although these initial efforts produced very few publications, they led to the enlistment of several established printers into the service of the Russian government, most notably Ilia Kopievsky, an elusive figure who worked for Peter in Amsterdam, Danzig, and Moscow before disappearing in 1709. Peter also hired two other printers of note: Fedor Polikarpov, a graduate of the Likhud brothers' school in Moscow, who directed the *pechatnyi dvor* through most of Peter's reign, and V. A. Kiprianov, who became Moscow's leading cartographer and book merchant during the reign.

Peter's program called for more than talented individuals, however. As part of his administrative reforms, he founded several new institutional publishing houses, including the St. Petersburg Press in 1711, which soon became the leading organ of the government in the new capital; the Senate presses in both Moscow and St. Petersburg in 1719; and the new Naval Academy press in 1721 to print schoolbooks and books on naval science. In addition, the old *pechatnyi dvor,* which at some point came to be called simply the "Moscow Press" (*Moskovskaia tipografiia*), gained several new printing presses and employees.

Each of these new presses came into being directly because of Peter's orders, and all of the new institutional presses were intended primarily for governmental use. Certainly the church had easy access to the Moscow and St. Petersburg presses, but the demands of the state came first. Even the single new monastic press, established at the Alexander-Nevksii Monastery outside St. Petersburg in 1719, came into being largely to serve as an organ of one of Peter's leading ideological supporters, Archbishop Feofan Prokopovich.

Another aspect of this secularization in the service of the state was the introduction of the new civil orthography in 1707. Peter believed that the old orthography was too archaic to allow for an easy rendering of new technical or educational books. The publication of modern knowledge required something simpler, more latinized, and with fewer obscure vowels and notations. By law, therefore, all secular books were thenceforth to be set in the new type, while books of faith would continue to use the old orthography. Thus, type itself was introduced as a visible symbol of statism and, more specifically, of the separation between the government's publishing program and the church's.

In practice, however, matters were more muddled, since it took the publishing houses several years to acquire enough new printing presses and type fonts to complete the transition. Between 1707 and 1725, fully a third of the titles printed in the old orthography were secular books or laws and notices initiated by the state. Conversely, some of the books that came out in the new orthography were religious. As the governmental publishing houses acquired more printing presses, they gradually abandoned the old type, so that by the early 1720s the vast majority of governmental publications did employ the new orthography. The church, by contrast, had only limited access to the new materials, and its publications consequently did not undergo significant orthographic revision. The point, however, is that a strict orthographic differentiation of secular and religious books took place only at the very end of Peter's reign. Thus, the secularizing effects of Peter's reform of the alphabet, if indeed there were any effects, could have appeared only after his death.

Paradoxically, the rigid state control probably limited printing's ability to act as an agent of secular or at least lay culture, since Peter denied access to any but the most highly placed individuals within the church and officialdom. Spontaneous expressions from Russian society simply had no place in this universe. Even Kiprianov, the only private publisher of the Petrine era, required a special privilege to operate his press, and even then he printed exclusively what the government ordered.

The formal lines of authority through which both new and old presses functioned further underscored the primacy of official business. In 1701, Peter placed all Russian presses, formerly directed rather loosely by the Department of Printing (*Prikaz knigopechataniia*), under the newly revived Department of Monasteries (*Monastyrskii prikaz*) and its chairman, Ivan Musin-Pushkin. As a civil office, the Department of Monasteries brought all publishing, including monastic, directly under civil control, a control that continued after the Department of Monasteries was merged into the Holy Synod in 1722.

Structuring and revitalizing the press in so centralized and hierarchical a manner suited Peter in numerous personal and political ways. It permitted him to play an intimate role in nearly every aspect of book printing. The increased printing capacity gave him the potential to issue as many copies of as many books as he chose. By making Musin-Pushkin directly and personally responsible for overseeing printing, moreover, Peter was ensuring that a loyal and trusted friend would be in charge, and through Musin-Pushkin he could exercise control over how each press functioned editorially.

Peter's personal involvement in publishing went well beyond consultation and ordering that new presses be established. He oversaw translations, contracted with printers, approved copy, and demanded periodic progress reports from publishing houses. . . .

Such direct participation, in addition to satisfying Peter's fancy to do everything himself, reflected his determination to use the press as a tool of reform and as a means of getting his message out in a manner that could reach any conceivable audience. In the seventeenth century, official publications had been limited to only the most important new laws, and print runs were rather low. Thus, the communication of information from the government to the nation had normally depended on public announcements or on the circulation of hand-copied versions. Under Peter, however, hundreds of laws and notices came out in print runs that often ran well into the thousands. By the latter part of his reign, laws and notices were appearing at a rate that exceeded one printing a week. The government then disseminated them (or at least attempted to) at little or no cost, posted them in public places, and ordered the parish clergy and local officials to read them aloud. In theory, therefore, the entire population could read or hear official pronouncements about as often as they heard prayers.

To understand fully what it meant to Russian society to receive the word of the state in such a continuous fashion requires a better understanding of the actual communication of the laws and of popular culture than currently exists. In light of the haphazard education of the parish clergy and its lack of familiarity with the new orthography, it is not even certain, for example, that local priests were capable of transmitting the laws. But some points are clear enough. Peter had come up with a use of printing that, if properly executed, would obliterate the barriers between literacy and illiteracy and between the capital and the nation. In principle, everyone could now know the will of the tsar and the state; everyone could now see an official copy with the tsar's seal; and everyone could hear the tsar's words. One might plausibly hypothesize that Peter's new policy engendered in the populace a clearer vision of the connection between the (mostly disagreeable) changes that they were experiencing and the will of the tsar. At any rate, it most certainly brought the voice of the state to the provinces with an intensity that hitherto only the church had achieved. To that extent, it was a powerful instrument of secularization.

Here, then, was Peter's design: The emperor would take over printing, expand it, and use it to circulate whatever useful information he wanted, to whomever he wanted, in whatever quantities he wanted, and on whatever terms he chose. As a result, Peter's will simply dominated the output of the presses. Between 1708 and January 1725, official pronouncements accounted for approximately 60 percent of all published titles. The tremendous print runs of many of these pronouncements suggest that they accounted for an even higher percentage of the total volume of printed material.

As emperor, Peter could, and often did, order that the government disseminate publications either to a particular audience or throughout the society. Circulating the word of the state was intended as more than a simple informational service, however, for it soon came to serve an unmistakable ideological function as well. Peter was hardly the first Russian ruler to see the importance of explaining the virtue and necessity of obedience in the face of unpleasant changes, but the expression and distribution of that message did change quite dramatically in his reign.

Most significant, of course, was the change in the ideology itself. Peter was now the emperor — instead of simply the tsar — as well as the first servant of the state. Obedience, therefore, took on a more statist and hence a more secular cast, not an easy notion for people who were raised believing in the "holy tsar." Obviously, the broad circulation of laws and public notices gave the new basis of authority some immediate and concrete meaning, but the laws and regulations could hardly legitimate themselves. Such legitimation had to come from other, more traditional and respected sources of authority, such as icons, panegyrics, propaganda, theological tracts, and sermons, all of which depended on wide circulation to be effective. . . .

But what about at the level of dissemination and reading? Prerevolutionary scholars tended to draw rather deprecatory conclusions concerning the circulation of Petrine books, but contemporary Soviet specialists see things differently. Luppov argues, for example, that Peter did succeed in circulating secular books, despite numerous financial and organizational problems — in part because he was prepared to give thousands of volumes away, but more fundamentally because his new secular books corresponded to the needs and interests of his literate nonclerical subjects.

As we already know, the seventeenth-century book received wide circulation among various groups of the Russian population. What, then, was new in this regard in the eighteenth century? . . . The basic feature of the Petrine era in comparison with previous periods is connected with the fact that the secular books, of which there were few even in the second half of the seventeenth century, had an especially wide circulation. Another feature of the Petrine era consisted of the fact that in that period the number of lay book owners significantly increased.

To support this position, Luppov and several other Soviet scholars have produced and synthesized a wide array of numerical and qualitative evidence which appears to show an extensive circulation network, relatively high sales for certain secular books, and a broad-based popular receptivity to these new books. But their interpretation of the numerical sources, which they concede are riddled with gaps, unexplained discrepancies, and questionable bookkeeping methods, is highly problematic. Too often these difficulties have been disregarded or have been resolved only through employing several broad and often dubious assumptions.

Beyond the numbers, however, there are questions concerning the process of distribution. Luppov believes that secular books found their way to readers in all social groups and throughout the empire. But the evidence for this position is quite thin; much of it is episodic, coming from occasional references in letters and petitions. As a consequence, we cannot completely rely on him for information about the mediating steps from printing to reading or what one might call the infrastructure of publishing. . . .

The preponderance of the evidence on circulation and reading argues for the view that for St. Petersburg and Moscow alike, traditional and religious works remained comparatively attractive. For the rest of the nation, religious works continued to predominate even more completely, since, other than the laws and notices which people had to listen to at least occasionally, only prayer books, alphabet books, and calendars were distributed in sufficient quantities to have much of a chance of reaching into the provinces in any significant numbers. In fact, once one left the major cities, hand copying was very likely to be more prevalent than printed books of any sort.

In the last analysis, therefore, the history of Peter's reshaping of the press is a classic demonstration of the strengths and limitations of an aggressive, governmentally controlled, instrumental publishing system. With relative ease, Peter was able to gather the necessary physical means to improve printing and was able to print more or less what he wanted and as much as he wanted. To some extent, he even succeeded in exposing his subjects to his output. He certainly made the voice of the state a more immediate presence than it had been before. But with the exception of a relatively small group of students and [noble] servitors, Russian society seems to have assimilated very little of it. Both the quantity and the character of book-buying in 1725 was, as best as can be determined, not radically different from what it had been in 1702.

Peter's failure, if one can call it that, certainly involved matters unrelated to printing, such as the lack of success of his primary schools and low literacy. But explanations of a general social nature miss a crucial point: the command basis of Petrine dissemination was ill-equipped to respond to demand or to create a readership. Bookshops were as rare in most of the empire in 1725 as they had ever been, and provincial peddlers hardly ever carried secular printed books. One cannot say how many people actually did read in Petrine Russia or what they would have liked the presses to publish, but the thriving trade in manuscripts and woodblock prints suggests that book printing was not responding to the existing type or level of demand. Thus, Peter failed completely to establish a basis for mutual communication between publishers and readers, and secular printing, although far more widespread and visible than before, was dependent largely on the tsar's will and massive subsidies to keep going. It is no wonder, then, that immediately after Peter died in 1725, his entire publishing network nearly ground to a halt.

Eighteenth-century Russian woodcut depicting a barber cutting the beard of an Old Believer. The barber is dressed in the style introduced by Peter I, and is shown executing Peter's much-resented decrees against the wearing of beards. (Ryerson Library, Art Institute of Chicago)

Peter and His Opposition

M. S. Anderson

Peter the Man: Character and Personality

Owing to the unprecedented volume of written material left by Peter himself and by numerous contemporary observers, both Russian and foreign, we know more about him personally than about any previous ruler in Russian history. In this excerpt M. S. Anderson provides a glimpse of the remarkable, in some ways amazing, and often contradictory personality that emerges from this material. Anderson suggests in conclusion that Peter's personality directly influenced major developments of his time: indeed, that "of no ruler in the history of Europe can it be said with greater truth that his work was the outcome of his own essential character."

No figure in modern history presents more starkly than Peter the juxtaposition in the same man of great virtues and almost equally great defects. Yet throughout his life his character was of a piece, changing

From M. S. Anderson, *Peter the Great*, 1978, pp. 157–167. Reprinted by permission of Thames and Hudson Ltd.

little in essentials. He was consistent above all in the wholeheartedness with which he adopted and applied policies, in his belief in the rightness of his own judgment and his own scale of values. His faults were often glaring; but they were the faults of excess, of rashness, of haste, and of too uncritical a self-confidence. They were never those of mediocrity, of indecision, or of a shirking of responsibility.

Some of his leading characteristics include his almost boundless physical energy, his insatiable practical curiosity, and the deep and genuine sense of personal responsibility for Russia and its people which he felt at least from his middle or later twenties onwards. The first of these marked him indelibly throughout his life. Faced with any situation which seemed to call for action, his overmastering instinct was to act at once, often almost without thought and in the most direct and personal way. Disturbed at dinner in January 1699 by the news that fire (the ever-present danger in a land of wooden houses) had broken out in the palace of one of the boyars, he sprang from table and [in the words of an eyewitness], "running headlong to the place where he had heard the fire was raging, not only gave his advice, but actually employed his own hands in putting out the flames, and was seen laboring away among the very tottering ruins of the house." A quarter of a century later precisely the same impetuous response to a visible and concrete emergency was to precipitate his own death.[1] But this urge to act, this will to be up and doing, went even deeper than such incidents indicate. It lay at the very roots of Peter's character. More than anything else it explains the impatience with which he regarded the passivity, the lack of ambition, of so many of his subjects. "What do you do at home?" he irritably asked his companions on one occasion. "I don't know how to stay at home with nothing to do." Few of his recorded remarks illustrate his character more simply or more clearly.

This lavish outpouring of physical energy, this obsessive activity, caught the attention of contemporaries more than any other aspect of his personality. "That was a tsar, what a tsar!" said an unknown peasant of Olonets. "He did not eat his bread for nothing but worked like a peasant." Peter's passion for working with his own hands took a wide variety of forms in addition to his labor as a shipwright about which so

---

[1] In December 1724, in St. Petersburg, Peter waded into ice-cold water to save several people from drowning. — Ed.

much has been written. Throughout much of his life he tried to spend some time each day woodturning, and when his second marriage was solemnized the decorations included "a sconce with six branches of ivory and ebon-wood" which he had himself made. "He told me," the British minister in St. Petersburg remarked, "it had cost him about a fortnight's time and no one else had touched it; the piece is indeed curious for the workmanship, as well as the hand that made it." To the end of his life, and even after his health had clearly begun to give way, energetic handicrafts, such as metalwork involving much hammering of sheet iron, continued to absorb a surprising amount of his time.

In Paris in 1717, as in London two decades earlier, he gave to many observers the impression of an energetic, intelligent, and endlessly inquisitive visitor from what in many ways was still another world. A naive (and therefore all the more revealing) witness saw him then "with short hair and no wig, with a plain face, large eyes, his body quite heavy and his behaviour gross . . . fleeing from being seen or visited by women, since he has neither seen nor received any that were not unavoidable during his visit to Paris of a month and thirteen days. [He is] thought to be well informed in literature, curious about all rarities and things worth seeing, making notes on all he sees and always carrying a pencil with him, seeking out practitioners of all the arts and trades and hiring them to go to his kingdom to establish themselves there, where a number have already gone."

A realization of the responsibility imposed upon him by the power which he wielded over Russia and its people took time to develop in him and become fully effective. During the later 1690s, however, the irresponsibility, even selfishness, of his early life rapidly disappeared. It was replaced by a deep-seated feeling that he was a trustee obliged to foster the well-being and improvement of the country entrusted to his care. The manifesto of 1702 which invited foreigners to work in Russia stressed his desire to rule so that "all our subjects, under our guardianship, will for the general good advance further and further towards the best and happiest condition." This is the first clear statement from him of such an objective. Once adopted, however, this attitude stayed with him for life and became the driving force behind all his work. Almost two decades after the 1702 declaration he could speak in very similar terms, in a speech celebrating the signature of the treaty of Nystad, of the obligation laid upon him to work for the general good and the benefit of his country. It was precisely the lack in Tsarevich Aleksei of any active public spirit of this kind which made the conflict between father and son so irreconcilable.

The combination of great physical and mental energy with a profound sense of responsibility meant that Peter worked hard at the business of government, probably harder than any other monarch of the age. Of this there are convincing proofs. In the preparation of the *Naval Statute* of 1720, for example, he labored for five months, four days a week, from 5 A.M. to midday and from 4 P.M. to 11 P.M. A large part of the manuscript of this very long and detailed decree was written in his own hand, and the rest was corrected by him. The drafts of different schemes for the new administrative organization of 1718–1719 bear many insertions and corrections by him; and many important decrees — for example, that of 1714 on the indivisibility of estates, and that of 1722 fixing the duties of the procurator-general — were worked out in detail by the tsar in person. The more intelligent and farseeing contemporary observers were often as much impressed by Peter's capacity for work as by that which he showed for drinking and crude horseplay. "His Majesty might truly be called a man of business," wrote a Scottish doctor who had over a decade's experience of Russia and had seen much of the tsar during the Persian campaign of 1722; "for he could despatch more affairs in a morning than an houseful of senators could do in a month. He rose almost every morning in the wintertime, before four o'clock, was often in his cabinet by five o'clock, where two private secretaries, and certain clerks, paid constant attendance. He often went so early to the Senate as to occasion the senators being raised out of their beds to attend him there."

All this paints a picture of seriousness, of sustained and constructive effort, which is in many ways very attractive. Peter's real devotion to duty becomes all the more admirable in the context of his constant disappointments with inefficient or corrupt subordinates, experiences which wrung from him the bitter though trite reflection that "There is little truth in men, but much cunning." There were, however, blemishes on his character which, though they did not vitiate his good points, were nonetheless important.

He was not, at bottom, a cruel man. Except for moments of genuine crisis — in the destruction of the *streltsy* [royal musketeers] in 1698, perhaps in some of the details of the punishment of Tsarevich Aleksei and his associates two decades later — he showed little deliberate brutality and no taste for cruelty. His sparing use of the death penalty for political offenses and his relatively moderate treatment of religious dissenters bear out this point. The sufferings which he inflicted on tens of thousands of humble and helpless people he never desired for their own sake. They were an inevitable result of his efforts to wrench Russia out of what he saw as stultifying conservatism and humiliating weakness. As such they had to be accepted and enforced. But they were always incidental to his real objectives.

If he was not cruel, however, he could certainly be violent — sometimes ungovernably so, in fits of rage. Physical assault, with cudgel, cane or even bare hands, on the unfortunate object of his anger was a commonplace; here again the urge to immediate and often unthinking action is visible. His huge stature (he stood about six feet seven inches tall) and the marked facial tic which afflicted him at moments of stress must have made this treatment even more frightening to the recipient than would otherwise have been the case. The most striking examples of this kind of behavior again date from the very tense later months of 1698. Then, on one occasion, Peter struck Menshikov a blow so severe that blood "spouted abundantly from the wound" and on another, hurled Lefort himself to the floor and kicked him.[2] But behavior of this kind, which was often followed by an immediate return of good humor, remained characteristic of Peter to the end. There is much force in the parallel which a great Russian historian has drawn between the tsar's associates and travelers admiring the view from the summit of Vesuvius while all the time awaiting the eruption of the uncontrollable forces under their feet.

Allied with this lack of self-control was an unmistakable vein of coarseness, even grossness, in his tastes and much of his everyday behavior. Some of this, for example, his liking for dwarfs, giants and physical abnormalities of all kinds and his pleasure in their display in pseudo-ceremonies, could easily be paralleled at other European courts in what was by present-day standards a highly insensitive age. In some respects he displayed unexpected sensibilities, as in his genuine fondness for gardens and gardening, at least in his later years (he appears to have had a particular liking for carnations). Yet we are left, in spite of his indisputable intelligence and range of interests, with the impression

---

[2] Both Alexander Menshikov and the Genevan, François Lefort, were special favorites of Peter. — Ed.

of a large substratum of uncouthness. The obscene and blasphemous ceremonies associated with his "Most Drunken Synod" are an example of this. The heavy drinking which continued to the end of his life was carried to lengths which even contemporaries, themselves far from abstemious, found astonishing or shocking. To be forced to take part in prolonged and brutish carouses with the tsar and his boon companions became from the 1690s a recognized hazard of the lives of foreign diplomats in Russia. In 1701, for example, a Prussian official begged not to be sent there as resident since "he could not stand strong drink, especially in excess"; while in 1714 Frederick William I chose Count von Schlippenbach for a diplomatic mission to Peter partly because of his taste for drinking. "He's no proud man, I assure you," wrote an English merchant from Archangel to his brother in 1702, "for he'll eat or be merry with anybody. . . . He's a great admirer of such blunt fellows as saylors are. He invited all the nasty tars to dinner with him where he made 'em so drunk that some slop't, some danced, and others fought — he amongst 'em. And in such company he takes much pleasure." The rigors of the tsar's hospitality are illustrated by an account given by the Hanoverian envoy of the hospitality offered by Peter, in the later years of his life, at the new palace of Peterhof, on the Baltic fourteen miles from St. Petersburg. Each guest, already hardly able to stand after a long drinking bout, was forced to empty a bowl containing a full pint of wine, "whereupon we quite lost our Senses, and were in that pickle carried off to sleep, some in the Garden, others in the Wood, and the rest here and there on the Ground." They were, however, soon awakened and forced to follow the tsar in cutting down trees to make a new walk to the seashore. At supper they drank "such another Dose of Liquour, as sent us senseless to Bed"; but an hour and a half later they were roused once more to visit Prince Cherkassky (himself in bed with his wife), "where we were again by their Bedside pestered with Wine and Brandy till four in the Morning; that next day none of us remembered how he got home." At eight o'clock they were invited to breakfast, but given brandy instead of tea or coffee. This was followed by a fourth drinking bout at dinner, after the guests had been forced to ride wretched horses, without saddles or stirrups, for the amusement of the tsar and tsaritsa. When the party sailed back to St. Petersburg they were overtaken by a dangerous storm; and by taking charge and himself steering the ship, this allowed Peter to show at once the courage and leadership which made him a great monarch. Yet when the party landed, "after being tossed about seven Hours," they could find neither dry clothes nor beds and had to make a fire, strip naked and wrap themselves in sled-covers while their wet clothes dried.

We are here not merely geographically distant from the courts of Europe but in what was still, in many essentials, a different world. Nor did the tsar's taste for drunken jollifications pressed to almost grotesque lengths weaken with the passage of time. In the summer of 1724, only a few months before his death, a drinking party to celebrate the consecration of a church at Tsarskoe Selo, near St. Petersburg — where Peter had just built a new palace — lasted for several days and consumed three thousand bottles of wine.

The simplicity of the tsar's own tastes; the fact that so much of his reign was spent in traveling, frequently outside Russia; a constant shortage of money and the imperative demands of the armed forces for what was available — all these factors combined to ensure that there was little elaborate or highly organized court life. Peter was certainly not indifferent to some kinds of outward appearance and some types of ceremony. This can be seen in his liking for firework displays and for complex ornamental waterworks (tastes he shared with many other rulers of the age) and in the elaborate triumphal processions, based on Roman models, which marked his most important victories. But, for imposing buildings, rich furnishings, handsome clothes, elaborate meals, material luxury in almost any form, he had in general little use. In April 1694, when he accompanied his half-brother Ivan in the Easter procession, he took part for the last time in a traditional court ceremony in the Kremlin. Thereafter he made almost no use of the palaces there, several of which had been extensively redecorated in the 1680s and early 1690s. Though handsome, the palace which he built at Peterhof was by the standards of Europe relatively small and unpretentious; another at Strelna, also near St. Petersburg, had scarcely been commenced at his death. The first Winter Palace in the city itself, begun in 1711, was a small two-story building which bore no relationship to the magnificent present-day structure of that name. Even the second Winter Palace which replaced it in 1716, though modestly attractive to judge by the plans (it was pulled down ten years later), was far from imposing by contemporary European standards. Like virtually every monarch of the age, Peter greatly admired Louis XIV, whom he regarded as a model of kingship. But he never succeeded in creating a Versailles of his own.

So far as the mechanics of daily life were concerned, the simplicity of his tastes contrasted startlingly and impressively, in the eyes of many observers, with the immensity of the powers which he wielded. He never appeared, noted a foreigner admiringly, "in a dress-suit of cloaths," except on important festivals and holidays: and "when he was dressed, he wore the order of St. Andrew; at other times he had no badge, or mark, of any order, on his person." In St. Petersburg he used an open two-wheeled chaise, attended by two soldiers or grooms and by a page, who often sat in the chaise with him and drove it. In winter he used a sledge drawn by a single horse, with the same small number of attendants. His impatience with ceremony and complete lack of courtly manners frequently created surprise or embarrassment on his foreign travels — at the Prussian court in 1712, at that of Denmark in 1716, on his visit to Paris in the following year. When his second wife, Catherine, made him a new coat of blue material trimmed with silver braid he evidently thought the braid too extravagant and wore this fine garment only once, at Catherine's own coronation in May 1724. Normally he wore merely a shabby old coat, into the pockets of which he was in the habit of stuffing official papers. Even his closest associates rarely dined or supped with him in St. Petersburg; Menshikov was the only one who was allowed to do this more than very occasionally. Finally, as perhaps the most convincing of all demonstrations of how far his tastes diverged from those of most of his fellow monarchs, he neither hunted nor gambled.

The indifference to appearances, to luxuries and even to ordinary comforts, which marked much of Peter's behavior can, however, be overstressed. He did not grudge expenditure on lavish public ceremonies when the occasion seemed to justify this. Thus, for example, when in August 1722 the small boat in which he had first learned to sail in 1688, and which he called the "Grandfather of the Russian Navy," was brought to St. Petersburg from Moscow, it was received with great ceremony. Three salvos were fired by the guns of the fortress and the assembled fleet, no fewer, it was claimed, than two thousand in all. This was almost certainly the most massive use of artillery for ceremonial purposes hitherto seen anywhere. (The day ended, typically, with a ten-hour banquet at which the tsar became drunk to a degree, according to observers well qualified to judge, scarcely precedented even for him.) Peter also allowed his second wife, Catherine, to maintain a retinue much larger and a style of life much more expensive than his own. Her establishment included, among other forms of display, pages in red and green with trimmings of gold lace, and even an orchestra in green uniforms; here we see a foreshadowing of the ostentatious luxury which was to mark Russian court life in generations to come. In the same way Menshikov and some other favorites were actively encouraged to live in a luxurious style in St. Petersburg.

More important politically was the tsar's willingness to spend money, and to encourage its expenditure by others, when this could heighten Russia's prestige abroad or popularize his policies at home. He was consistent in his concern that his country and his own achievements should present the best possible face to both foreign and domestic observers. In 1707, for example, he gave strict instructions to Menshikov, then in Poland, to keep up an appearance of pomp and luxury so long as he remained there in order to impress the population. He not only employed hack journalists to publicize his achievements in Europe but also did his best to suppress the publication of hostile pamphlets and other material there. Similar methods were used to influence domestic opinion. As soon as he heard of any important Russian victory Peter would demand reports of it "which can be printed and distributed." These would then appear either separately or in the *Vedomosti*, a government news-sheet published irregularly from 1703 onwards which is frequently referred to as the first Russian newspaper. Descriptions of the capture of Narva and of the battles of Lesnaia and Poltava were printed as placards and displayed in the streets of Moscow, St. Petersburg, and other towns — while 6,000 copies of the ratification of the peace of 1721 were produced for propaganda use of this kind. For the great illiterate majority, official accounts of Russian successes were read out to the congregations in the churches after thanksgiving services.

Even the portraits of Peter painted at various times by European artists were pressed into service for similar ends. Two in particular — that by Kneller, painted when he was in England during the Grand Embassy of 1697–1698, and that by Carel de Moor, painted in Holland in 1717 — seemed to the tsar to convey the idea of himself which he wished to disseminate; the result was that they were much more frequently engraved than other, and to the historian equally interesting, likenesses of the tsar. Engravings made from them were widely distributed; and miniature copies were made, first by French and later by Russian artists, to be given away in considerable numbers as presents and rewards. His posthumous reputation also preoccupied Peter. He dreamed of erecting a great memorial to himself, a concrete and visible perpetuation of his fame for posterity, though these plans were never realized while he was alive. A scheme for a great triumphal pillar surmounted by his statue and covered with bas-reliefs representing the main events of his reign (probably inspired by descriptions he had read of Trajan's column in Rome) had no result; and a projected bronze commemorative statute of him was not cast until after his death and was not mounted on its pedestal until 1800. Peter thus presents a picture of extreme simplicity in personal expenditure coupled with a willingness to tolerate, and even vicariously enjoy, the expenditure of those close to him. He would also spend quite lavishly where his own or Russia's prestige seemed to be involved.

Family affections and ties did not, in general, play a large part in his life. His sister Nataliia, only a year younger than he, remained until her death in 1716 his consistent admirer and supporter. But, to Peter's achievements she contributed little: she probably understood many of his objectives only imperfectly. The same is true of his sister-in-law, the Tsaritsa Praskoviia, wife of Ivan V, a formidable lady of the old Muscovite school who was also an admirer of the tsar until her death in 1723, and of his niece, the Duchess of Mecklenburg. All these meant something to Peter. It was to Nataliia that the little Tsarevich Aleksei was entrusted after his separation from his mother in 1698; and Praskoviia took charge of Peter's young children by his second wife when their parents traveled to Germany in 1716. That second wife, Catherine, was, however, the only woman who was truly close to him (at least after he broke with his mistress, Anna Mons, in 1703) or on whom he seriously relied.

Catherine's story illustrates strikingly Peter's freedom in his personal life from the prejudices and proprieties accepted by other monarchs of the age. The daughter of a Lithuanian peasant, orphaned and destitute while still a child, she was taken to Moscow in 1703 after the Russian capture of Marienburg, where she had been in effect the servant of a Lutheran pastor. In Moscow, as a member of the household of Menshikov, she met and attracted Peter. Though illiterate, she was pretty and good-natured; her first child by the tsar was born in the winter of 1704–1705. In 1707 they were married privately in St. Petersburg; but it was not until 1712 that the marriage was publicly solemnized. Even then the fact that Peter's first wife, Evdokiia, was still alive, and that there had been no divorce, made Catherine's status, and that of her children, extremely doubtful. By many contemporaries the marriage was seen, quite reasonably, as further evidence of the tsar's willingness totally to disregard conventional restraints of all kinds. "I suppose," wrote the British minister to Russia to one of the secretaries of state, "you will have already heard that the Czar has married his mistress and declared her empress; it is one of the surprising events in this wonderful age." Nevertheless the marriage was remarkably successful. Catherine bore her husband no fewer than twelve children, though of these only two girls (Anna, who in 1724 married Charles Frederick of Holstein-Gottorp; and Elizabeth, who was to become empress in 1741) lived beyond early childhood. Cheerful and comforting, she could soothe Peter when he was angry and encourage him when he was despondent. To be with him she braved difficult and uncomfortable journeys; she accompanied him on the disastrous Pruth campaign [against Turkey, in 1711], to Pomerania and Denmark in 1716, and even to Persia in 1722. His letters to her show a domestic and even tender side which is hardly evident elsewhere in his correspondence. He was not faithful to her physically. In that age, however, such fidelity was certainly not expected of a ruler; and none of his affairs (some of which were entered into with her knowledge) ever threatened the real hold of "Katerinushka" on his affections. Her coronation in Moscow in May 1724 — an almost unprecedented event — finally consolidated her official position. Peter placed the crown on her head with his own hands; and one motive for paying her this public honor was almost certainly to increase her chances of succeeding him should he die suddenly.

Apart from Catherine, the tsar's closest collaborator during much of his reign, and the one with whom the association proved most durable, was Alexander Danilovich Menshikov. After service in one of Peter's first regiments and as his personal adjutant, he accompanied the tsar as a volunteer on the Grand Embassy of 1697–1698. In spite of his humble birth, his intelligence, liveliness, almost brutal energy, and capacity for the sort of rough merrymaking that Peter enjoyed rapidly earned him not merely favor but also real affection. After the death of Lefort [1699] the rise of the new favorite was spectacular. Governor of the newly captured Schlüsselburg in 1702, he soon became Governor General of Ingria, Karelia, and Estonia, and in 1705 a Prince of the Holy Roman Empire. In 1707 Peter gave him the title of Prince of Izhora, with the right to be addressed as "Highness"; and in the following year made him governor of the St. Petersburg province. His influence over the tsar seemed so complete that even members of the old Moscow aristocracy as important as Field-Marshal Sheremetev now begged for his support. In the triumphal procession in Moscow after the battle of Poltava he rode in the place of honor on the tsar's right hand. . . .

Menshikov was in many ways an unattractive character. Ruthless, a dangerous foe, above all intensely avaricious, he made a host of enemies. Indeed, a good deal of noble opposition to Peter and his policies was inspired not so much by the tsar himself as by the favorite who seemed, in the eyes of so many Russians of good family, an arrogant and greedy upstart. In the spring of 1711, and again in 1714–1715, serious accusations of peculation and corruption were brought against Menshikov. On the second occasion he was heavily fined; and perhaps only the support of Catherine averted a more severe penalty. In 1723–1724 he was accused of concealing over 30,000 runaway serfs on his great estates in the Ukraine, and of illegally extending the boundaries of one of these estates. An investigation into these charges was still in progress at Peter's death. During the last decade or more of the reign, therefore, his old intimacy with the tsar was at an end. Yet no one took his place; and the memory of past friendship and past services was too strong to allow Peter ever to take really severe measures against a man who, for over a decade, had bulked so large in his life.

The blots on the tsar's character were thus considerable: irascibility, lack of self-control, grossness, and insensitivity carried to the pitch of outright brutality. Yet against them must be set even greater virtues: courage, energy, self-sacrifice, and a capacity for true and lasting friendship. Under all the crudeness, the impatience, the lack of feeling for outlooks or ideas different from his own, can be seen an essential truthfulness and simplicity. Both Peter's faults and his good points were direct reflections of his deepest nature, undistorted by hypocrisy, calculation, or artifice of any kind. Of no ruler in the history of Europe can it be said with greater truth that his work was the outcome of his own essential character.

James Cracraft

Some Dreams of
Peter the Great

The following work, first published in 1974 and considerably abbreviated here, is an "experimental" exercise in historical dream-interpretation aimed at a "deeper understanding of the life of a man who for sound historical reasons is worth studying closely." As such, the essay raises questions of interest not only to students of Peter the Great but to anyone concerned with the relationship, still problematic, between history and psychology.

In 1884 the historian M. I. Semevsky published the more or less fragmentary records of twelve nocturnal dreams experienced by Peter the Great between November 1714 and November 1716, to which were joined the records of two dreams that occurred to Peter's second wife, the future Catherine I, on two successive nights in January 1719. The records were found among the papers of the so-called *Kabinet* of Peter the Great, that vast and still not fully organized collection of documents now housed in the Central State Archives — TsGADA — in Moscow. Evidently Peter's dreams — his recollections of them — were written down by Peter himself soon after waking and were then transcribed by various attendants, although only one of the dream-records was (or is) extant in Peter's original as well as in a contemporary copy. Catherine's recollections of her dreams were taken down by a private secretary (she was illiterate). . . . We have positive evidence, in other words, not merely that Peter and his wife dreamed (a fact of no inherent interest), but that they were careful to record some of their dreams, the by all accounts rather stupid and indolent Catherine no doubt following in this her husband's example or even perhaps his direct order. And that, surely, is something worth noting. Can anything like it be found in the life of a ruler, whether of Russia or of any other state in Europe, particularly at this time? Indeed, it seems reasonable to conclude that Peter's action in recording his dreams, even his evident interest in

Reprint of James Cracraft, "Some Dreams of Peter the Great: A Biographical Note," in *Canadian-American Slavic Studies*, vol. 8, no. 2 (Summer 1974), pp. 173–197.

them, was exceedingly rare anywhere in Europe between Classical times and the nineteenth century, when the serious study of the dream revived. We are confronted here with historical evidence of an altogether extraordinary kind.

Possibly a reference to the only similar case which my research has so far uncovered will make this basic point clearer. A Pakistani historian has recently translated from the original Persian and published the thirty-seven dreams of Tipu Sultan of Mysore which the latter recorded in his "Book of Dreams" between 1785 and 1798. The dream-records survive in the dreamer's own handwriting; and in almost every instance, as with Peter, the dreamer recorded his dreams without commenting on them. There are other intriguing parallels in the careers and even the outlooks of Peter and Tipu Sultan. But my purpose here is to stress the geographical and especially cultural distance that separated the two. For Tipu Sultan was a devout Muslim and as such nurtured in a civilization where the dream was both ubiquitous and the subject of intense concern: in a "great tradition" which was thoroughly penetrated by the importance of dreams. This was not true of the Christian civilization of Europe, at least not at its upper levels — and particularly not in the early modern period, when in effect older religious prejudices conspired with an emergent rationalism to leave the science of dreams in those nether regions of society and culture to which it had been largely confined. On the face of it, I would urge, a comparison of Peter and Tipu Sultan in this respect serves to illustrate that the former's behavior regarding his dreams was not only rare, but most odd.

Yet granted the highly unusual nature of the evidence, what, as students of Peter, are we to make of it? Semevsky published his material because, as he says, it is "not without interest" that Peter was intrigued by some of his dreams, that he wrote some of them down, perhaps discussed them with others, and had them preserved. Semevsky emphasizes that Peter acted "only out of curiosity," that he was the "enemy of superstition and prejudice," that he attached no importance to the dreams nor saw in them "any hidden, significant meaning": that Peter was, in short, no pharaoh seeking in his dreams signs or portents to guide his future policies. Indeed he was not. But possibly this second basic point also needs expanding. For what did Peter understand by "superstition" and "prejudice"? What, more exactly, was Peter's attitude towards dreams, and why did he bother to record some of his own? A resolution of these questions should tell us something more positive about the man than what Semevsky's remarks convey. And while to my knowledge Peter left no direct or explicit clues in the matter, there is I think enough circumstantial or indirect evidence on which to base an answer.

Elsewhere I have argued that if Peter never abandoned his basic religious beliefs, what I called his "simple soldier's faith," nevertheless in maturity he clearly did not possess that quality of ardent, reverential, churchgoing, even mystical piety (*blagochestie*) which characterized the religious life of perhaps the majority of his subjects — as it had that of his father, the "Most Pious" Tsar Aleksei, a man "strict in his devotions and a savourer of his religion," in the words of his English physician. I argued that Peter had come to have, in the words of an Englishman in *his* service, a "more rational sense of God and religion": that he had come to believe, in his own words, that "reason is above all the virtues, for without reason virtue is nothing [. . . *ibo vsiakaia dobrodetel bez razuma — pusta*]." This aspect of his general outlook, surely, had several effects which are of some relevance here.

There is, firstly, Peter's religious tolerance, which was as universally praised by Europeans as it was deprecated in his own country. And although, in official practice, his tolerance had somewhat arbitrary and fixed limits, he was as a person remarkably open-minded on religious matters, on what today we should call ideological or philosophical questions. He had, as was said by yet another contemporary Englishman, the Anglican chaplain at St. Petersburg, "rub'd off the rust of that bigotry to his own religion which his people seem generally to have contracted; and . . . was both an impartial and excellent judge of any controverted points in religion." In fact, as a man, and to some extent as tsar, Peter was usually quite *intolerant* of any expression of the institutionalized prejudices of the Russian church. It can also be shown that Peter was most definitely a determined enemy of "superstition," which was defined for him by his closest ideological collaborator, Feofan Prokopovich (Peter supervised the relevant texts), as the attributing of a "power to do good or evil to persons or things which in truth have no such power": as (this in a major legal pronouncement) the sum total of those accumulated "fictions" and "frauds," "wicked practices or deeds," "false miracles" and "old wives' tales," or "ridiculous" and "shameful" carryings-on, all of which, "in a word, can be described as superstitious: that is, anything which is superfluous and unnecessary for salvation . . . and like snowdrifts impedes progress along the straight path to truth." It was Prokopovich, the first authentic voice in Russia of the Early Enlightenment, who once said of Peter, most admiringly: "he made it his business frequently to inform erroneous and doubtful consciences, to free them from the bonds of superstition, and to lead them to knowledge of the truth." And together they made every effort to enforce their views.

It is more difficult to establish Peter's attitude towards dreams. But, indirectly, there is no evidence whatever that he shared — as did, for example, Archpriest Avvakum (died 1681) or, more discreetly, St. Tikhon of Zadonsk (died 1783) — that complex of views which might be described as "medieval" and whereby dreams are regarded with a definite credulousness, as "visions," as the work of God or the devil, as indisputably prophetic or didactic, as "real" in the sense of being symptomatic or revelatory of otherwise inaccessible areas of reality (areas whose existence we might doubt): as things the significance of which points outwards, rather than inwards to the dreamer himself (and to his society and culture). More directly, we know that Peter's measures against "superstition" included the prosecution of a peasant woman who claimed to have had "visions" of Christ and his angels and of a monk who had spread "tales" of his visions of St. Zacharius, for which he was horribly punished (the woman was sent home, having been made to promise that if she had further visions she would not tell anybody). The Holy Synod, the bureau Peter created to deal *inter alia* with such matters, once declared that "these and similar superstitions [*superstitsii*] . . . were brought to Russia by Greeks." This is a little of what could be adduced to show that Peter and his closest associates had abandoned the mystical, the oriental, the past, in favor of the Latin (Catholic or Protestant), the rational, the — what should we call it? — the "modern." And such attitudes are not consistent with a "medieval" conception of dreams. Such attitudes, such an orientation, such manifestations indeed of that general outlook which was suggested above, could not have coexisted with such a conception: not in one man's mind. But perhaps the best, though admittedly quite indirect proof of this are the carefully preserved, unelaborated dream-records themselves; their content (no saints or angels: none of Avvakum's golden ships on the blue Volga or Tikhon's shining lights and Virgin Mary); and the complete absence of any evidence that Peter ever acted in any way in accordance with what he "saw" (as the Russian expresses it) in these or any other dreams.

Then why did he do it? Semevsky has asked us to agree that it was "only out of curiosity, as an amateur of all things peculiar." And, yes, the open-minded, impatient Peter was before all else extraordinarily inquisitive — not just about the theories and practices of other Christian confessions, but about nearly everything. Today in Leningrad one can view the remains of this omnivorous curiosity in half a dozen or more rooms of the Hermitage, in the Naval Museum, the Library of the Academy of Sciences, the *Kunstkamera*, the Summer Palace, and at Peterhof. But the trait was well known then, too, and by the most forward of Peter's contemporaries was highly esteemed. Leibniz, who talked with Peter several times in June 1716, was awestruck by "la vivacité et le jugement de ce grand Prince," as he wrote shortly thereafter: "he summons experts [*des habiles gens*] to him, and in conversation astounds them with the knowledge he shows of their affairs . . . all the mechanical sciences . . . seafaring . . . astronomy and geography." Closer to home, Prokopovich once explained to the Russian reading public that the translation and publication of a certain book on Classical mythology had been undertaken because Peter, in his "noble curiosity," had wondered about the origins of the "superstitious polytheism of the pagans, and if there were a pagan work on the subject." We hear echoes everywhere. What the duke of Saint-Simon and others who observed him during his six-week stay in Paris in the spring of 1717 most admired was Peter's "extreme curiosity" — the same words used by the sagacious Charles Whitworth, English ambassador in Russia, when describing Peter in 1705, in 1707, and again in 1710. It was by his "curiosity" as well as by his diligence, Whitworth maintained in the earliest of these references, that Peter had overcome his lack of a good education and "acquired almost an universal knowledge." Indeed John Perry, the English engineer and disciple of Newton who spent some fourteen years in Peter's service, was sure that it was this "early genius and curiosity to enquire into the reason and causes of things, which method . . . he still [c. 1715] uses with indefatigable application in the minutest things," that lay at the heart of Peter's manifold and, to their way of thinking, beneficent activities.

"Curiosity . . . in the minutest things." I submit that these dream-records are in the first instance evidence of Peter's extraordinary curiosity. But this is not to agree that he acted "only" out of curiosity, as Semevsky, perhaps not quite deliberately, has put it. For the adverb "only," like today's connotations of the word "curiosity," in Russian as in English, might seem to trivialize, quite misleadingly, Peter's motive here. In early modern Europe such "noble and solid curiosity," in a phrase of the day, was a positive virtue, as my quotations above from Peter's admirers might have indicated. "The great scientists of the sixteenth and seventeenth centuries wanted, above all else, to satisfy their own curious minds."[1] In short, it could be argued, if one allows personal motives to play any role, that a sustained and lively curiosity about nature and all its phenomena was an important factor in bringing about the Enlightenment or, more particularly, the so-called Scientific Revolution, with its complex of characteristically "modern" modes of thought. Curiosity such as this, "the disinterested desire to know," was perhaps "the central impulse which . . . led men to engage in scientific work and to clear the scientific point of view from encumbrances."[2]

For historians, therefore, what may be most striking about this material is the simple fact that Peter had the "curiosity" to record at least a dozen of his dreams and in this way to provide for their preservation. Preservation for what? For study, along with most of the myriad other "curiosities" that he collected? We cannot say for certain. But even so, not merely was such behavior rare, and most odd, for that time and place; it was, by any standard, astonishingly "modern." And it tends to oppugn, I should also like to urge, that persistent characterization of Peter as a kind of insensible boor, a sort of royal *bricoleur* "designed by nature [as was said by a passing acquaintance] rather to be a ship carpenter than a great prince"; as a "*bogatyr* [or rude folk hero] in the literal sense of the word," as the historian Bogoslovsky once put it; or as a man of "practical intelligence . . . raised to the level of genius": "his range of interests . . . in many ways narrow": "always and essentially a technician" (M. S. Anderson). But perhaps the most objectionable thesis, once again, is that of Kliuchevsky, in his influential history lectures, where he serenely declares that "In his mental makeup Peter was one of those simple, straightforward people [*odin iz tekh prostykh liudei*] who can be understood at a glance."

This does not exhaust the implications of the evidence, however. There remain the contents themselves of the dream-records and the possibility that they might tell us something more about Peter (and his wife). But

[1] A. G. R. Smith, *Science and Society in the Sixteenth and Seventeenth Centuries* (New York, 1972), p. 30.
[2] G. N. Clark, *Early Modern Europe* (London, 1966), p. 104.

here the historian is aware of moving suddenly to the frontiers of his discipline — to that region, still not successfully mapped, where history and psychology meet. It is enough to engender the greatest caution. For, obviously, there are formidable conceptual and technical difficulties in the way of deriving any useful historical knowledge from the contents of these dream-records, which is possibly one reason why they have been ignored by everyone else who has written on Peter except, of course, Semevsky. And his further editorial comments are not helpful, concluding, as they do, with the statement that "we leave it to others to interpret this interesting material." It was perhaps understandable reluctance on the part of a scholar who wrote some sixteen years before Freud's *The Interpretation of Dreams* was first published and well before elements of the master's synthesis had for better or worse become, in Lionel Trilling's expression, part of the slang of our culture.

But this is not the place to deal with the methodological and other general problems that are raised by an attempt to make something more of this evidence. Here it may be sufficient, before embarking, to point out that at the most basic level a degree of conviction or, minimally, a suspension of disbelief is needed if we are to proceed at all. That is to say, the historian must be willing to accept at the outset that dreams have meaning, that they can be interpreted, and that they perhaps are, in Freud's well-worn aphorism, the "royal road to the unconscious." He must accept, more generally still, that the "unconscious" itself, as the term is usually employed by depth psychologists, exists and is, or can be viewed as, a source of motive for "conscious" actions. A historian of such persuasion might then be prepared to see in these dream-records precious vestiges of Peter and Catherine. He might be willing to consider the discovery and detailed study of evidence such as this as a kind of archaeology: as an exercise, more exactly, in a kind of proto-biography which may lead to a deeper understanding of the life of a man who for sound historical reasons is worth studying closely. For what in any case is being essayed here is not history proper but something ancillary or, perhaps better, preliminary to it.

As for the more technical difficulties to be encountered, they are related, on the one hand, to the more or less fragmentary, often isolated (in time, from one another), imperfectly edited, or sometimes linguistically obscure nature of the dream-records themselves and, on the other, to the problem of applying modern dream analysis to history (to the dream-reports of people who are, in a word, dead). I hurry to add that these difficulties are separable for expository purposes only, and that they precipitate questions which cannot, again, be gone into in this paper. But on the first set of difficulties it might be noted that the undoubted authenticity of the dream-records, as well as the length, actual content, and linguistic intelligibility of several of them, encourage us to dispense with reservations on this subsidiary point and to get on to the main problem — that of applying the techniques and, more relevantly, the findings of modern dream psychology to historical evidence without doing violence to either, but especially not to the latter. And perhaps the best that can be said in this connection is that lacking few if any direct precedents (I mean examples of historical dream-interpretation by historians — by scholars bringing historical knowledge to bear for primarily if not exclusively historical ends), principled or *a priori* objections to an attempt to make something more of this evidence must be largely hypothetical. For instance, the historian of orthodox Freudian leanings may object that since of course neither Peter nor Catherine can be asked to free-associate to these dream-records, or that since neither has left any comment on them, it is impossible to move forward. The objection, once it has been ascertained that Freud (all of Freud) has not been misunderstood on this point, could be answered at several levels: by emphasizing the very different objectives of historians and psychologists (supposing the latter to be interested at all in the matter); by referring to the actual example of Freud and others in commenting on the dreams of historical persons; by suggesting that post-Freudian developments in the physiology and content analysis of dreams, and in dream symbolism, would tend to make such an objection obsolete or, at the least, not entirely operative: that perhaps especially in this area even Freudian psychoanalysis need not be regarded, by non-practitioners anyway, as a set of either immutable or permanently interfused doctrines: as something that must be swallowed whole. Objections like this are debatable. The point is, given the highly unusual nature of the evidence, and in the absence of specific guidelines or models, even negative ones, the matter should not be prejudged. Nor should, I hope, the worth of the enterprise itself be decided on the basis of what happens here.

In other words, the remainder of the paper is intended to be introductory, exploratory, even "heuristic," or, to put it most neutrally, experimental. It is meant to open the question of what historians might learn from studying Peter's dream-records, not to close it. The idea is to engage the historian's peculiar combination of specialized historical knowledge, sensitivity to evidence, general intellectual awareness, and common sense in an effort to shed some little light on material that might otherwise have remained reproachfully dark and mysterious; and when that is not enough, when the meaning (or *a* meaning) of a particular dream-record is not transparent, then to refer to the modern masters of dream-interpretation — to the works, in particular, of Freud and Jung and their students. The method involves among other things tracing correspondences between elements of a given dream-record and things we know to have figured in Peter's conscious life, and drawing analogies between components of a dream-record or a whole dream-record and whatever may seem relevant — similar if not identical — in so to speak the typology of dreams that is emerging from more than half a century of scientific study. But in this paper, again, references to the psychological literature will be kept to the minimum. The aim is to elicit possibly useful information or "leads," not to propose a new and comprehensive psychology of Peter.

Some of Peter's dream-records are more interesting to the historian, or more accessible, than others. Those that have been selected for study here are divided into what I call Peter's "symbolic" and his "Turkish" dream-records (Catherine's also fall into the "symbolic" category). By "symbolic" is meant records where the language is plain enough but which contain images or symbols that must be deciphered to some extent before even a partial and provisional interpretation of the dream can be hazarded. "Turkish" simply refers to the subject matter of a second group of dream-records. Those of Peter's dream-records that are not studied here have been excluded because they are excessively isolated or fragmentary, or obscure linguistically. One, whose content is quite clear but in itself not very interesting, is used to help add a further possible dimension to an interpretation of another.

Here, in my translation, is the first of the symbolic dream-records left by Peter. On January 28–29, 1715,

> *being in Moscow, [he] had a dream in the night: the lord colonel was walking along the bank of the Bolshaia river, and with him were three fishermen. And the river became rough, and great waves arose. And a wave would come and then recede. And so it was with the waves that covered them. And the river retreated, but they did not. And little by little the water returned to its former place.*

The "lord colonel" of this dream-record obviously is Peter himself. One of his major and self-appointed roles in life was that of colonel of the Preobrazhenskii regiment of guards, which he had founded in his youth and publicly had led as recently as January 6, 1715. We know from a mass of correspondence that he and his intimates frequently addressed one another by their military rank. It would have been natural for an attendant to employ such a title when transcribing or recording the tsar's dream-report: psychoanalysis in any case assures us that the dreamer's own ego makes its appearance in every dream, and plays the principal part, even if it knows how to disguise itself completely as far as the dream's "manifest content" is concerned. And at a very general or even "collective" level of significance, this may be no more nor less than a classic dream of birth, or of death and birth, a theme which (it appears) such contact with water almost invariably represents: "either we are falling into water or clambering out of it, saving someone from it or being saved by them, i.e., the relation between mother and child is symbolized. . . . We give birth or are being born."[3]

But we might quite legitimately press the content of this dream-record for a more personal and hence, for historians, a more helpful meaning. We know from various records that on the night of January 28–29, 1715, Peter was not actually "in Moscow," as the dream-record reads, but in St. Petersburg, where in the course of the month he had personally signed and even lent a hand in drafting several important pieces of legislation. He had also been present that month at various public festivities, most notably, on January 16 and 17, at one of those grandiose masquerades in which he often indulged and whose aftermath lasted, not unusually, for almost a fortnight. We know, further, that on January 27, 1715 (the dream took place, again, on January 28–29) one of Peter's naval officers was married "in His Majesty's House"; that on January 29 "His Majesty was at the Admiralty and [then] at the baths and [then] at [the officer's house]" — to continue, presumably, the wedding celebrations; and that on January 30 "His Majesty was indisposed and stayed at home all day." In January 1715, in fact, Peter had not been in Moscow for nearly four years, and would not be again for another three.

---

[3] Freud, *A General Introduction to Psychoanalysis*, trans. J. Riviere (New York, 1970), pp. 160, 168–169. Similarly, J. Jacobi, *Complex/Archetype/Symbol in the Psychology of C. G. Jung*, trans. R. Manheim (Princeton, 1959), pp. 143–145.

Thus in spite of the appearance in the dream-record of a "Bolshaia river" — which was not the name of a river in Moscow but rather of the *Bolshaia Neva* in St. Petersburg (and such a confusion of detail appears commonly to happen in dreams) — for Peter "being in Moscow" must have been part of his dream. Bearing in mind the universal theme of birth, or of death and rebirth, educed above, things now combine to suggest that in this dream-record we have evidence that in the midst of work and exhausting festivities in his new capital Peter knew an inner, possibly repressed nostalgia for the old, for the city of his birth. This additional interpretation of the dream-record does not so much contradict as it seriously qualifies the familiar allegation (based only on circumstantial evidence) that Peter disliked or even hated Moscow: now we might wish to say that he was ambivalent about it. And in this connection it might be remembered that beginning in 1717–1718, with the virtual cessation of hostilities in the Baltic area, Peter was to spend his remaining winters in Moscow and was to have been there again, in December 1724, when he succumbed to an attack of the disease which in the following month killed him.

As for the three fishermen who appear in the dream-record, any symbolic significance the number itself may have is probably eclipsed for us by the fact that fishermen were precisely the kind of plain nautical folk among whom Peter, to the astonishment of the uninitiated, was quite at home. Thus, among many such instances, we might cite Bergholz, the well placed diarist of Peter's last years, who in the fashionable Summer Garden in St. Petersburg once "observed with surprise some foreign shipwrights. . . . They were sitting with the Emperor, who was lodged among them, they with their hats on their heads and he talking with them without any ceremony. His Majesty treats very graciously with such persons and with great pleasure passes the time with them conversing about sailing and trade." Indeed, at that "grand masquerade" of January 16–17, 1715, which was occasioned by the wedding of Peter's aged mock-patriarch with "a buxom widow of thirty-four," Peter himself, according to an eyewitness, "was dressed like a boor of Frizeland, and skillfully beat a drum in company with three generals." By "Frizeland" (or Friesland) our witness meant the Dutch province of that name or very likely Holland itself, many if not most of whose sons were fishermen or sailors; and ever since Peter had first donned such clothes in the shipyards of Amsterdam, nearly twenty years before, they had been a favorite costume of his: as late as January

1724 he was to be seen wearing them at a court masquerade. Taken in conjunction with what has already been said about the dream-record in question, the appearance of the fishermen would seem to suggest for it a still more personal and immediate significance. That is to say, we can now see a link, perhaps even a causal link between the various festivities of January 1715 in St. Petersburg and their debilitating consequences, and the latent nostalgia that we have presumed to detect in the dream-record of January 28–29. In the wake of the former Peter quite naturally yearned secretly for peace, security, "home," the womb: for oblivion; and for, more positively, a kind of purification or rebirth. We had not appreciated this before and might now want to look for more definite evidence both of Peter's ambivalence towards Moscow and of a weariness of his way of life.

This dream-record also suggests, though the point may be too banal, that Peter's notorious love of sailing contained an opposite, an unconscious, perhaps deliberately repressed, yet altogether natural fear of death by drowning. At any rate, this aspect appears to be the dominant theme of another of his dreams, one which is otherwise of little interest — as far as we know of it — and took place in November 1716. According to the dream-record, Peter

> had a dream, when [we] entered Pomerania: [I] was in a galliot, whose mast and sail were not in proportion; [we] sailed off in it and it tipped to one side and became bogged down with water; [we] fell in and swam to the other side and turned [the boat] towards home and went [there] by easy stages; and at home [I] ordered the water to be poured out. . . .

Here it would appear certain that for Peter the phrase "when [we] entered Pomerania" was part of the dream. But the significance of the phrase, or indeed any connection between the dream-record's content and Peter's circumstances either in the spring of 1716 (when he did in reality pass through Pomerania) or in the following November (when the dream apparently took place), is not at all clear. We have comparatively little knowledge of Peter's personal life at this time. Possibly the dream was triggered by some sort of sailing accident that occurred in the spring or in November, immediately before the dream was "seen"; or perhaps such accidents — which Peter, who sailed so much and with such feckless courage, was wont to have — happened both in the spring and in November, the one reminding him of the other. In any case, a latent fear of such accidents, of death by drowning, and perhaps even a "wish" for the same, are evident in this as in the preceding dream-record. And when it is remembered that it was Peter's involvement in a stormy sailing mishap some eight or ten years later which precipitated the crisis that led to his death, the dreams take on a premonitory aspect, a quality of certain dreams which some modern interpreters — though not Freud — still recognize. It is being suggested, not that the nature of Peter's death was foreordained, but that he had, unconsciously at least, some sense of it and therefore, more remarkably, some sort of inner compulsion regarding it. It may be as good an explanation as any of why he waded into the water on that cold December day in 1724 to rescue the crew of a capsized boat.

The record of a second of Peter's symbolic dreams reads as follows. On April 26, 1715, he

> had a dream. It was as though an eagle were sitting in a tree, and beneath it had crept or crawled some sort of large wild beast, like a crocodile or a dragon [na podobie krokodila ili drakona], onto which this eagle immediately leapt, and gnawed its head from its neck — that is, chewed away half the neck and killed it. And then, while many people gathered to watch, another such beast crept up, whose head this eagle also gnawed off, it seemed in plain view of everybody.

The horrible, nightmarish quality of this dream may be able to tell us as much about the distance that separates us from Peter, our immediate culture from his, as it can about Peter himself. For while Peter, unlike his father and brothers and one or two of his intimates, was wholly uninterested in hunting or in blood sports of any kind, and so might never have witnessed any such scene in real life, he had at the same time been exposed to beasts and monsters to a far greater degree than would be usual among his modern students. Thus in looking for possible sources of these striking dream images we might remember that among the wall paintings of the Annunciation Cathedral in the Moscow Kremlin, which was the domestic church of the tsars, the child Peter would have found an abundance of wild animals and monsters: beings like those he would have seen, there and elsewhere, in the ikons especially of the preceding century, with their frequent portrayal of the Last Judgment and other apocalyptic scenes.

Very likely, too, the child as well as the adult Peter would have known of the similar monsters and scenes that figured in those *lubki* or broadsides — usually crude woodcuts — which circulated at the time. Or again, among the illustrations of the splendid *Aleksandriia* (a mythical history of Alexander the Great) which was made for Peter in his childhood by craftsmen of the Moscow Armory, there are many of various monsters and more or less imaginary beasts, including unicorns, lions with horns, eagles with women's heads, elephants with enormous tusks but especially, a huge, horrible, eagle-like creature and, at two other places in the book, a sort of crocodile with four clawed feet. Examples of mythical monsters are also represented in the illustrated primer used by Peter's son Aleksei and daughter Elizabeth, which had been originally published (in 1694), if not actually compiled, at Peter's instruction. And the basic book of symbols used by Peter and his associates when designing their elaborate fireworks, naming ships, etc., a book that was probably commissioned by Peter and certainly was printed at his order (in 1705), contains many "emblems" in which wild beasts and birds — particularly eagles and eagle-like creatures — are prominently portrayed, often in violent settings. The possibilities could be multiplied. I only want to suggest that it is not at all surprising, at first glance, that wild beasts and monsters should figure not only in this dream-record of Peter's, but in two others which survive in extremely fragmentary form, the first dated January 23–24, 1715, and reading

[I] had a dream: of wild beasts — of a lion and a beaver.

and the second, dated February 25, 1715, noting only that

[I] dreamt of bulls and the sun.

But what do the contents of these dream-records signify? Obviously, it would not be enough simply to interpret the two brief fragments on the basis of what students of dream-interpretation or of symbolism have established is the usual significance of certain animal images: to read "passion" or "aggression" for "bulls" and immediately conclude that on February 25, 1715, for instance, Peter's dreaming was instigated by deep-seated evil impulses with which he was unconsciously dealing. To elucidate even these fragments, it seems, we must move on to the longer dream-record, that of April 26, 1715, with its eagle attacking the beast. And here we might note a more specific, more proximate, and altogether more probable source of the latter's imagery: a picture on the "most magnificently adorned" triumphal arch that was erected in St. Petersburg in September 1714 to celebrate the

Russian victory off Cape Hango. As an eyewitness reported it, "among divers emblems was to be seen the Russian eagle seizing an elephant, with this inscription: *Aquila non capit muscas* [the eagle does not catch flies]," the elephant of the emblem symbolizing the captured Swedish frigate, called the *Elephant*, which was brought in triumphal procession up the Neva. Since this emblem was the only one on the arch to have caught our witness's eye, it must have figured prominently; and it is not too much to suppose that Peter saw it too or even that he, in his omnicompetent way, had helped to put it there. A direct correspondence between Peter's dream imagery and a powerful symbol of his conscious life is now, perhaps, established.

Peter had led the triumphal procession up the Neva, just as he had personally commanded the victorious Russian fleet off Cape Hango. Moreover in the spring of 1715, when the dream occurred to him, he was engaged among other things in the preliminary stages of formulating what was to be a master plan for bringing to an end the long war with Sweden. Still, it would seem wholly inadequate to interpret this strangely vivid and violent dream as nothing but a symbolic reenactment in Peter's unconscious mind of a victory, or victories, over the Swedes. The content itself of the dream-record, whether viewed in the context of Peter's other dream-records or in the light of what we know of dreams generally, demands something more. Thus, at a much deeper level, what we may have here is the core of an archetypal "dream of the bad animal" such as the Jungian psychologist Jacobi has analyzed at length and in a most sophisticated, indeed at times moving, way — in a way that precludes any such attempt at analysis in this paper. But I might stress that apart from any universal symbolic role it may have, the eagle was the official Russian — indeed Tsar Peter's personal — emblem; that the "bad animal" of our dream, as in that of Jacobi's subject, may be one of those mythical monsters which represent the instinctual, dark, "lower world," or, "in psychological terms . . . the world of the instincts and drives, i.e., of the psyche that is associated with biological life"; and that in such a dream, as Jacobi concludes, "the dreamer is confronted with an inner reality that far exceeds [his] powers of understanding."[4] What may well be symbolized in Peter's dream-record, in other words, is an intense, not to say savage struggle waging within him

---

[4] Jacobi, *Psychology of Jung*, pp. 139 ff. See also Freud, *Introduction*, p. 165 and J. A. Hadfield, *Dreams and Nightmares* (Baltimore, 1967), pp. 175 ff.

between his baser and nobler selves, a struggle that is being acted out, as was everything in his conscious life, before a crowd of people. Such an interpretation certainly accords with what from the widest array of sources we know of Peter's overt behavior: of its erratic alteration, to put it briefly, between acts of the vilest cruelty and others of heroic kingship, or even of personal kindness.

And the impression that something very basic in Peter is at issue here gains further ground when we reflect that the *raskolniki* [Russian religious dissidents], who were always a most troublesome problem for Peter, were wont to depict him, in both word and picture, as the "crocodile," as he no doubt knew. It was one of the ways in which the more aggressive of these dissidents taunted and reviled him, to which he would respond, with equal vigor, by denouncing them for ignorance and superstition, for obstinacy and plain wickedness, and by persecuting them in one way or another, sometimes violently. The lofty, imperial eagle pounces with horrifying and deadly swiftness on the neck of the monstrous crocodile — while a crowd watches. By means of this dream-record we can perhaps penetrate — and the depth of the insight takes the breath away — to the core of Peter's being. It would follow that in a future effort to come to terms with his personality some sort of fundamental inner conflict must be postulated and its ramifications traced.

The third of Peter's symbolic dream-records to be considered here is less violent in content but no less striking in its imagery. On January 28–29, 1715, seemingly, Peter dreamed that he was "in Iavorov," where he

> came upon a high tower; and from this tower hung down a rope, which [he] took hold of. And [he] went up the tower and wanted to go up the spire [shpits], but it was smooth, and his feet could not hold and climb. And so, having made some snowshoes [lyzhi: perhaps "skis"], he went up that spire on those snowshoes. And on the tip of the spire had been put an apple, and on the apple, on one side, was the tsar's emblem of the two-headed eagle; and in the center of the apple was its core. Then with his left hand he fixed a flag in this core.

In basic psychoanalytic terms the meaning of the impressive dream recorded here is plain: it is a symbolic reenactment of sexual intercourse or, perhaps better, of sexual conquest (of imperial sexual conquest!), which perhaps ultimately recounts, were the point to be pressed, a "primal scene" of Oedipal dimensions. Such dreams, such symbolic representations of sexual intercourse, are not, one gathers from the specialized literature, common. And its appearance here may at one level serve to emphasize, if it needed emphasizing, the passionate, indeed the aggressive and often violent nature of Peter's personality.

But for Petrine specialists, noting the specifically Petrine significance of some of the images, there perhaps is, again, a little more to it than that. The personal import of the two-headed eagle is obvious. Hardly less so is that of the flag and especially of the spire or *shpits* (from the German *spitze*), an architectural form that was quite distinct from the traditional Russian domes or cupolas or the tent-shaped *shatër*. In fact, the spire of this dream-record may provide a clue to an additional interpretation of the dream's meaning. For Peter could only have seen such a thing on one of the few European churches then extant in Russia, on the church of the Peter-Paul Fortress in St. Petersburg which he had just built in the new style, or in Europe itself, in his travels through the Baltic provinces, North Germany, Holland, England, Austria, and Poland (he had not as yet been to Denmark and France).

Thus it may be significant that the action of this dream takes place as it were in Europe, "in Iavorov," a small town not far from Lviv, in the most Polish part of the Ukraine, where the Polish king maintained a residence and the Polish *Senatus-Consilium* occasionally met. In the spring of 1711 Peter himself had spent more than a month in Iavorov, where he had been engaged principally in preparing for his upcoming campaign against the Turks, an enemy against whom he had long sought support in Europe. But it had not been all work. His beloved Catherine, whom it was his habit at this time to call "Mother" (i.e., *Muder*, in Dutch, or sometimes, in Russian, *Mat* or *Matka*), had joined him there, and had been treated as if she were already formally tsaritsa (they were not publicly married for another ten months). With Peter she had frequently attended the banquets and balls and soirees that were given for them by various Polish grandees, as she informed a correspondent early in May. It was at Iavorov, too, that Peter had arranged for his only son to marry a German princess, a sister-in-law of the Austrian emperor, a marriage in which he placed great hope. It had been in one way or another a memorable time in his life. And when viewed in this context, I am proposing, the content of this dream-record might also symbolize Peter's special attitude towards Europe: it might provide an unprecedented glimpse of the depth and quality of as it were his lifelong urge to surmount or conquer its culture — to master, above everything else, its way of making war.

Catherine's two dream-records, which are also of a highly symbolic kind, are of interest chiefly for what they may reveal about her relationship with Peter — which is both convenient and appropriate, since Catherine herself is of interest to historians primarily because of her connection to him. And because we know relatively little about Catherine personally, a function of her illiteracy but also no doubt of her humble background and essentially subordinate role, almost any source of possibly new information about her is on the face of it welcome.

In the words of a secretary, to whom, necessarily, she would have had to dictate her dream-report,

> On [the night of] January 13–14, 1719, her Sovereign Majesty the Tsaritsa was pleased, before dawn, to have a dream. It was as if in the garden of a palace a wild beast, in white wool, like a lion and very angry, was encountered. [The beast] attacked with his teeth the legs of her Majesty's team of six lightly-colored bay horses. At the same time there were ministers and a multitude of people in the garden. And the women's skirts were raised by the wind up to their heads; and there were white banners, which they said were signs of peace. And this angry beast often screamed [the word] "saldoref! saldoref!" But another such beast went up to a bull in some sort of courtyard; only this beast was very affectionate. On its head was a crown and on the crown three candles. And it went up to his [sic] Majesty and was affectionate to him.

Elements of the content of this dream-record — the angry beast and its violent actions, the royal sense of being surrounded by a crowd — are similar to elements we have already observed in the content of one of Peter's dream-records. The sexual significance of others is transparent. Thus initially, perhaps, we might want to consider the dream recorded here as in part an archetypal "dream of the bad animal" and in part a highly sexual fantasy. That is to say, the dream-record provides evidence that Catherine was deeply troubled by an inner reality with which she could not cope, one which far exceeded her modest powers of understanding and was somehow connected with her sexual life —

with, since he actually appears in the dream, her relations with her husband, the tsar.

Yet when all of the elements of this remarkably detailed dream-record are taken into account, the dream might be made to yield a more specific and comprehensible meaning. There is for example the obviously crucial image of the beast in white wool. Semevsky suggests that it was prompted in Catherine by the two white bears which she and Peter had recently acquired as pets: their previous owner, Prince Romodanovsky, had trained them to serve huge cups of vodka to his guests and, as Catherine would have known, to molest those who might have declined the offer — an impressive, if not terrifying sight for anyone. But if Semevsky is right in this, he has found the source of the image, not its significance. And it is equally likely that if the image had been prompted in Catherine by her pet bears, she would have said as much; when recalling her dream she would have said to her secretary "a white bear" rather than "a wild beast, like a lion, in white wool."

The image of the beast in white wool, or rather of the two beasts, the one angry and violent and the other, with its crown and candles, affectionate: this image must be the clue to a fuller and more informative interpretation of the dream. And if we assume, mindful of the central role in dreams played by the dreamer himself, that the beast in fact represents Catherine, such an interpretation begins to unfold. The angry or violent beast, precisely the "bad animal," symbolizes Catherine's darker side, the evil impulses of the *id*, of the world of the instincts and drives, of the infantile or animal self. The beast is covered with the protective white wool of respectability, even of majesty, that Catherine has won as Peter's mistress and then wife, as the "Sovereign Tsaritsa." But it is only a covering. For the beast gnashes viciously at the vulnerable legs of the team of bays, a straightforward symbol of sexual attack in which Catherine herself, because they were her horses, is not only active but passive, not only aggressor but victim, just as the women in the surrounding crowd are the victims of a lascivious wind. The attack on Catherine, in which she herself is a culprit, as well as the milder treatment accorded the women of the court, are witnessed by the "ministers," evoking not only the realities of court life but, more personally, the critical time in her life when the homeless prisoner-of-war, the winsome "Katerina," was transferred from the bed of her captor to that of Menshikov (the tsar's favorite minister) and thence to the tsar's. Thereupon, with the appearance of the white banners, which

Catherine has to be told are signs of peace, a sort of truce intervenes; and the angry beast, screaming a certain word, is upstaged by, or transformed into, the affectionate beast, a beast as good as the other is bad. The candles on the good beast's crown, which are arranged in a primordial triad, would stand for purity, honor, innocence, meekness, the graces; the crown itself, of course, for the royal dignity; the whole image, the good beast wearing its crown with candles, for the virtuous, noble, divine being that Catherine has become through the exercise of her charms on his Majesty the bull, an obvious symbol of aggressive, even violent male sexuality.

So far, perhaps, so good. The interpretation, as it unfolds, seems to correspond with what we knew or might have suspected about Catherine and her relations with Peter, at the same time offering unprecedented insight into the character of this obscure and pathetic woman who was for twenty years Peter's intimate companion and for two years, after Peter's death and until her own, empress of Russia. But it is the apparently mysterious word that the bad animal screamed which provides the clue, perhaps, to a still more central meaning of the dream, a suggestion that is strengthened by the fact that it is this word which links Catherine's first dream to her second, the one she experienced the next night and of whose content only a fragmentary record survives:

> *On January 14–15 of this same year, 1719, before dawn, the Sovereign Tsaritsa, in a dream, heard them scream the aforementioned word, "saldoref!"*

To the dreamer, clearly, the mysterious word had an ominous, even oracular significance. And it could very well be an obsolete or ungrammatical form of the verb *saldirovat* (from the German *saldieren* or the Dutch *saldeeren/salderen*, from the Italian *saldare*), a verb meaning "to balance," as in an account between creditor and debtor. The mysterious word might very well refer to a common commercial expression in the various languages meaning to balance or to settle or to square an account. If so, its significance in these two dream-records, where it plays such a pivotal role, becomes intelligible. It is a desperate cry of warning, a threat, a calling to account uttered by the bad animal only to be echoed the next night by "them." In other words, it is an impulsive and as it were public admonition of the primeval, instinctual, self-preserving "conscience" (as distinct from the superimposed conscience of civilized values) to beware.

But to beware of what? Why the anxiety which now in retrospect seems to pervade the dreams, to be there regardless of whether we have deciphered the mysterious word correctly? The answer — or an answer — may lie in the fact that in January 1719, when the dreams occurred to Catherine, she had been having an affair for more than two years with a gentleman-in-waiting of her court, William Mons, a German of Muscovite upbringing who had entered Peter's service in 1708 and had won his affection. At the time of the dreams, by all that we know, Peter was still not aware of the liaison, and was not to find out until late in 1724, only a month or two before he died and after Catherine had been solemnly crowned empress. Rather, to judge from their private correspondence and public appearances, relations between Peter and Catherine remained, from the beginning of the affair until its end (when Mons was arrested, tried, and executed — ostensibly for taking bribes), as close, as fond, and as earthily humorous as they had ever been. Yet there can be no doubt that Catherine was aware of the unhappy lot that had befallen the woman who preceded her as Peter's mistress when she had proved unfaithful to him, if only because that woman — Anna Mons (she died in 1714) — was the sister of her lover. Nor can she have remained ignorant of the fate of Peter's first wife, whom he had compelled to enter a convent in 1698. Equally, Catherine would have known from years of experience the violence of Peter's temper, which she had become the principal means of assuaging. And by 1719 Mons, it seems, was growing bold to the point of foolishness in his relentless influence-peddling and unscrupulous self-aggrandizement.

So it is not surprising to discover in these records of Catherine's dreams evidence not only of an inner and unresolved conflict between her two selves — a conflict so basic and pervasive that she could not, in spite of the grave danger, control her actions — but signs of profound feelings of guilt and anxiety as well. A new dimension, at least from Catherine's side, has perhaps been added to our knowledge of this critical relationship at the heart of the Petrine system.

Lastly, we turn to Peter's Turkish dream-records, the first of which, chronologically, is preserved only in exceedingly fragmentary form. On April 24, 1716, while in Gdansk (Danzig),

The Sovereign dreamt that on the drums of the Turks there were pearls.

Yet the significance even of this fragment begins to emerge when it is studied together with the records of Peter's other two Turkish dreams. On October 9, 1716, in Copenhagen,

> His Majesty the Tsar had a dream. He had sent to Fieldmarshal Sheremetev and ordered him to go quietly past the towers with his army, doing nothing to disturb the peace with the Turks. But then, when his Majesty himself approached the towers, he saw that they had been made by a fine architect and were adorned by the Turks with banners. And when he went into one of these [towers], it appeared that inside they were also decorated with pictures and other things. And he saw Turks in the dress of various nations and speaking in various tongues, among whom one spoke with his Majesty in Dutch. Their adornment was exceedingly rich, with precious stones on their swords and belts. And some of them had been slain. He [Peter] began to speak to the Field-marshal, as though in anger: why had he taken this tower and thus broken the peace with the Turks? To which he [Sheremetev] said: because the Turks had not been willing to let them pass. To which he [Peter] said: so they would not let him pass without a fight, and therefore he was forced into battle with them. Still, though there was a battle, not many were killed.

And one month later, on November 9, 1716, in Schwerin (duchy of Mecklenburg, North Germany),

> His Majesty the Tsar had a dream about the Turks. He saw many of them in rich dress on a field in [St. Petersburg], among whom was a [the] vizier, who came up to his Majesty, said nothing, and then held up [his sword] in the form of a Latin cross, as the others who were standing behind the vizier did with their swords. And their swordbelts were inlaid with many rich gems. And after the vizier and the others had taken off their swords with the richly inlaid belts, they surrendered them to his Majesty.

Certain elements of these dream-records that may call for some comment can be dealt with quickly. Peter's mention — in the second dream-record — that he spoke Dutch with one of the Turks probably signifies no more than his pride in being able to speak the language (which we know he could) and perhaps also an awareness of the fact that it was only in Dutch, the only foreign language that he knew, that he could converse directly with foreigners. That Peter should have de-scribed, in the third of the dream-records, the upheld Turkish swords as "in the form of a Latin cross" will not be puzzling when it is remembered that Russian crosses had more than one crossbar or in other ways could not have represented the submissive gesture of an upheld Turkish sword hilt that Peter wished to convey. And his observation on entering the Turkish tower, again in the second of the dream-records, that "some of them had been slain," or later that "though there was a battle, not many were killed," betrays perhaps an inner feeling of remorse or even of guilt for the blood that was shed in his wars as well as a natural fear of — and familiarity with — death in battle. Such observations also accord with a certain gallantry towards the enemy that Peter had come to show in his military campaigns and with the solicitude for his soldiers that he often demonstrated. But these details, while they make interesting points in themselves and serve to remind us that Peter's Turkish dreams are of a relatively coherent or prosaic kind, do not bring us closer to the dreams' meaning.

On the other hand, the repetition in the two longer dream-records of details such as the jewelled swordbelts and the rich dress of the Turks suggests a context within which even the fragmentary recollection of drums with pearls begins to make sense. That is to say, the reappearance of details such as these in three dreams which occurred over the space of several months in 1716 suggests that at some earlier point in his life Peter had been impressed with the splendor, with the wealth or the power, of the Turks. The suggestion is corroborated by the dreamer's further observation (or recollection) that the Turkish towers were well made and elaborately decorated both inside and out. For Peter had been an avid student of the art of fortification since childhood, as he himself tells us; and the Turkish fortifications at Azov, which he had besieged in 1695 and 1696, were most probably the first modern fortifications he had ever seen. We have here, then, an aspect of Peter's outlook or of his feelings which we were not previously aware of.

But more than that, if the campaigns against Azov had constituted Peter's first face-to-face encounter with a Turkish force, the battle on the Pruth, in June 1711, had constituted his second and only other before the Turkish dreams took place. And it is entirely likely that the memories of these two personal encounters with the Turks, the first having ended in victory (the first of his career) and the second in defeat, should have been deeply embedded in Peter's unconscious mind, as these dream-records also contrive to suggest. It is another aspect of his mental life which has not before emerged so clearly. Nor can the matter be left there. For in the second of the dream-records we find Peter, his ego undisguised, ordering Sheremetev (commander of the advance guard at Pruth) to do nothing to disturb the peace with the Turks, and concluding that the ensuing battle had been forced by them on the Russians — just as in his conscious life he had both in his communications with the Turkish government and in his public proclamations repeatedly blamed the Turks for the worsening of relations between them and for the onset of hostilities. "If the [peace] be broken and human blood spilt," Peter had warned the sultan in January 1711, "we shall be able to justify ourselves before God and the whole world, since we had no intention of breaking [it]." In his "Manifesto" of February, which on Peter's orders was published in Polish, French, German, Latin, and Turkish as well as in Russian, he had gone on to prove in great detail that the war was the fault of the Turks, that the Russians had had no choice but to take up arms against this "perfidious enemy." And four years later, after losing the battle on the Pruth and concluding a new peace with the Turks (in June 1713), Peter had addressed another manifesto to the sultan's Balkan subjects, to those same Christian peoples whom he had previously promised to liberate from their Muslim masters: only this time, now, in July 1715, he had urged them to restrain themselves and to do all in their power to keep the peace with the Turks.

The second of Peter's Turkish dream-records, in short, would also provide evidence that in 1710–1711 Peter had genuinely sought an accommodation with the Turks or, better perhaps, that he had wished to believe and, at the time of the dream, continued to wish to believe that he had genuinely tried to keep the peace; evidence, moreover, that he was sensitive to the possibility that the Pruth campaign was an ill-conceived, even reckless venture for which he must bear the principal blame; evidence, finally, that after 1711, and perhaps particularly in the autumn of 1716 (when the dream occurred), he was genuinely anxious to maintain the new treaty. Thus, in the dream, Peter's orders to Sheremetev "to go quietly" and to do "nothing to disturb the peace with the Turks," and his initial anger at Sheremetev for having taken the tower "and thus broken the peace with the Turks." If nothing else, the dream-record thus constitutes a valuable reminder of the realities of Peter's diplomatic situation. For as L. A. Nikiforov[5] has remarked, Russia's relations with Turkey in the years after Pruth have been undeservedly

[5] Soviet diplomatic historian. — Ed.

neglected by historians, since they were of such critical importance to Peter's activities in the north. As Nikiforov puts it, "throughout the entire Northern War the Russian government was obliged to keep one eye on the southern flank, to try to preserve peaceful relations with Turkey, for the sake of success in the war on the Baltic."

But still more, at the battle on the Pruth Peter had undergone perhaps the most difficult time of his life, as he himself described it soon thereafter in a letter to one of his intimates. On July 9, after several bloody engagements, and on realizing that he was surrounded as well as outnumbered, he had sued for peace: he had sent his envoy under a white flag into the camp of the grand vizier of the Turkish empire (who was commanding his troops in person) with instructions to negotiate away all of Russia's conquests on the Baltic as well as in the south, if need be, except the province of Ingria, where St. Petersburg was located. At one moment, while his envoy was across the field dealing with the Turks, Peter had feared that he might be taken prisoner or even killed, as he confessed to his Senate in a letter dated July 10. A few days later, after accepting with minor revisions the grand vizier's terms, he had informed Admiral Apraksin in St. Petersburg — to whom "I should never have wanted to write about such a matter" — that "this deadly banquet is now ended," that it was a "grievous thing to be deprived of those places where so much labor and blood have been expended." By the latter Peter had meant Azov, Taganrog, and certain forts on the lower Dnieper, all of which had been taken from or ceded to him by the Turks and their allies but which now, together with his Black Sea fleet, he was obliged to surrender or destroy under the agreement worked out between him and the grand vizier at Pruth and formally ratified by his and the sultan's representatives at Adrianople in June 1713. Altogether the occasion had been not only a memorable one for Peter, but one the memory of which was most painful, and therefore probably repressed — especially since in his activist's way Peter had immediately turned his attention back to the north and a resumption of the war with Sweden.

It was the painful memory of the battle on the Pruth that triggered Peter's Turkish dreams of 1716. Yet it will have been noticed that in the two longer dream-records Peter is victorious over the Turks. In one a tower is taken, recalling Peter's successful siege of Azov in 1696. But in this same dream the Russian troops are commanded, as they were in the Pruth campaign, by Sheremetev, who had played only a peripheral part at Azov; and he was acting, it seemed at first to Peter, contrary to his own orders, which had been to do nothing to disturb the peace — a policy which we know Peter did in fact pursue, broadly speaking, both before and after the Pruth campaign but not before Azov. The significance of this apparent confusion by the dreamer of two events — or of the memories of two quite separate events — becomes clear when we go on to consider the content of the third of these dream-records, where the vizier and his men are seen surrendering to Peter in his capital. When the Freudian doctrine of wish-fulfilment in the process of dreamformation is allowed for, it would seem that having triggered the dreams the painful memory of the Pruth disaster was promptly transformed by them (by the "dream-work"), drawing perhaps on the memory of the successful siege of Azov, into visions of victory and Turkish surrender.

Thus in 1716 Peter dreamed of a reversal of what had in reality happened along the Pruth in 1711, at the same time revealing that he had been impressed by the splendor or might of the Turks and had been, and remained, anxious lest his treaty with them be broken by his side precipitously or unjustifiably. These findings do not, perhaps, unduly bend the mind. But is it possible that Peter's Turkish dream-records can tell us even more, something, in particular, about the future direction of his policy, or rather, tantalizingly, about what might have been the future direction of his policy? For it is doubtless not merely a coincidence that when these dreams took place (April, October, November 1716) Peter was in Europe (Danzig, Copenhagen, Schwerin) and at the conscious level wholly preoccupied, so far as we know, with Baltic affairs: with the affairs of Mecklenburg, whose duke had just married his niece (April 1716) and whose territory was now occupied by Russian troops; with the beginnings of a serious rupture in the northern alliance against Sweden, Peter's troops having been excluded by his allies from the capitulation of Wismar (April 1716), the last Swedish stronghold on the continent and a prize that Peter had promised to the duke; with, in the words of one specialist, a growing awareness of the "diplomatic isolation which threatened him despite the great military successes of Russia or indeed precisely because of them."

Perhaps a little more detail will help to clarify this last point about Peter's Turkish dreams. By the spring of 1716 not only were the former Swedish provinces of Ingria, Karelia, Estonia with the city of Reval, and Livonia with Riga under Russian control, but with the fall of Kaenborg (in April) the whole of Finland had been conquered. Russian troops were in Pomerania as well as in Mecklenburg. But while his allies became increasingly apprehensive of Peter's power in the eastern Baltic, Russian documents show that apart from protecting the interests of his niece's husband Peter concentrated on forcing the unyielding Charles XII to accept defeat and to conclude peace on the basis, naturally, of the *status quo post bellum*. This Charles would not do, and Peter had decided that the only means to this end was an allied invasion of Sweden itself. And it was to this end that he had gone personally to Europe in 1716 and had spent that spring and summer in negotiations and preparations for what proved to be an abortive campaign. For by the end of the summer it was apparent even to Peter that his allies were not inclined to cooperate, and in the autumn it was decided to postpone the whole project. Thereafter, in November and December 1716 and on into 1717, Peter continued to plan for a final campaign. In spite of all that had happened he continued to believe that joint allied operations against Sweden proper were still possible and that this was the only way to end the war.

Accordingly, it is fair to say that by 1716, when Peter experienced his Turkish dreams, the long war with Sweden was regarded by him as essentially over: that in his eyes it was now a problem of compelling Charles to accept what was and to make peace. The fact that it would be two more years before direct Swedish-Russian peace negotiations were opened, and another three before they were concluded, has perhaps obscured for later observers this fundamental change in the nature of the conflict. And it is in this light that another, possibly deeper meaning of the dreams in question begins to take form. They suggest that Peter was already starting to turn his attention, or that he wished to turn his attention, back to the south and to his problems with the Turks. They suggest, when taken together and in their entirety, that Peter harbored a secret ambition to reverse the humiliating denouement of the Pruth campaign and to triumph once more over the Turks: that if he had had his way, if circumstances had been propitious, he would have sought an opportunity to resume direct hostilities with the Ottoman Empire. Here we have evidence, perhaps, of something like a deeply felt need for revenge.

But of course here we are dealing, again (and again, it is hoped, objectively), with subjective phenomena: with the deeper springs of Peter's motivation; with, it may be, precious if not unique, although admittedly fragile clues to his conscious behavior. And like the various lines of inquiry that are opened by an examination of the content of his other dream-records (and of those of Catherine), this is one that might be usefully pursued in a future, properly historical study of Peter the Great, one where explicit and provable statements will be made about his personality and about (this is the point) the connections, direct if not causal, between it and the events of his time.

James Cracraft

Opposition to Peter the Great

In this essay the question of opposition in Russia to Peter I is systematically surveyed. It is argued that the subject can tell us much not only about Peter personally, but also about the motives underlying various of the major reforms discussed elsewhere in this book.

The subject of opposition in Russia to Peter I "the Great" has not been ignored by historians. References to it abound in the extensive literature on the Petrine period while monographic studies have been devoted to major oppositional figures, "affairs," events, and movements, and to the governmental organs created to adjudicate cases of opposition. Yet with one or two partial and quite limited exceptions, no single study has focused on the whole phenomenon of opposition to Peter's government and policies and to Peter himself, although links between various of its occurrences have been posited. This neglect, if it may be so termed, is understandable. Indeed, it is a thesis of this essay that opposition to Peter in Russia was both constant and pervasive, and that it therefore cannot be adequately described and assessed without detailed reference

From James Cracraft, "Opposition to Peter the Great," in Ezra Mendelsohn and Marshall S. Shatz, eds., *Imperial Russia 1700–1917: State, Society, Opposition: Essays in Honor of Marc Raeff*, 1988, pp. 22–34. © 1988 by the Northern Illinois University Press. Used with permission of the publisher.

to the main developments of the time. The history of opposition to Peter is in effect the history of his reign; or so, with qualifications, it will be argued here.

Of course, the problem is in the first instance one of definition. Which of all the known instances of unrest, dissatisfaction, violence to persons or property, or hostility to the authorities, whether active or passive, whether by deed or by oral expression, are to be considered manifestations of opposition to Peter's government and policies or to Peter personally? Which, in other words, can be seen as having immediate political significance? One approach to answering this question is to adopt the view of contemporary Russian officialdom. But the difficulty with this method is that the basic legal provisions against political offenses enacted under Peter exhibit a transcendent breadth and vagueness, reflecting, it might be suspected, less a lack of legal finesse than the breadth and complexity of the problem itself.

Thus a Senate decree of 1714 specified that by the traditional phrase *slovo i delo gosudarevo* ("the sovereign's word and deed") was to be understood anything written or spoken that related adversely to the "health of His Majesty the Tsar or to the high-monarchical honor" or that comprised "any [act of] rebellion or treason." By the tsar's own decree of January 25, 1715, "all true Christians and loyal subjects" were to report directly to him or to the appointed officials anything relating to "grave matters . . . namely, the following: 1. Any evil design against the person of His Majesty the Tsar or treason; 2. Any sedition or rebellion; 3. Any spoilation of the treasury, and other such matters."

Again, under the *Military Statue* of 1716, which declared that "His Majesty is an absolute monarch who need not account for his actions to anyone on earth, but as a Christian sovereign has the power and authority to govern his realm and lands in accordance with his own will and good judgment," we find that any act or even unfulfilled intention that might have infringed on the tsar's freedom of action or discomfitted the authorities was considered criminal. In addition to straightforward acts of treason or rebellion, the *Statute* required punishment of anyone "who transgresses by abusive words against the person of His Majesty, censures his actions or intentions, or discusses same in an unseemly [*nepristoinyi*] manner." Also proscribed here were "all unseemly and suspicious meetings and gatherings." Whole chapters of the *Statute* were similarly devoted to often trivial offenses that were nonetheless thought to be connected, somehow, with treason to the fatherland. And while the *Military Statute* was meant to apply to persons in the armed forces, the decree ordering its dissemination extended its norms to practically everybody else.

As well it might have. In the continued absence of an updated legal code the officials charged under Peter I with adjudicating political offenses could refer only to the *Sobornoe Ulozhenie* [law code] of 1649. There, both the death penalty and confiscation of property were prescribed for anyone who harbored designs against the sovereign's life, raised an army for the purpose of taking over the state, consorted with or in any way aided the tsar's enemies, treacherously surrendered a town, or "banded together and plotted" against the tsar or any of his officials and caused "pillage and massacre." The same punishment was provided for anyone who concealed knowledge of such crimes or designs.

The *Ulozhenie* of 1649 was the first code in the history of Russian law to designate political offenses as the most important form of criminal activity. But its inadequacies in this respect required that the actual definition of a political crime, particularly in the earlier years of Peter's reign, be worked out in judicial practice, and by officials obliged to handle what seems to have been an unprecedented degree and variety of hostility to the regime. And it is to this practice, especially the operations of the Preobrazhenskii Prikaz, that we now turn in an effort to discover the nature and extent, as well as the historical significance, of opposition to Peter I.

The Preobrazhenskii Prikaz emerged in the 1680s as the administrative office (headquarters) of the guards regiment founded by the youthful Peter I at the royal retreat, near Moscow, of Preobrazhenskoe. In the 1690s, following riots in Moscow, the regiment was assigned the basic police and garrison duties in the capital formerly carried out by the royal *streltsy* (musketeers), who had become increasingly restive under Peter's regime. In 1696 the Preobrazhenskii Prikaz was given jurisdiction over political offenses committed anywhere on the territory of the Russian state, regardless of the offender's rank and regardless of where the case might previously have been tried.

Peter's decision to endow the headquarters of his favorite regiment with such sweeping powers appears to have been inspired by several factors: by the growing number of political offenses requiring adjudication; by the jurisdictional confusion engendered by his own previous but only partial grants of such authority to the Preobrazhenskii Prikaz;

by the fact that the Prikaz, his own creation, was headed by one of his most senior and trusted lieutenants, Prince F. Iu. Romodanovsky; by distrust of the *streltsy* (finally disbanded in 1698); and by Peter's concern, evident in other decrees of the time, to counteract the shortcomings of established judicial procedure. His decision also reflected a deeper trend in Russia toward judicial centralization and accretion of power by the monarch going back at least fifty years.

Between 1697 and 1708 the Preobrazhenskii Prikaz heard hundreds of cases either brought to it directly or referred by other offices. These included plots against Peter's life, outright rebellion, espionage, pretensions to the throne, despoiling of the tsar's image, distortion of his titles or abuse of his name; "unseemly utterances" touching not only on Peter, his personal conduct, or his relations with his entourage but on his wife, children, and other family members; and complaints against persons suspected of having dealings with Peter's half sister, Tsarevna Sofia, deposed as regent in 1689, or of sympathizing with other of his opponents. In these years, as its records show, the Prikaz handed down convictions in some 507 such cases, prescribing for each punishment ranging from death by dismemberment and decapitation to mutilation, floggings of one kind or another, terms of hard labor, banishment to a monastery or distant settlement, and — in the case of some female convicts — obligatory spinning for the state. These convictions do not include the many hundreds more for participation in the *streltsy* revolt of 1698 and in the Astrakhan uprising of 1705–1706. Nor do these numbers include, obviously, the hundreds of additional cases found *not* to involve a political offense. Indeed, so large had become the volume of business at the Preobrazhenskii Prikaz that by a Senate decree of 1714 the initiators of cases that did not in fact touch on the "health" or "honor" of the tsar or "comprise any rebellion or treason," but dealt with "simple matters," were themselves made liable to harsh punishment, which in practice usually meant flogging with the knout. After promulgation of this decree, and apparently as a result of it, the number of such "simple" cases handled by the Prikaz sharply decreased.

The actual practice of the Preobrazhenskii Prikaz in these earlier years of Peter I's reign reveals, then, that for his government, and indeed for hundreds of ordinary plaintiffs, political crimes included virtually any "word or deed" which infringed, however slightly it might seem to us, however innocently, on the absolute power of the monarch or which tended to undermine, however indirectly, the existing state order. The operations of the Prikaz also reveal that over the years the authorities had developed norms for distinguishing political from other offenses and for specifying, with respect to the former, the degree of punishment due. Moreover, it appears on close inspection that in the final analysis the author of these norms was Peter himself. Not only did he take a most active part in the work of the Preobrazhenskii Prikaz, but as tsar he was of course the ultimate source of both law and justice and could settle cases not covered by existing law or judicial practice. Officially and formally, the final and often the initial factor determining what constituted politically significant opposition to Peter I's regime was Peter himself.

For Peter, on the evidence once again of the records of the Preobrazhenskii Prikaz, the most serious political crimes were treason and rebellion (*bunt*). By the latter he understood, like his predecessors, any mass undertaking against the authority of the tsar or of his deputies or any conspiracy aimed at killing the tsar or overthrowing the government. The usual penalty for such crimes was death, the form depending on the degree of guilt; in some cases, however, as with lesser participants in the "Shaklovity affair" of 1689, the punishment was flogging and mutilation followed by perpetual banishment to Siberia. But Peter also considered *any* joint action against the authorities equivalent to rebellion and liable to similar punishment, even when this amounted to no more than the submission of a collective petition of grievances, a petition that in at least one instance he did not even bother to read before condemning the petitioners.

Under Peter, moreover, acts of treason to be punished by death came to include defecting to the enemy, divulging military secrets, spying, giving aid to the enemy, and engaging in any antigovernment agitation that led others to leave the country. "Unseemly utterances" and other individual actions reflecting adversely on the tsar's dignity or policies were in general treated as lesser crimes; yet even here, depending on what was said or done and on who might have seen or heard it, and sometimes also on the offender's social class, death or the harsher forms of corporal punishment were prescribed. Such "unseemly utterances," the records indicate, were by far the most common form of political offense tried at the Preobrazhenskii Prikaz between 1697 and 1708; and for the various grades of these and all other political crimes (and for false accusations of same) some thirty different punishments were defined under Peter I's supervision and systematically applied. It is worth noting that in supervising the Prikaz's work Peter himself showed a preference for work sentences or for banishment to a distant or new settlement, as distinct from the death penalty or the more severe forms of mutilation. He is reported as having once said, "Of course crimes and disorders must be punished; but at the same time my subjects' lives must be preserved as far as possible" — preserved, there can be no doubt, for service to the state.

Our knowledge of the operations of the Preobrazhenskii Prikaz in these years (1697–1708) prompts several tentative conclusions. The first is that in thus adjudicating hundreds if not thousands of political offenses Peter's government devised various penal and procedural norms that were later applied elsewhere. The relevant provisions of the *Military Statute* of 1716 (referred to previously) would be one such instance; elements of the treatment of religious nonconformists (decrees of 1718), another; the use of inquisitorial process in suppressing banditry (1710), a third; some of the material gathered in preparing a new law code (1720s), a fourth. A second, related conclusion is that in granting, late in 1696, comprehensive jurisdiction over political offenses to a single office, the Preobrazhenskii Prikaz, and in thus subordinating all other governmental agencies to it, Peter took his first decisive step on the road to greater administrative centralization and functional delineation. Here the history of the famous reorganization of the state properly begins. Third, the range of offenses judged by Peter's government to be of a political nature and requiring trial and punishment was obviously wide, wider than ever before in Russia; and this fact, coupled with the volume of such cases handled, indicates that from early on in the reign opposition to Peter was on an unprecedented scale. Finally, the records of the Preobrazhenskii Prikaz strongly suggest that opposition to Peter's regime was also widespread in society, since actionable political offenses were committed by persons of every rank and social condition: by members of the boyar class and service gentry, *streltsy*, clergy both high and low, simple townsmen and peasants, and officers as well as ordinary soldiers. Qualitatively if not quantitatively, it would seem, Peter I faced by 1708 a kind of national resistance.

The Preobrazhenskii Prikaz was not the only bureau charged by Peter with adjudicating political crimes. There was also the Secret Chancellery or, in its full title, the "Chancellery for Secret Inquisitorial Affairs," a title that distinguished it from such lesser inquisitorial offices as those concerned with irregularities in recruitment or with routine "schismatic affairs." An examination of its activities tends to confirm the conclusions just noted with respect to the operations of the Preobrazhenskii Prikaz.

The Secret Chancellery emerged in 1718 in connection with the trial of Peter's son and heir, Tsarevich Aleksei, and as part of the office of P. A. Tolstoi, one of several such personal chancelleries founded under Peter and entrusted by him with various missions. Tolstoi had earned Peter's special favor by having retrieved the wayward tsarevich from his haven in Italy, and during the first six months of its existence the Secret Chancellery, headed by Tolstoi, was concerned almost exclusively with prosecuting the tsar's case against his son. There is, it seems, little of substance to add to the printed documentation and secondary literature on the whole Aleksei affair. But with reference to the problem before us the trial of the tsarevich — undoubtedly the single most important political trial carried out under Peter I — is significant in at least several major respects.

In the first place, Aleksei's trial was relatively open. After the usual secret and lengthy inquisitorial process had done its work, and the evidence had been gathered, the case against the tsarevich was presented for judgment to an assembly of 128 notables specially convened for the purpose. Then, following Aleksei's condemnation by the assembly, a substantial selection of the evidence against him was published both at home and abroad, with the intention, clearly, of justifying the tsarevich's condemnation, of discrediting his sympathizers, and of warning the tsar's enemies whoever they might be. Such actions by Peter's government bespeak an anxiety that the conspiracy surrounding Aleksei was but the crest of a wave. Indeed, although relatively few persons were denounced in the course of the trial and eventually punished, the circle of the tsarevich's tacit or potential supporters against his father, to judge only from the evidence presented, was wide, and threatened the destruction not only of Peter's grand projects, such as St. Petersburg or the fleet, but of Peter himself.

Second, the trial of Tsarevich Aleksei — his arrest, interrogation under torture, open condemnation for treason, and mysterious death before sentence could be imposed — itself became a cause of further opposition to Peter I. There is considerable evidence, for example in the records of the subsequent activities of the Secret Chancellery, that Peter's treatment of his son was generally perceived as a great scandal.

More immediately, several prominent churchmen had been implicated to one degree or another in the conspiracy surrounding Aleksei; in the case of the metropolitan of Rostov, the association led to his execution. And there is no doubt that this revelation precipitated Peter's decision to abolish the ancient headship of the Russian church and to incorporate its administrative apparatus in the administration of the state. Finally, the Tsarevich Aleksei affair gave rise to the Secret Chancellery itself, which thereafter expanded its operations under Peter and in fact was to endure, in one form or another, until the nineteenth century.

Its records show that apart from the Aleksei affair the Secret Chancellery investigated some 370 "grave matters" between 1718 and 1725, sharing jurisdiction in this respect with the older Preobrazhenskii Prikaz. (The exact relationship between the two offices is a subject of scholarly dispute, but it seems that under Peter I the Secret Chancellery retained the character of an extraordinary commission, the Preobrazhenskii Prikaz that of a permanent bureau. In 1722, it too was designated a "chancellery" and between 1718 and 1725 it adjudicated roughly two thousand political cases.) By far the majority of the "grave matters" investigated during these years by the Secret Chancellery — upward of 75 percent — involved political offenses as these had come to be understood, although by now the term included, its records show, such crimes as "unseemly utterances" against senior officials and Peter's second wife, Catherine, and expressions of sympathy for the deceased tsarevich. Moreover, in the first three years of its existence some 70 percent of all cases lodged at the Secret Chancellery were referred to it directly by the tsar, some following an arrest that he had personally made. It would seem that nearing the end of his reign Peter was increasingly occupied with the problem of opposition to his regime even as he pressed forward with new and far-reaching reforms — administrative, military, economic, cultural — and in no way modified his conduct to placate his opponents. The possibility that Peter had become obsessed with what he took to be opposition, indeed that he had long since, perhaps from the beginning, exaggerated its importance, should be considered.

In other words, the records of both the Preobrazhenskii Prikaz and the Secret Chancellery suggest that the problem of Peter I's opposition is also the problem of Peter himself: of his motives, ambitions, and desires, if not of his whole psychological makeup. This might be the moment to place in evidence, as an example of what is at issue, Peter's "dream of the bad animal." On April 26, 1715, as the written record, evidently dictated by Peter himself, relates, he

> *had a dream. It was as though an eagle were sitting in a tree, and beneath it had crept or crawled some sort of large wild beast, like a crocodile or a dragon, onto which this eagle immediately leapt, and gnawed its head from its neck — that is, chewed away half the neck and killed it. And then, while many people gathered to watch, another such beast crept up, whose head this eagle also gnawed off, it seemed in plain view of everybody.*

It was suggested elsewhere, after referring to the psychological literature and after establishing correspondences between the content of this dream-record and known facts of Peter's conscious life, that what may well be symbolized here was an intense, not to say savage struggle raging deep within him between his baser and nobler selves — a struggle that was being acted out, as was everything in his conscious life, before a crowd of people.[1] Peter's dream record (one of twelve to have survived) presents evidence of a fundamental inner conflict whose projection onto the outer world, one might add, facilitated his readiness to identify and punish opponents. Indeed in that earlier study, discussing possible sources of this dream's imagery, it was also suggested that

> *The impression that something very basic in Peter is at issue here gains further ground when we reflect that the* raskolniki *[schismatics], who were always a most troublesome problem for Peter, were wont to depict him, in both word and picture, as the "crocodile," as he no doubt knew. It was one of the ways in which the more aggressive of the religious dissidents taunted and reviled him, to which he would respond, with equal vigor, by denouncing them for ignorance and superstition, for obstinacy and plain wickedness, and by persecuting them in one way or another, sometimes violently.*

Turning to more conventional texts illustrative of a possible obsession with his opposition, we might consider Peter's directive to the clergy requiring them to violate the traditional and canonical secrecy of confession whenever they heard anything therein that could be construed as treasonable. In the spring of 1722, under Peter's direct supervi-

---

[1] See the previous reading (pp. 243–246). — Ed.

sion, the Holy Synod added to the recently promulgated *Ecclesiastical Regulation* a provision that reads in part:

> *If during confession someone discloses to the priest an unfulfilled but still intended criminal act, especially [one] of treason or rebellion against the Sovereign or State, or an evil design against the honor or health of the Sovereign and the family of His Majesty, and disclosing such an evil intention shows that he does not repent of it but indeed justifies his intention and does not forsake it, and confesses it not as a sin but rather to be confirmed in his intention by the assent or the silence of his confessor, which [fact] may be discovered in this way: if the confessor orders him in the name of God wholly to desist from his evil intention and he is silent and apparently dubious, or justifying himself appears unchanged in this respect; [in such cases] the confessor must not only not grant him absolution and remission of his openly confessed sins, but must promptly report him at the prescribed places. . . .*

These "places," as the document specifies, were the Secret Chancellery and the Preobrazhenskii Prikaz, where "such crimes are tried" and where, at the time of trial, the confessor himself was to appear and "declare everything he has heard about this evil intention explicitly, without hesitation, and concealing nothing." The authors of this injunction went on to argue that in so acting priests did not really violate the secrecy of confession but rather fulfilled a larger Christian duty. And in a supplementary "Announcement" to the clergy of May 1722 the Synod, again with Peter's personal participation, recounted several "actual cases" in this connection for the purpose both of instructing (or admonishing) confessors and of justifying the Synod's injunction. One such case had arisen in the course of Tsarevich Aleksei's trial, when it was revealed that "during confession he had told his confessor that he wished his father were dead; and this confessor forgave him in the name of God and said that he too wished he were dead, which this former confessor himself admitted under inquisition . . . ; and for this evil deed he [the confessor] was put to a well-deserved death." The second and most recent case cited by the Synod in its "Announcement" had come to trial in March of that same year (1722), because

> *a certain malefactor, on arrival at the town of Penza, publicly uttered many evil things against the most high honor of His Most Illustrious Imperial Majesty, and most pernicious words against the State, about*

> *which an inquisition is now under way in the Secret Chancellery. But from this inquisition it has already appeared that this malefactor had intimated these evil words to his priest in confession, who did not in any way forbid them but indeed assented to some of them, as now this unfrocked priest himself has confessed under inquisition.*

The "malefactor" in question was later executed, essentially for the crime of publicly calling Peter the Antichrist. His trial also resulted in the informal trial by the Holy Synod of its own president, Metropolitan Stefan Iavorsky, who was alleged to have remarked to the defendant that Peter was not the Antichrist, but an "iconoclast" — a contemporary euphemism for "Protestant." And the third such case cited in the Synod's "Announcement" to the clergy of May 1722 involved "the criminal Talitsky," who

> *intimated to his priest in confession his most wicked intention, namely: to write a letter by means of which he wished everywhere to incite sedition, insisting that it was right and not to be forsaken; and the priest, although this [intention] disgusted him, nevertheless gave him communion, and did not report it to the appropriate authorities . . . and this criminal proceeded to carry out his intention. And should he not have been caught in the act, what blood and disasters would have issued therefrom! And to what wickedness the sacrament of penance had been put by Talitsky and his confessor!*

This passage was written by Peter himself, as was another denouncing Talitsky in similar terms that Peter inserted into a Synodal admonition to religious dissenters that had been promulgated a few months before (January 1722).

In fact, we now know that in the spring of 1708, at the height of the Bulavin rebellion, Peter issued a secret order to the clergy obliging them in the course of their duties, including that of confessor, to be on the lookout for signs of treason or rebellion among other criminal acts or designs and to report them to the authorities. Here Peter cited instances in which clergy had been remiss in this regard in the revolts of the *streltsy* of 1682 and 1698, the Astrakhan rebellion of 1705–1706, and the case of Talitsky. Talitsky, it should be noted, had been tried and executed back in 1700–1701 for composing a leaflet in which the proximate end of the world was predicted, Moscow was called Babylon, Peter himself was denounced as the Antichrist, and the people were bidden not to serve the tsar or to pay his taxes. Talitsky evidently had planned, with a following thus aroused and with the help of disaffected *streltsy*, to depose Peter while he was away campaigning and to replace him with a certain, presumably sympathetic, boyar. Seventeen persons were named by Talitsky as his supporters and were also summoned to trial at the Preobrazhenskii Prikaz. Five of these were also executed in consequence; eight were condemned to flogging, mutilation, and banishment to Siberia; and one, the bishop of Tambov, was deposed and banished to the Solovetskii monastery in the far north, while his diocese was virtually abolished (by merger with the Moscow diocese). Observing how Peter would cite the case once in 1708 and twice again in 1722, it might be thought that Talitsky had become in his mind the personification of all who opposed him, and the touchstone of his obsession.

In any event, it was the Talitsky affair and other such cases of opposition to Peter I's regime, whether collective or individual, large-scale or apparently trivial, and spanning the whole of the reign, that gave rise to the judicial activities of the Preobrazhenskii Prikaz and the Secret Chancellery, to the death of the heir to the throne, and to some of Peter's more radical and far-reaching "reforms." Opposition to Peter's regime, as we see, was neither an isolated nor, in the eyes of the regime itself, a negligible phenomenon. But what exactly inspired such opposition? How much of it is to be attributed to the actions of Peter and his government, and how much to events before his time or to factors over which he had little if any control? No very precise answers can be given to these questions. Yet a sampling of the fairly abundant evidence at our disposal in this connection yields, again, several tentative conclusions.

The first is that at least some of the opposition to Peter I derived from obvious structural, inevitable, or accidental causes. These would include the displacement, as in the palace revolution of 1689, of certain grandees and their kinsfolk, clients, and friends (who then plotted to regain, while it still seemed possible, their lost power and privileges); the incompetence or depredations of particular officials; the hostility of the official church toward nonconformists (a policy initiated before Peter's time); or the burdens of serfdom (an institution about which Peter did, and perhaps could have done, essentially nothing). But it is also apparent that much of the opposition which surfaced during Peter's reign was directed against policies that were either initiated by him and his government or in some way intensified or expanded by them. Among the causes of this more specific opposition may be mentioned the unprecedented exactions of all kinds occasioned by Peter's continual wars and building projects; the official and sometimes forcible promotion of such practices as smoking tobacco, shaving the beard, and calculating the year from the birth of Christ (instead of from the creation of the world), all hitherto proscribed by custom or by law; the official preference granted foreigners, almost uniformly scornful of Russians and their ways; the often drastic curtailment of the clergy's rights and immunities, sometimes without any justification; the imposition of new responsibilities on the service gentry; not just the suppression of rebellious *streltsy* but the abolition of the *streltsy* as such; and the intensified persecution, albeit in moderated form, of religious nonconformity.

All of this is fairly well known, even if it has yet to be studied in a systematic and comprehensive way. But the evidence under review also reveals that still more of the opposition which manifested itself during the Petrine period was directed against Peter himself. It was aroused not only by the factors just mentioned, but by Peter's own "unseemly" words and deeds: by his smoking and drinking; by his often shabby, unregal, or un-Russian dress; by his frequent indulgence in extravagant jokes and pranks; by his flouting of the sacred rites; by his divorce from Tsarevich Aleksei's mother (a member of a prominent Muscovite clan) and then marriage to a lowly foreigner; by his treatment of Tsarevich Aleksei; by his perpetual, public, and seemingly unconcerned revelation of the many follies, vices, and frailties of the tsar himself, hitherto a sacrosanct figure.

Indeed, the most common of the complaints lodged against Peter's regime, the common thread running through the endless depositions and denunciations brought to the appropriate offices, cutting across rank and social condition, was that in his personal conduct, as much as or even more than in his policies, Peter had early revealed himself to be a false tsar. He was a "tyrant," "impostor," "servant of Antichrist," or "Antichrist" himself; "heretic," "blasphemer," "Latinizer," or "iconoclast"; the "Gog" of Ezekiel's prophecy; really a "German" or a "Swede," even a "Musulman," in disguise. These charges were repeated again and again as each new impropriety (*bezchinnost*), each fresh imposition, added fuel to the fire. We are back to Peter — and to the realization, once again, that without him the history of his times would have been unimaginably different.

Yet in closing this introductory and necessarily brief survey of the problem of Peter I's opposition, the difficulties in reaching any final conclusions should be stressed. The lack of access to certain archives is one such difficulty, obviously, as is the necessarily heavy reliance on official sources. The need also to rely on the testimonials of foreign observers, primarily Europeans whose hostile and uncomprehending bias against natives and native institutions or customs was endemic, is a third. But more difficult perhaps than any of these is the voice of the opposition itself. How is the historian to translate or interpret hostility that is frequently expressed in terms that are not just unfamiliar, but utterly alien to his own sensibility? Too often the secondary literature reveals not so much an awareness of this difficulty as a willingness to put words in the mouths of Peter's opponents, a readiness to decide that what actually is being said manifests some underlying cause or some unconscious motive that historians themselves have invented.

To be aware of these difficulties, however, does not preclude advancing a kind of unifying hypothesis. We have perhaps isolated here a fundamental syndrome of action and reaction, of opposition to Peter I's regime engendering in turn innovations or even major "reforms" as well as its own punishment. Opposition to Peter's regime, continual and pervasive, manifesting itself in various ways and arising from various causes, was both cyclical and cumulative, and bore as much relation to what happened of historical significance during the era as any other factor, whether it be the incursions of foreign enemies or the Europeanizing ambitions of the ruler. To study the whole phenomenon is to become increasingly skeptical of the view which holds that the sole or even the main agent of change in Petrine Russia was a dynamic governing elite and which depicts the rest of society, whether intentionally or not, as largely inert or passive. And it is likely that when the full history of Peter's opposition has been written, our picture of a basically benign, enlightened, or at least progressive regime — of an era of great reform — will be fundamentally modified. However we might ultimately evaluate his achievements (another question altogether), it may well turn out that Peter became "the Great" as a matter less of conviction than of simple self-preservation.

Bronze bust of Peter I by Marie Collot, St. Petersburg, 1770. (Russian Museum, Leningrad; photo by editor) This head was the model for that of the famous equestrian statue of Peter I by Etienne Falconet, which was erected in St. Petersburg in 1782 and soon became known as the "Bronze Horseman."

 In Retrospect

Nicholas V. Riasanovsky

The Image of Peter the Great in Russia

The figure of Peter the Great, it is generally conceded, has dominated the development of Russian political and social thought as well as Russian historical writing. In this conclusion to his extended study of Peter's "image" in Russian history and thought, Professor Riasanovsky, of the University of California at Berkeley, succinctly sums up the major forms this image has taken over the centuries — from that of an enlightened autocrat, first propagated by members of Peter's own entourage, to the "complex bipolar image" current in the Soviet Union today.

Peter the Great left a remarkable impress on Russian history and thought. The original image of him and his role, drawn by the reformer himself as well as by such members of his admiring entourage as Feofan

Prokopovich, blended wonderfully well with the concept of the enlightened despot of the Age of Reason. The first emperor brought light into darkness, converted barbarism into civilization, even created a rational state and society *ex nihilo*. The new Russian power and international significance confirmed brilliantly his accomplishment. The Russian educated public, itself a product of the Petrine reform, kept believing in this overwhelming image of its originator and kept mounting his praises, without a fundamental change in this point of view, for some 125 years. Catherine the Great [reigned 1762–1796] made the claim that she represented a still higher stage of the Russian Enlightenment, and different Russian intellectuals, reflecting personal tastes or the ideological current of the moment, placed different emphases on the first emperor's many virtues and achievements, but they did not question his primacy or his supreme significance. Criticism was limited to an occasional mention of costs, to some aristocratic unease, to an infrequent sentimental regret of things past, and, only toward the end of this long period, to a more radical reading of the Enlightenment than the established Petrine image allowed for. Much more common was an absolute endorsement of the reformer and an enthusiastic defense of him and his activity, character trait by character trait and incident by incident, in the generally accepted terms of the Age of Reason. The identification of the modern Russian educated public, between the years of 1700 and 1825 or thereabouts, with the modern Russian monarchy found splendid expression in the Russian Enlightenment image of Peter the Great.

A new situation emerged only in the 1830s. The Russian government had lost all its liberal promise, having consciously chosen extremely conservative policies. The world, after the French Revolution, Napoleon, the Congress of Vienna, and repeated disturbances, was divided and seemed threatening. Inside Russia, too, the simple Enlightenment beliefs in education and progress appeared to bear little relationship to reality. Moreover, the ideology of the Age of Reason itself had been challenged and, in part, replaced by traditionalist doctrines and by German idealistic philosophy and Romanticism in general. In these circumstances, three basic images of Peter the Great arose in Russia. The Enlightenment image split in two. The government and its supporters retained faith in Peter the Great, the victorious creator of the Russian Empire and its might, the sage organizer of the state, the lawgiver of modern Russia. But they rejected any further imitation of the West, dynamic development, progress. The Westernizers, by contrast, hypostasized precisely that other part of the original Petrine image as the true aim and hope of their country and their people. In addition, a third Petrine image, the first full-scale negative one to emerge in the midst of the Russian educated public, was postulated by the Slavophiles.[1] They declared the entire Petrine reform a perversion and a disaster and clamored for a return to the true Russian principles, reflecting, one may surmise, the difficulty — some would say the failure — of the Russian adjustment to the modern world that followed the Petrine turn Westward. The unity between the government and the educated public, as well as the unity within the educated public itself, were no more. The celebrated debate between the Westernizers and the Slavophiles was carried on not in the quasi-empirical framework of the Age of Reason, but in a metaphysical one, that of German idealism to be more exact: for both schools of thought, Peter the Great possessed transcendent power and importance; only the first endowed him with a plus, and the second with a minus, sign.

The third period in the history of the Russian image of the reformer, from about 1860 to 1917, exhibited less unity than the second, not to mention the first. Utilitarianism, pragmatism, positivism, scientism, and an emphasis on precise scholarship were less favorable to overarching schemes than earlier weltanschauungs. Also, Russian society and culture were becoming more pluralistic, and that led to a greater differentiation of attitudes toward Peter the Great as toward other topics under discussion. Still, certain trends in regard to the Petrine image should be noted. The decline of metaphysics and the new vogue of "scientific history" led to Soloviev's outstanding treatment of the Petrine reign: the original Westernizer metaphysical structure was used to render meaning, pace, and power to an extensive and thoroughly scholarly factual exposition.[2] With the eventual disappearance of that structure, the way was opened to P. N. Miliukov's presentation of the reign as catastrophe and confusion worse confounded and to M. M. Bogoslovsky's supreme devotion to detail. Furthermore, whereas the new Petrine scholarship surpassed by far in quantity and quality earlier contributions, it also became evident for the first time that important modern Russian history could be focused on other subjects than the first

---

[1] Westernizers and Slavophiles were ideological opponents in Russia in the 1830s–1850s. — Ed.

[2] S. M. Soloviev (1820–1879) is often considered Russia's greatest historian. — Ed.

emperor, such as the gentry or serfdom. The ideologues also provided different approaches. The government continued to uphold its statist image of Peter the Great although with less emotional commitment and enthusiasm than before. Most liberals sailed in the wake of the original Westernizers. On the radical left, opinions split: one could consider the reformer, cruelty and all, as the true Enlightener; or one could emphasize Petrine autocratic oppression. Some anarchists and populists were not only inimical to the first emperor, but also little concerned with him. Finally, the Petrine theme was revived in the so-called Silver Age (strictly speaking, a separate intellectual period): its ramifications, like the age itself, pointed in different directions and await further study.

The October [Bolshevik] Revolution [1917] was followed by a denunciation and denigration of Peter the Great together with other Romanovs. The first dominant school to emerge, that of M. N. Pokrovsky [1869–1932], took a strikingly negative as well as personally hostile view of the reformer and his historical role. Yet when Stalin came to power and the Soviet system received its definitive form in the 1930s, Pokrovsky's schema was replaced by a much more complex bipolar Petrine image, which remains the established Petrine image in the Soviet Union today (even if it is at present less xenophobic and less insistently linked to the Marxist classics than formerly). That image emphasizes both the positive and the negative in the reformer and his reform in an extreme and contradictory manner: positive in strengthening the state, in war, diplomacy, industrial development, education, organization, and administration; negative in its furtherance of gentry domination and in the increasing oppression of the people. Although the parts are disparate, the totality exhibits a striking bipolar symmetry. An outstanding example of conflict between a national and a class interpretation, the image has other aspects besides. Thus, contemporaries quickly noticed parallels between Peter the Great and Stalin as to leadership, methods, and costs, as well as the international setting and the alleged primacy of the struggle for survival. Critics of the Soviet system censured not only Stalin but also Peter the Great, either for the emperor's betrayal of Russian principles or for his having been a fine example of the recurrent autocratic blight in Russian history. Yet, at the age of about fifty, the dominant Soviet Petrine image is clearly second in duration only to the Petrine image of the Russian Enlightenment.

What will the next Russian image of Peter the Great be like?

B. H. Sumner

Peter's Imperial Legacy

B. H. Sumner (1893–1951), a British historian who specialized in Peter I's campaigns against Turkey, outlines here the longer-term results of Peter's transformation of Russia's foreign relations, which he considered the most important aspect of the Petrine legacy. The book from which this reading is excerpted was written by Sumner in the wake of World War II and amid widespread concern in the West about the emergence of Russia, now the Soviet Union, as one of the world's two great powers. Sumner traces the roots of this transcendent development to the wars and diplomacy of Peter the Great, "who revolutionized both Russia and, ultimately, Europe by forcing Russia into the Western world."

What was the legacy of Peter? How much of it survived?

First and most obviously, he transformed Russia's foreign relations. For a century before Peter, Muscovy had been tentatively and spasmodically linking herself closer with the West. Now henceforward Russia played her part as one of the main participants in European history. One dry, prosaic fact speaks for much: on Peter's accession he found his country with only one regular mission abroad, in Warsaw; on his death he left his representatives accredited to almost all the courts of Europe. For a long time Russia's part was confined to diplomacy, politics, and war. Within ten years of Peter's death, she decided the issue of the Polish succession; within forty years, the issue of the Seven Years' War in Europe; within ninety years, the issue of Napoleon. Later her contribution was enlarged to cover the arts and sciences; and in this century it has been transformed by the Soviet revolution into one of the greatest world influences of our day.

Peter left no will, and his so-called testament is a much exagger-

From B. H. Sumner, *Peter the Great and the Emergence of Russia* (New York: Crowell Collier, 1962), pp. 188–200. Reprinted with permission of Collier Books, an imprint of Macmillan Publishing Company.

ated, and in part fantastic, diatribe against Russian foreign policy in the eighteenth century. It was concocted originally by Napoleon's propagandists for the campaign of 1812, probably on the basis of a somewhat earlier analysis made by an émigré Pole. On the other hand, it is true that Peter initiated policies toward Poland, Sweden, and Turkey which his successors systematically developed.

For the first time in her history Russia was now indisputably stronger than her old enemy Poland. It was Peter's aim to use that strength so as to keep Poland internally weak, divided, and subject to dominant Russian influence, and to make of Courland a Russian preserve. This policy was continued after him with success, together with his practice of marching Russian troops at will through Polish territory for action in Germany. Later, Catherine the Great was led on to the policy of partition (1772, 1793) and finally to the total dismemberment of Poland by the three eastern powers (1795) — a crime and a tragedy which has made the Polish question ever since one of the most intricate and intractable of European problems.

It was likewise Peter's policy after the Peace of Nystad [1721] to keep Sweden internally weak, to encourage supporters of the Holstein line of succession, and to prevent any other foreign influences from gaining ascendancy in Stockholm. As in Poland, Russian designs aimed at the maintenance of the oligarchical constitution in Sweden as the surest safeguard against a revival of her power. This policy his successors were able to continue for nearly fifty years, though with varying success. Twice Sweden struck back at Russia, vainly hoping to recoup her loses in the Northern War (1741–1743, 1788–1790). By the end of the century, when the power of the monarchy in Sweden had been restored, Russians were considering the possession of Finland to be essential for the security of St. Petersburg, and Alexander I not only conquered Finland but, unlike Peter, retained it (1808–1809).

At Stockholm, Peter's successors had to counter French diplomacy working steadily against them. The same was true at Warsaw and Constantinople. In his earlier years Peter had found the old French combination with Sweden, Poland, and Turkey directed against him. In his last years his efforts at a close understanding with France achieved only partial and temporary success. The continued efforts of the empress Catherine I [reigned 1725–1727] were fatally rebuffed by Louis XV's government, with the result that Russia turned to the Hapsburg rivals of the Bourbons. Within eight years of Peter's death France was supporting in arms Charles XII's former protégé, Stanislas Lesczyński, for the vacant throne of Poland against the Russian candidate; within fifteen years she was stirring up Sweden to attack Russia and was intervening to such effect in Constantinople that Russia came virtually empty-handed out of a successful war against Turkey [1736–1739].

Although Empress Elizabeth [reigned 1741–1762], enthused with French predilections and a sentimental hankering for Louis XV, was assisted to the throne by the intrigues of the French ambassador, little political advantage thus accrued to France. The long and fruitful sway of French culture that now began in Russia stands in striking contrast with the almost continuous opposition or coldness of the two countries on the political plane down to 1789 (except during the Seven Years' War when they fought on the same side). The persistent French support of Turkey, Sweden, and Poland remained an insurmountable obstacle to good relations. The French Revolution and Napoleon gave deeper cause for hostility. Almost continuously until the closing decades of the nineteenth century, Russia — the country that had become the bastion of autocracy and reaction — stood opposed to France — the progenitor of revolution and socialism and the inspirer of nationality.

The struggle in the Baltic brought Peter to the edge of open war with George I. Peter himself did all he could to divide Great Britain and Hanover, and was prepared to offer much to British commercial interests, believing rightly that in the end these would gain the upper hand in London. Great Britain was far and away Russia's biggest customer, and the large excess of Russian exports to her over imports from her was an invaluable source of much-needed specie. The refusal of Great Britain to accept the advent of the newly risen power in the Baltic played into the hands of her Dutch and Prussian trade rivals, and proved ineffective in attaining her essential aim, the safeguarding of the supply of naval stores, now largely in Russian hands.

When both George I and Catherine I died in 1727, policy was reversed and Peter's forecast proved correct. Russia and Great Britain drew together in close and very profitable economic relations. Those ties remained the central strand in their mutual relations until the close of the century, even though the two countries fought on different sides, though not against each other, in the Seven Years' War. Thereafter the American War of Independence, Catherine the Great's armed neutrality, and incipient British alarms at her threatening expansion against Turkey ushered in a new period that took shape in the nineteenth-

century contest over "the sick man of Europe" and "the threat to India."
Peter the Great's establishment of Russia on the Baltic produced no
contests between the bear and the lion comparable to those engendered
by Catherine the Great's establishment of Russia on the Black Sea.
Constantinople and the Straits were to range them in opposition to each
other to an extent that Copenhagen and the Sound never did.

Peter's Baltic legacy included his innovation of German marriages
for his family. The consequences proved very far-reaching, though
largely unintended. The innovation became the regular rule for all
succeeding rulers of the Romanov dynasty. Save for Empress Elizabeth,
who never married, they all took foreign, and with one exception,
German wives. From the accession of Catherine the Great (1762) onwards the dynasty was in blood Russian only by virtue of Catherine's
husband, Emperor Peter III, being the son of Peter the Great's daughter
Anna, who had married the duke of Holstein. The result was that the
upbringing of the Romanovs and the character of the court came to be
largely German, and that dynastic and family considerations played a
conspicuous part in Russian foreign relations.

Already under Peter, Holstein, Mecklenburg, and Courland
caused endless difficulties. Once his controlling hand was removed,
these German connections involved Russia in a further influx of German princelings, courtiers, and adventurers, who entered upon a ran-
corous struggle for power with each other and with the Russian
aristocracy (the so-called "period of favorites," 1725–1741). The reign
of Empress Anna (1730–1740) became a byword for the predominance
of her Courland favorites, and led to a nationalist resurgence in favor of
Peter's daughter Elizabeth as empress and to an anti-German revulsion
which opened the floodgates to the dominance of French cultural influences. Within a generation of his death, Peter was looked back upon as
a Russian patriot and beneficent despot who saw to it that Russians were
not sacrificed to foreigners.

Under Elizabeth it was professedly in the name of what her foreign
minister called "the system of Peter the Great" that she abandoned what
had been a cornerstone of Peter's Baltic-German policy, friendship with
Prussia. The reason for this change lay in the decisive and alarming
successes of Frederick the Great, who proceeded to rival the exploits of
Peter the Great and, like him, to place his country in the center of the
European stage. Prussia was now held to be "by reason of her proximity

and of her great and threatening strength the primary and chief danger to Russia." Thus Russia joined in alliance with Austria, and in conjunction with France to attempt the abasement of Prussia in the Seven Years' War (1756–1762).

Of all the major powers of Europe, Austria was the most consistently antipathetic in the eyes of Peter the Great. From his time dates the two centuries long rivalry of Russia and Austria in the Balkans. Yet with him was also initiated the attempt at common action against the Ottoman Empire. Peter began by alliance with Emperor Leopold against the sultan (1697), but the treaty was scarcely signed before Leopold's victories enabled him to make peace on his own. At the very end of Peter's reign signs could be seen of a rapprochement with Vienna. The final collapse of Russian hopes of a French marriage and the withdrawal of French support for Russia in Constantinople led Empress Catherine I to reinsure against the Turks by alliance on very favorable terms with Austria (1726).

The alliance, in varying forms, lasted for the greater part of the century, with one long break after the Seven Years' War. Twice Russia and Austria fought side by side against Turkey (1737–1739; 1787–1791); once against Prussia (1756–1762). While Empress Maria Theresa bewailed Russian inaction in the War of the Austrian Succession and had only too good cause to complain of desertion in 1762, Russia had heavy counts against Austria in 1739 and 1791. The western commitments of the Hapsburgs, and above all mutual suspicion and rivalry, prevented the alliance from ever being firmly cemented or from leading to a partition of the Balkans such as was proposed by Empress Anna and later by Catherine the Great.

Peter himself had no such definite aim. But while in his own lifetime he accomplished so little against Turkey (in striking contrast with the victorious achievements of Austria) and is chiefly remembered for his disaster on the Pruth, he nevertheless set his stamp on Russian policy towards Turkey by bequeathing new ideas and new claims which shaped it for the rest of the eighteenth century and far into the nineteenth.

He was the first to initiate successful offensive action against the Crimea, to strike south against Azov, to build a fleet, and to demand freedom of navigation and access to the Black Sea. Anna followed in his footsteps (1735–1739), in the end to little advantage; Catherine the

Great did likewise (1767–1774, 1787–1791), with triumphant results. The southern steppes and the Crimea passed into her hands, and the Black Sea ceased to be a Turkish lake.

Peter was the first to strike direct for the Danubian Principalities of Moldavia and Wallachia. In every single one of the seven following Russo-Turkish wars, right down to 1878, Russian armies did likewise. He was the first to summon the Balkan Christians to rise against their Turkish masters and join hands with their Orthodox liberators. His descendants renewed the summons in diverse forms on diverse occasions. He was the first to demand that the Orthodox, not the Catholics, have the custody of the holy places in Jerusalem, a claim with a long subsequent history which figured prominently among the antecedents of the Crimean War [1853–1856]. He was the first to demand a guarantee of religious freedom for the Orthodox in the Ottoman Empire, a claim which was in part realized by Catherine the Great and was to prove one of the main causes of the Crimean War.

It is only too apparent that the importance of Peter's legacy is in inverse ratio to the actual gains that he was able in the end to hand on after his catastrophe on the Pruth. He succeeded only in repudiating any tribute to the Crimea, in securing the right to diplomatic representation in Constantinople and to pilgrimages to Jerusalem, and in barring the Turks from the Caspian. This last result was the one permanent outcome of his Persian venture, which had such ramifying consequences for Russian foreign relations during the three closing years of his life.

The involved struggle in the very unhealthy Caspian provinces, which Peter wrenched from a Persia in collapse, was extremely costly and highly unpopular in Russia. After his death other counsels gained the day in St. Petersburg, and within the next ten years Russia handed back Baku and the other occupied regions to a revived Persia and withdrew to her former frontier. Nonetheless, Turkey was kept from the Caspian. Not until half a century later was Peter's Caucasian advance renewed, as a result of which Catherine the Great and then Emperor Paul brought Georgia into the Russian empire (1801), and Alexander I conquered and this time permanently retained Derbent and Baku (1813).

In his southern policy Peter with his intrepid vision and over-sanguine energy sketched the outlines of a rough program that would take generations to fill in. However, he disregarded one vital factor:

colonization. Unlike Austria, Russia was not effectively contiguous with Turkey; the two empires were still separated by the debatable Black Sea steppe lands, across which neither power could strike sustainedly. Impatient for the offensive, Peter did not follow his predecessors in pressing forward defense lines or attracting new farmer-settlers to the frontier. He struck against Turkey with a leap as it were. He struck against Persia by sea. To a large extent the later successes of Russia against Turkey and in the Caucasus depended on the fact that under Anna and Elizabeth, Catherine the Great and Alexander I, new defense lines were formed and an active colonization policy was pursued. To the extent that the southern steppes gradually became more like a base and less like nomad grazing and hunting grounds, it became possible for Peter's projects to be attained or furthered.

Colonization of a kind Peter did promote (and with his usual ruthlessness), but it was forced labor for his southern fleet, for his northern fleet and the construction of St. Petersburg, or for the Ural mines. None of the burdens he laid upon Russia were more onerous or bewailed, unless it was his conscription levies. There seemed indeed to be no end to the prodigious strains of every kind imposed on all classes for thirty years on end, no end to the series of shocks administered by the glowering taskmaster with his Pontic urge and ever-compulsive will. That was the deepest count of his subjects against him, and almost the only one that was felt alike by all. Russia needed some easing of unremitting toil and unsparing pace. With Peter's death alleviation came and for most of the next thirty years Russia took a breath; but his work, though warped or for the time being laid aside, was not in the main undone.

The fate of Peter's legacy depended primarily on the dominant landowning class, the serf-owners. They had their counts against him, and the old, aristocratic families were for the most part deeply opposed to him; yet even to them Peter gave high and responsible posts, and the essential basis of his rule could never cease to be the common bond of the maintenance of serfdom. The adoption of European ways deeply antagonized the masses, but far less generally the upper class, among whom a number even of Peter's opponents favored Western literature and culture.

Further, the serf-owners were much divided among themselves. Some of the grievances of the magnates against Peter found little or no echo among the smaller landowners, the army officers, or the lesser officials in state service, who could find ample opportunity to mount Peter's ladder of service and had no desire for a diminution of autocratic power by a reconstitution of the old Muscovite council of magnates such as was attempted in 1730 by an oligarchical clique of old, noble families. Hence it was that the main essentials of Peter's reorganized absolutist state, with one great exception, survived the struggle for power among court factions and the disputed successions to the throne that filled the political canvas of the dismal "period of favorites" (1725–1741).

The exception was compulsory state service for the serf-owners. Already there was mitigation under Empress Catherine I: the army and navy were heavily reduced. In the following reigns the obligations to serve were progressively whittled away, until in 1762 Emperor Peter III issued an edict completely freeing the serf-owners from service. Thus within little more than a generation one of the most important and unpopular features of Peter the Great's rule was erased.

On the other hand, there was no lessening of the bonds of serfdom; on the contrary, Peter the Great's extension of serfdom suited the serf-owners only too well, and thereafter their power over their serfs became almost untrammelled. At the same time, however, entry into the privileged class of serf-owners, which had been facilitated by Peter, was being made increasingly difficult. The Russian serf-owners were becoming more and more confined to a hereditary estate of the nobility somewhat equivalent to that in central Europe and France, an estate which was reorganized as such by the Imperial charter of 1785.

These victories of the serf-owners were not extended to the abolition of Peter's legacy of a standing army. At the time of his death it numbered 210,000, apart from Cossacks and various irregulars. For some years it was diminished in numbers, and the worst features of Peter's quartering of the army throughout the country were eradicated. But his system of conscription levies was retained, and it was not long before military service again weighed all too heavily on the peasantry. In the army itself, however, there was a strong core of patriotic pride. Peter prized his soldiers, and as their songs bear testimony they in return prized him and his heritage. He was the creator of the redoubtable Russian military tradition, the founder of Russia as a great power in arms. For the last two and a half centuries the world has had all too good cause to know the legendary endurance and peasant toughness of the army that Peter first fashioned.

He was even more the founder of the Russian navy, for Muscovy had possessed no fleet at all. His first attempt, the Azov fleet, foundered utterly, after costing an immense outlay in labor and money. It was reserved for Catherine the Great to create Russia's Black Sea fleet; and this she did after land campaigns and the acquisition of the Crimea (1783) — not by striving, as Peter did, to build up a fleet for the subjugation of the Crimea in the landlocked, harborless sea of Azov.

On the Baltic, on the other hand, Peter not only innovated, but built securely. When he died, the Baltic fleet establishment was sixteen to seventeen thousand strong, and there were some twenty-five men-of-war fit for sea, in addition to the galley fleet. The navy was soon left to dwindle for some time, but despite the continued unpopularity of naval service there was in fact no question of abandoning Peter's handiwork. Russia with her new Baltic coastline could but match the habits and practice of other states.

Nor was St. Petersburg abandoned as the new capital. For a few years indeed (1728–1732) the seat of government was moved back to Moscow, but the old aristocracy failed to maintain this success of theirs. The empress Anna, with her Western tastes and her crowd of German favorites, returned to the Neva. Elizabeth, as the daughter of Peter, naturally remained there, combining in a curious amalgam glorification of her father with Russian nationalism and a passion for French millinery. Not until 1918, when the Bolsheviks feared a German swoop on Petrograd, did Moscow once again become the capital. Thus the St. Petersburg period in Russian history is coincident with the Imperial period, and each owes its origin and name to Emperor Peter the Great.

Marc Raeff

Peter's Domestic Legacy: Transformation or Revolution?

In this comprehensive assessment of Peter's domestic legacy, Marc Raeff raises questions about our understanding and interpretation of the whole of modern Russian history, from the seventeenth century to this day. While dwelling at length on the long-term results of the Petrine administrative reforms, he also considers their social consequences, and particularly the "identity crisis" bequeathed by Peter to Russia's educated classes and the ever-widening gulf between them and the mass of ordinary people. In so doing he draws on a lifetime of work in the field and brings together many of the points made by others in the preceding readings. Raising questions of such scope and significance, and stressing the often incomplete, paradoxical, or ambiguous nature of the Petrine achievement, Raeff's essay is controversial in the best sense of the term.

Marc Raeff recently retired from teaching at Columbia University, where he was the Boris Bekhmeteff Professor of Russian Studies.

The tsardom of Muscovy, having built the unity and extended the boundaries of Russia and having survived the trauma of the "Time of Troubles" (1598–1613), attained its final political and cultural form by the middle of the seventeenth century. These achievements in turn gave rise to new problems that ushered in a period of change and maladjustment: reconstruction of the ruling elite, social and economic disarray, dynastic difficulties, reorientation of foreign policy from a southeastern to a southern and northwestern focus, and active military, diplomatic, and economic relations with eastern and northern Europe. Last, but not least, there was religious schism, which had a profound impact on the cultural consensus and national identity that had been the foundation of Muscovy. Piecemeal adjustment, limited reforms, and selective imports of foreign technology and personnel proved incapable of absorbing these changes through the institutional, economic, and cultural means available to the Muscovite polity. By chance, a new political culture in the West provided tools and a model, while the accession of a particularly dynamic and original ruler, drawing on the readiness of some members of the elite, enabled the tsardom to strike out in new directions and to transform itself into the All-Russian Empire of St. Petersburg.

What was the new foreign model that could be adapted to bring Muscovy out of its crisis of stagnation? Since the sixteenth century central and western Europe had been engaged in a radical transformation of its political culture. The medieval notion of political action had been a negative one: the purpose of government was to maintain security and preserve the conditions that enabled men to prepare for the hereafter. This outlook stemmed from the conviction that the world God had created was finite, its productive potential limited. But geographical and scientific discoveries, as well as a quickening of the intellectual and scientific pace, gradually gave rise to the notion that God's universe was infinite and its productive potential limitless. Furthermore, man had the ability to discover the laws that regulated nature and, based on this knowledge, he could apply his will to maximize resources in both the material and the cultural realm. An increased productive potential would first benefit the state and its rulers, but eventually also augment the prosperity and happiness of all, or most, members of society. The eighteenth century further concluded that there need not be a term to productivity and, therefore, that it was possible to enjoy limitless progress.

Such results could best be achieved by an educated elite of administrators under the guidance of a sovereign (whether a monarch or an enlightened elite) who would "discipline" the population for productive work through the regulatory and planned action of a central authority. Officials in the service of the sovereign — they soon came to constitute a bureaucracy — were to engage in a "rational constructivism" (Friedrich von Hayek's phrase) to create the conditions necessary for a successful implementation of the goal of maximized productivity. This new political culture is usually called the "Well-Ordered Police State" ("police" referring to administration) and its practices collectively labeled "cameralism."[1]

In the course of the last third of the seventeenth century Muscovy's elite became acquainted with the concept of the Well-Ordered Police

---

[1] For cameralism, see also the reading by Claes Peterson, especially page 101. — Ed.

State and with cameralist policies thanks to increasingly frequent and effective contacts with central and western Europe, mainly through the educational establishments of the newly incorporated Ukraine as well as through the foreign specialists and traders settled in Moscow's so-called German Suburb. The tsar's advisors recognized the military, political, and economic benefits for the state while the cultivated members of the elite sought the more challenging and dynamic cultural life that the new political notions and practices would bring in their train. But it required an energetic and innovative sovereign to give concrete Russian expression to the European model. It was the last-born son of Tsar Aleksei, Peter, who assumed this historical role.

Peter's personality must be stressed: his creative energy and his determination to breathe into Russian society a vitality comparable to that of the West strongly marked *his* revolution. Like a force of nature, he was able to overcome every obstacle that stood between him and his objectives. Avid for knowledge and always on the lookout for whatever was new, he imparted to his reform program his own intensity and feverish energy. Yet his loudly proclaimed desire for change and his determination to achieve tangible results whatever the cost and in spite of stubborn resistance yielded many superficial changes and reforms that hung suspended in midair and eventually proved to be ephemeral; his helterskelter activity concealed a lack of rigor. The effect of Peter the Great's reign was to tear Russian society apart, leaving behind a legacy of uncertainty and insecurity that ultimately led to an identity crisis among the Russian elite.

More positively, however, Peter's personality and energetic reform program attracted precisely those members of the elite (as well as some more modest subjects) who were hungry for action and eager to use their energies to enhance their country's wealth and power as well as their own. Peter found plenty of willing collaborators in his work, which shows that in late seventeenth-century Russia many people — groups as well as individuals — were eager to throw off the bonds of traditional Muscovite culture, with its static and isolationist outlook. Peter's misfortune was his failure to involve large numbers of common people in his efforts — partly because he could not, partly because he would not do so. To mention just one example, the Old Believers — many of whom were determined, tireless men, eager for action — rejected the very foundations of the Petrine state.

Here we may disregard the structural detail of Peter's institutions and the twists and turns of his legislation. We may summarize the eventual results of his reforms as follows: the ruler's person was separated from the government; henceforth the ruler viewed himself, and came to be considered by many of his subjects, as the servant of the interests and welfare of the *state* — a new concept, which in reality covered a congeries of institutions. The areas of governmental concern were extended to cover nearly all aspects of national life and many phases of personal life. Through its administrative institutions and its officials the state frequently took the initiative in establishing and promoting new fields of public and private endeavor, so that for several generations it became the principal industrial and commercial entrepreneur, the chief educator, and even a leader in the country's cultural and social life. Such an extension of governmental concern led to the creation of many new administrative and cultural institutions of all types, a tremendous increase in the number of government officials, and the elaboration of rules to guide the actions of both institutions and officials. The rules were drafted either in imitation of Western models or on the basis of rational and theoretical considerations. There could no longer be an appeal to tradition or custom ("as done in olden times"); the new rules could be justified only by appealing to some abstract concept or value — hence the rationalist and universalist character of Russian legislation in the eighteenth and early nineteenth centuries. It is easy to see how the army could serve as the most readily available and most easily understood model for the civil administration to emulate, and it inspired not only Peter I, whose prime concerns during most of his reign were the needs of war, but his successors as well. The obvious danger was that form would outweigh content in administrative practice. Rationalist, abstract, formalistic legislation and administrative procedures tended to remove government from the realities of national life; it led officials to see their tasks in terms of shuffling papers and to forget the concrete human or particular local circumstances. Even after the appeal to rational concepts and foreign models (rather than to divine law and tradition) had lost its force in the course of the eighteenth century, the new administrative practices introduced by Peter could never build a bridge to the traditional political and moral consciousness of the common people.

The necessity of organizing new institutions and of adapting to "rational" (in Max Weber's sense) procedures and rules of administration put the ruling elite under great pressure. Throughout the first three quarters of the eighteenth century, policies and institutions were in constant flux, in search of a harmonious adaptation of the new norms to existing conditions and in search of stability in the face of frequent changes of rulers and favorites. This is why the codification of existing legislation became such a vital problem. Codification was necessary not only to eliminate laws reflecting outworn traditions and precedents, but also to reconcile conflicting norms and procedures which *ad hoc* measures were constantly introducing. Not until the reign of Alexander I (1801–1825) did the administrative organization initiated by Peter receive its more or less permanent shape, and not until Nicholas I (reigned 1825–1855) was codification brought to a successful conclusion.

The new administrative institutions created by Peter the Great and his immediate successors required officials capable of acting on the basis of formal, general, rational regulations within the framework of a highly organized bureaucratic hierarchy. This meant a radical departure from the more traditional and personal methods of earlier times. Essentially, the issue faced by the elite immediately after Peter's death (and in a way the problem remained a live one until the end of the Imperial regime, in 1917) was whether to follow the personal or the formal, bureaucratic approach in dealing with the population. It is quite striking to note how slowly the elements of personal relationship disappeared from Russian public life. Naturally, the very fact that the sovereign ruled as an absolute autocrat helped to perpetuate the personal element in government. Indeed, as long as appeal to the emperor for his personal decision or judgment was possible, the exercise of political power retained something of its earlier patriarchal character, and the subordinate officials were seen, or considered themselves, as personal delegates of the monarch. It was difficult to give up this view of authority. In the first place, there was a rather simple political and sociological reason: the personal appeal to the ruler or his delegate provided the only protection against or redress from injustice, abuse of power, or persecution by subordinate officials who acted on the basis of vague and poorly understood regulations. And it was easy for the officials to take advantage of the monarch's remoteness and of the ignorance, poverty, and weakness of those they were supposed to govern, but in fact oppressed. In addition, the sovereign was the embodiment of ethical and religious values, which remained powerful among the people and which at times found expression among the educated classes in times of public crisis or personal tragedy. Of course, parallels to the personal character of political authority could be found in the chronicles of all monarchies, but in Russia it retained greater force much longer.

With the Westernization and modernization of the Russian state such a personal relationship between rulers and ruled could not, to be sure, remain the foundation of administration and policy decisions. Bureaucratic norms and procedures had to be worked out and, as always happens in such a case, they became the object of bitter resentment and hatred. Procedures seemed to have become mechanical; rules were frequently deemed arbitrary and unjust; the attitudes of clerks and officials were felt to be callous or capricious. How could one secure justice under such circumstances? And yet it was firmly believed by the people that the defense and enforcement of justice were the most important functions of political power. Thus the officials, the bureaucracy, came to be seen as an insuperable barrier separating an understanding and compassionate tsar from his people. It is irrelevant in our context that such a feeling might have been an illusion, a myth, or an unwarranted, retrospective idealization of a relationship that had never existed in this form even before Peter the Great. What matters is the survival of the ideal and the expectation that the authorities ought to act in accordance with it.

The conflict between personal and bureaucratic orientation was largely determined, and heightened, by the nature of Russia's administrative personnel. In a sense, the officials themselves prevented the formation of a genuine bureaucracy on the Western model. Not until late in the nineteenth century, and only in the upper ranks of the hierarchy at that, did there develop anything like a sense of professional responsibility, technical competence, an *esprit de corps*, and a set of ethical norms reflecting the social responsibilities of the bureaucracy. Of course, the maintenance of the autocracy was in itself the primary cause of the situation, for it robbed the officials of genuine responsibility and prevented them from feeling that they could give definitive solution to any matter of consequence, as the final decision depended on the autocrat or his personal favorites.

It should be kept in mind that in an autocracy the emperor is always surrounded by courtiers and court factions. A weak sovereign may easily become the prisoner of such factions. By their nature, court factions are interested only in securing immediate personal benefits for their members. The same may be said of the individual favorite, who may exercise great political influence, but still primarily for his own selfish ends. The harm done by court factions and favorites lies not so much in their selfish grabbing, for a rich country may be able to afford some amount of graft if it makes for smoother operations of the government. The greatest threat to a harmonious and beneficent relationship between the ruler and his people stems from the fact that such favorites monopolize access to the ruler's ear. The political instability at the top throughout the eighteenth century was largely the result of this situation.

The basic problem of Russian political and administrative life throughout the eighteenth and nineteenth centuries was the inadequacy of the channels of communication between the government and the nation. The central offices and policy-making officials in St. Petersburg depended entirely on the written reports of their subordinates. In view of the quality of these personnel, these reports were highly unreliable as well as incomplete. The emperor's subjects were normally unable to obtain a hearing by relatively high officials except by accident, through the intervention of well-placed friends, or with the help of bribery. Equally serious was the government's inability to inform the population of its true intentions and of the purpose of its decisions and legislation. Peter the Great had used legislation for civic education, to inform his subjects of his aims, and to impart to the people notions of rational government. His successors did not follow his practice, and in any event it is doubtful that even Peter had been very successful in his efforts. Cut off from direct contact with the country at large, imbued with only vague and general theoretical notions of government, high officials in St. Petersburg rarely conceived that it would be desirable to communicate with the people or allow the people to communicate with them. Many decrees, laws, and statutes were issued in such a way as to remain unknown (if not actually hidden) to the majority of the population concerned, including the educated classes. Even the lower officials were not always adequately informed of the legislation or regulations that they might have to enforce.

A second serious problem for the Russian government was the need for better coordination of decisions and policies. In principle, the sovereign was the source of all law and the final instance of appeal for all matters of administration and justice. But he could not possibly coordinate all facets of public life himself. This was especially the case when the ruler was not quite equal to the task, as happened all too frequently.

Perhaps of greater significance than lack of harmony in the laws was the absence of coordination in the administration itself. There was no single institution specifically entrusted with this function. Peter the Great had intended the Senate to play this role, but after his death the Senate's authority declined, and it eventually became primarily a supervisory body and high administrative tribunal. There were brief periods during which the Senate acted as the agent of centralization for the administration (but not as coordinator of legislative policy), as under Empress Elizabeth (reigned 1741–1762) and to some extent also under Catherine II (reigned 1762–1796). Throughout the eighteenth century and in the first years of the reign of Alexander I, efforts were made to restore to the Senate this function of coordination. But it was believed in high government circles that delegating functions of policy coordination to the Senate could give it an authority and power that might enable it to exercise some measure of control, and in so doing put a limit to the autocratic absolutism of the monarch. Thus, this solution was never accepted. Attempts were also made to secure greater coherence and consistency of policy by means of special councils that would assist the ruler while being completely under his control. Yet, again and again, universal fear of the rule or influence of an oligarchy prevented such plans from being implemented in full.

In a paradoxical way, perhaps, the lack of adequate coordination of legislation and administration made it possible to preserve the power of autocracy intact into the twentieth century. As the ruler's decision was required in so many matters, he was able to issue *ad hoc* legislation at will. No group of men could challenge the autocracy's supremacy by virtue of their regular administrative functions. Yet at the same time inadequate policy coordination paralyzed the monarch's autocratic power on a day-to-day level. Indeed, his will could easily be betrayed by subordinate officials, who were in a position to act arbitrarily without being called to account, as there was no effective system of coordination and control.

The rulers of Muscovy had succeeded in preventing the development of social classes into estates, and the population of Russia had been "atomized" quite early in its history. The absolute power of the autocrat had destroyed whatever feeble manifestations of an estate structure had struck roots among the nobility. The reforms and modernization of Peter the Great eliminated the last remnants of a decaying pattern. The elements of regional and class solidarity had never been strong among the peasant population because of the great mobility of its members. The feeble expressions of such solidarities were nipped in the bud by the spread of serfdom and completely destroyed by Peter's poll — or "soul" — tax, which turned the peasant into the property of an individual owner who could easily and arbitrarily disrupt at any time his serfs' attachments to a village or region. The clergy had never enjoyed the privileged status of its counterpart in the West. What did bind together members of the same class or group were family relationships. But for political purposes, ties or solidarities based on family connections are not so strong as the bonds among members of an estate. In a sense, family loyalties separate or oppose individual families quite as much as they bind together the members of the same family. In Russia individual families (or clans), particularly among the nobility, rose and fell as the tsar's favor was bestowed or withdrawn from their members, but these families were not able to act in unison to secure rights and privileges of benefit to each and all of them. The two opposed principles of birthright and service achievement helped to keep the nobility divided: nobles who advocated special status on the basis of individual service merits came into conflict with those who claimed status on grounds of birthright. Peter the Great's Table of Ranks gave the conflict a new form, but preserved the nobility's basic lack of cohesion. As rank was strictly personal and not transmissible to others in the family, it could not survive as a basis for estate solidarities and privileges and was even contrary to them. The paramount role of rank (*chin*) kept the nobility an open and divided class. Quite naturally, the sovereign was only too happy to preserve a situation that worked to his own advantage. The cities and their burghers were few, economically weak, and very much dependent on the sovereign's favors, and thus they could not be the mainstay of a strong third estate as in France.

Consequently, the individual Russian, including the members of the upper classes, faced the autocrat and the apparatus of the state alone. Naturally, he could not have a strong sense of security with respect either to his person or to his property and status. Needless to say, the situation was twice as bad for the peasant, who stood in the same isolated and insecure position with respect to his master.

Three basic elements, therefore, determined the efforts at governmental reform which we observe in the eighteenth and nineteenth centuries: (1) the desire to establish regular channels of communication between the government and the population; (2) the need to coordinate and harmonize more effectively the policies of the government; and (3) the wish to invest the relationship between the government and governed with security of person, property, and status for the latter.

One may liken Peter the Great to a man who is trying to erect a house while hurricane winds are blowing overhead. Part of the structure collapses almost immediately under the next gush of wind, and while repairs are made to it, there is no time to complete the other parts or to lay solid foundations. The government edifice Peter left at his death in 1725 resembled a cluster of more or less completed, more or less well-built structures, poorly integrated both among themselves and in relation to the landscape. Peter had rushed to complete as much as he could, breaking up a great deal of the old edifice, and in so doing completely disregarding the needs of individuals. He had driven everyone hard, no matter what the consequences: the pace had been furious, and the nation was exhausted. Not surprisingly, therefore, the first concern of the service noblemen Peter had helped to bring into being by means of the Table of Ranks was to catch their breath, consolidate their gains, and acquire some sense of security and stability.

The first years after the death of Peter were quite confusing; emperors and empresses followed one another in rapid succession, and their powerful favorites were more short-lived still. The sense of insecurity was at a peak, for every change in the power constellation at court or in government affected deeply the fortunes of many service noblemen. Loss of favor, moreover, meant not only removal from a position of influence but frequently loss of personal liberty and confiscation of property as well. An additional reason for profound insecurity stemmed from the fact that, while the old, traditional order of social relations, especially with regard to the upper classes, had been shattered or even completely destroyed by Peter's reforms, the new rules and relationships had not yet taken hold. In the absence of a feeling of stability, permanence, or coherence, individual members of Russia's nobility felt very much disorientated, socially as well as personally.

In the course of the eighteenth century Russian society, especially the upper class, underwent a profound transformation. This became manifest not so much in the structure and basic social character of the class as in the cultural outlook and activities of its members. In brief, Russian noblemen as a group (including newly-created nobles and a few professionals) had come of age: they were now individualized and Westernized. The nobleman was individualized in the sense that he had broken out of the closed framework of family and clan solidarities; each member was now on his own, and his position in society depended primarily on his personal achievements within the framework of governmental service. At the same time he had adopted Western customs and was beginning to acquire Western modes of thought. With respect to the latter, it is true, progress was rather slow, especially in the provinces, where the vast majority of the petty gentry was still quite uncouth and, indeed, uncivilized from a European point of view. But the leaders, the men who lived in the capitals and served in commanding positions in the army or administration, had become thoroughly Westernized. In our context the most important result was that for the elite, Westernization meant acquiring a sense of self-respect, worth, and dignity. When Catherine II finally prohibited the use of derogatory diminutives and humiliating epithets in official petitions to the ruler, she was wiping away an anachronism. The average educated nobleman no longer thought of himself as a slave (*rab*) or servant (*kholop*) of the ruler; he considered himself a loyal subject and, more important still, a "true son of the fatherland." Naturally, he expected to be treated accordingly, to be secure in his person and property, and to be given public recognition for his class's cultural accomplishments. In short, the Russian nobleman had finally become conscious of his "nobility"; he yearned for the public consideration largely enjoyed by his European counterpart; he was convinced that he ought to have special rights and privileges which could guarantee his status and worth as the cultural and moral leader of the nation.

In this perspective, the most important step taken by Peter's government, which had considerable impact on the future of Russia, was its thorough and methodical effort to establish a modern system of education and to bring European culture and technology, military as well as industrial, to the Russian people. The government's carefully planned and diligently executed policy was designed to shape a new, technologically advanced and highly productive society (in the short term, of course, these initial expectations were not entirely fulfilled). This new society, based on the exploitation of the material and intellectual wealth of the nation, did not call on the services of all its citizens but mainly on the ruling elite. The institutes, academies, and schools that Peter established were reserved for service nobles, clergy, and the children of certain commoners engaged in commerce, manufacturing, or the military. The elite that was tapped to rule Russia was supposed to be a new class based not on genealogy but on ideas, values, and manners. There is no denying the fact that, despite strong initial resistance, Peter and his immediate successors, systematically pursuing a common goal, eventually succeeded in changing the ethos of the Muscovite service class. After Peter died there was no talk of turning back, of giving up on efforts to educate the children of the service nobility in European science, technology, arts, and letters. European culture henceforth became a prerequisite for membership in the ruling elite. First court life and later public and social life changed dramatically, offering a striking contrast with the situation that prevailed in the Kremlin before Peter's accession.

Beyond that, Peter and his administration took steps to systematically exploit the material resources of the empire, doing the best they could with the existing state of the economy and the men and the equipment at their disposal. Explorations were made to scout out new mineral resources, timber, and arable land. Factories, roads, and canals were built; commerce was encouraged; new cities begun — among them the capital — and old ones restored. The ideal Petrine administrator was also a scholar: he was supposed to be competent in economics, science, and politics. One such man was Vasily Tatishchev (1686–1750), an exemplary representative of Peter's generation, whose career and ideas offer the best possible illustration of what Peter was trying to accomplish with the resources at his disposal.

The emperor tried to organize Russian society so as to encourage active and productive work in all areas, including intellectual activity and the private sector of the economy. To that end he used the traditional tool: his command of the state service. His attempt to involve the nobility in economic enterprises proved unsuccessful. It is reasonable to ask why the nobility resisted involvement in activities that would have made it more prosperous while continuing to squander resources in conspicuous consumption. Peter's attempt to change all this, his 1714 legislation to enforce single inheritance of land (repealed in 1731), proved a fiasco.

Peter also enlisted the aid of other social classes by means of state service. The Main Municipal Council (*Glavnyi magistrat*) provided institutional support for members of the urban classes who wished to set up commercial businesses and factories. But once again state interests took precedent over all other considerations: members of the council had to participate actively in the collection of taxes and the maintenance of security in the towns, and their talents and resources had to be placed at the disposal of the state. Much time and energy were wasted as a result, and members of the council ran serious risks since they were legally responsible for any losses incurred by the state treasury. The protection and encouragment offered to private initiative and individual creative energy were insufficient to yield the results that Peter's observations of western European methods had led him to expect.

Finally, society — or at any rate high society — was modernized and Europeanized by the importation of court styles from the West. This proved to be a complete success. Within two generations the court of St. Petersburg could rival any in western Europe for splendor and liveliness. By contrast, the persistent efforts of Peter and his collaborators to induce his people to shed the religious customs and prejudices that were inhibiting the development of a productive *vita activa* ended in almost total failure. In fact, Peter's persistence had the opposite of the desired effect, for it convinced the common people that the emperor and his acolytes were doing the work of the devil and that the sovereign himself was the embodiment of Antichrist.

To sum up: in Russia it was the state that took the lead in efforts to create a more dynamic society, better equipped to exploit available resources in a rational way. Broadly speaking, the state achieved its objectives in regard to the service nobility and the intellectual elite. But with the common people the government's failure was virtually complete, at least until the middle of the eighteenth century.

As a result, Peter's reforms never penetrated to the heart of Russian society or the Russian nation. By intervening here and there agencies of the central government achieved limited short-term results that ultimately changed little. One sometimes has the impression that innovations remained suspended in midair: somehow they always seemed temporary. For Russians of the time, and even more for foreign observers, instability was the most impressive characteristic of the new Russia. The service elites, on the other hand, responded enthusiastically to the cultural challenge and adapted so well to imported Western innovations that within two generations they were making contributions of their own to the new culture of modern Russia. Why did they fail to show similar enthusiasm and creative energy in the economic realm? The question is worth coming back to. For now, let us observe simply that they were overwhelmed by the burdens of state service, which, during the long years of war with Sweden and Turkey, was onerous, difficult, and highly unpredictable, a strain on a man's health and sometimes even a threat to his life. Given prevailing customs, recreational fashions, and the paucity of available resources, it was therefore impossible for a man to pursue economic objectives while also discharging the professional obligation to keep up with the latest cultural fashions, something that could be done while serving in the army or at court.

Accordingly, the elite showed (and would continue to show) a sincere interest in intellectual imports from the West and wholeheartedly adopted the new Russian cultural values. Cultivated Russians were soon able to deal as equals with cultivated Westerners. But popular culture, largely untouched by Peter's revolution, stagnated within the traditions of the seventeenth century. This not only opened an ever-widening gulf between high culture and popular culture but left the latter frozen and dull so that ultimately it withered. The popular mind fell out of step with the mind of the elite and those who identified with the elite. The consequences of this situation made themselves felt with great force in the nineteenth century, when the popular masses returned to the mainstream of Imperial life and culture.

Indeed, the issue became a crucial one from the middle of the eighteenth century, when the rules of compulsory state service for the noble elite were relaxed and then, in 1762, rescinded (although state service remained the normal pattern for the overwhelming majority of the nobility well into the nineteenth century). Service in the Petrine state implied receiving a Western-type education: at first rather primitive and limited to purely technical and military subjects, but gradually expanded in sophistication and breadth to become a general education in European literature, art, and thought. But as this development occurred in the eighteenth century, the Age of Enlightenment, such an education carried in its wake new moral and social ideas. Principal among them was the notion of individual worth and dignity, which underpinned the program of the Well-Ordered Police State. Also implicit was the belief that under proper legal and economic conditions all members of society should be free to pursue productive endeavors. Their combined effort, under the guidance and protection of a benevolent government, would then bring about favorable circumstances for unlimited cultural and material progress.

In the course of the eighteenth century the Russian service elite largely made this attitude its own. However, it was hampered in implementing these Western values by the ongoing existence of the arbitrary, personal authority of the autocrat as well as by the contradictions and insufficiencies of the administrative apparatus. It was difficult to break the fetters of serfdom and burdensome controls to release the energies of the peasantry and urban classes. It was equally difficult to bring about the security of person and property to insure the success of the program of economic expansion initiated by Peter I. The lack of common values between the common people and the elites, an awareness that Peter's legacy had given rise to "two nations," nay two cultures, did not make the task any easier, of course.

It is not surprising, therefore, that the enlightened, better educated, and morally conscious members of the service elite came to switch their loyalty from the state to the people. They became persuaded that genuine progress, the effective materialization of the Petrine program, demanded of them that they lead in educating, enlightening, and guiding the people, primarily the peasantry, in both their moral and material development. They were reinforced in these attitudes by a religious revival that had been much influenced by German Pietist individualism, spiritualism, and notions of social obligation. But their efforts were stymied by the rigid and autocratic establishment and unwieldy administrative structures that Peter had originally put in place. Frustration set in and led to a parting of the ways, a break between the service state and the most progressive elements of the service personnel. The moral commitment to guide and serve the people, and the resulting clash with political authority, gave birth to the "intelligentsia" — i.e., Western-educated members of the elite, critical of the status quo and demanding greater personal freedom and respect for individual dignity in the name of their dedication to the happiness of the Russian people, the enserfed peasantry in particular.

In the nineteenth century the intelligentsia would take the initiative in advocating a new and radical transformation of state and society. Paradoxically, therefore, in the long run Peter's reshaping of the service class resulted in the latter becoming the critic and opponent of the Petrine state. Thus indirectly the first emperor created the driving motor that was to topple the Imperial system for which he had laid the foundations. It was another illustration of the unforeseen consequences of the tension or discrepancy between ends and means — the crucial issue in the pursuit of any program of social and cultural transformation.

Last, the very ambiguity of Peter's legacy was the focus, and constituting element, of modern Russian national consciousness. Indeed, the Imperial Russia that emerged from the ruthless and impatient hands of the Tsar Transformer seems at first glance so different from the Muscovy he inherited that his reign has been perceived as a radical break in the nation's historical development, in Russia's very identity. In other words, is modern Russia by its culture Western? And if so, does this mean that it renounced its older, medieval, Orthodox self? These questions in turn have raised another, more general one: is there such a thing as a true, organic development in the history of a nation, a development that may be ignored only at the cost of losing something essential and producing a "distorted," nay diseased, subsequent evolution? Russia's educated elite and intelligentsia debated these questions throughout the nineteenth, and on into the twentieth, century. This debate is the foundation stone of the country's intellectual history and historiography. Best known outside Russia in more recent times is that aspect of the debate which concerns the "Russianness" or "organicity" of Lenin's Bolshevism and Stalin's Soviet system: do they owe their principal features, as well as their ultimate cause, to the legacy of Peter the Great — i.e., to Western, "alien" imports? Or is the Soviet Union of Lenin and Stalin a modern avatar of the tsardom of Muscovy? And so the debate continues, having acquired a new relevance, as well as virulence, in the context of *glasnost*, *perestroika*, and the question of Russia's place in the world of the late twentieth century.

No revolution is ever complete, and in this sense Peter I's reign was a revolution, if only in the self-image and consciousness of Russian society and culture.

Suggestions for Additional Reading

The figure of Peter the Great has inspired innumerable writers of every kind as well as myriad historians, with the result that by now, more than three centuries after his birth, the literature devoted to his life and times is vast. A critical review of this outpouring, which runs to hundreds, indeed thousands of titles, obviously cannot be attempted here. But an excellent survey of the literature in Russian, with some reference to that in other languages, is Nicholas V. Riasanovsky, *The Image of Peter the Great in Russian History and Thought* (New York: Oxford University Press, 1985). On this subject see also the earlier, more limited work by Xenia Gasiorowska, *The Image of Peter the Great in Russian Fiction* (Madison, WI: University of Wisconsin Press, 1979). Nothing like Riasanovsky's magisterial survey, or Gasiorowska's more limited study, has been published on the literature devoted to Peter in languages other than Russian.

Regarding the more strictly historical literature on the Petrine period, Hans Bagger, a Danish historian, has compiled a useful survey: *Peter den Stores reformer: En forskningsoversigt* (Copenhagen, 1979). Bagger provides an outline of the "problems" of the period as reflected in its historiography as well as a list of some 400 scholarly works published in Russian and other languages; an updated edition with additional commentary has since appeared in Russian: Khans Bagger, *Reformy Petra Velikogo: Obzor issledovanii* [The Reforms of Peter the Great: A Survey of the Scholarly Literature], trans. V. E. Vozgrin, ed. V. I. Buganov (Moscow, 1985). A work of similar scope has been published in German under the overall editorship of Klaus Zernack: *Handbuch der Geschichte Russlands*, vol. 2: *Vom Randstaat zur Hegemonialmacht, 1613–1856* (Stuttgart, 1986), pp. 214–369. In English, there is only Cyril E. Black, "The Reforms of Peter the Great," in Black, ed., *Rewriting Russian History: Soviet Interpretations of Russia's Past*, 2nd ed. (New York: Vintage, 1962), pp. 233–259, which is a critical survey confined to major works published in the Soviet Union before 1960. But see also the review essay by James Cracraft, "More 'Peter the Great'," *Canadian-American Slavic Studies*, vol. 14, no. 4 (Winter 1980), pp. 535–544.

A substantial sample of the major primary sources on Peter and his reign, well edited and translated, is in the second volume of George Vernadsky et al., eds., *A Source Book for Russian History from Early Times to 1917*, 3 vols. (New Haven, CT: Yale University Press, 1972). Complete editions of important contemporary writings include: William E. Butler, ed., P. P. Shafirov, *A Discourse Concerning the Just Causes of the War Between Sweden and Russia: 1700–1721* (Dobbs Ferry, NY: Oceana, 1973); James Cracraft, ed., *For God and Peter the Great: The Works of Thomas Consett, 1723–1729* (New York and Boulder, CO: Columbia University Press, 1982); L. R. Lewitter and A. P. Vlasto, eds. and trans., *Ivan Pososhkov, The Book of Poverty and Wealth* (Stanford, CA: Stanford University Press, 1987); Alexander V. Muller, ed. and trans., *The Spiritual Regulation of Peter the Great* (Seattle, WA: University of Washington Press, 1972); and Max J. Okenfuss, ed. and trans., *The Travel Diary of Peter Tolstoi: A Muscovite in Early Modern Europe* (DeKalb, IL: Northern Illinois University, 1987). An edition of both primary sources and secondary readings in French is Simone Blanc, *Pierre le Grand* (Vendome: Presses Universitaires, 1974).

Book-length scholarly studies of the Petrine period in English are as yet relatively rare: see, on the subjects indicated, James Cracraft, *The Church Reform of Peter the Great* (Stanford, CA: Stanford University Press, 1971); Cracraft, *The Petrine Revolution in Russian Architecture* (Chicago, IL: University of Chicago Press, 1988); Claes Peterson, *Peter the Great's Administrative and Judicial Reforms: Swedish Antecedents and the Process of Reception*, trans. Michael F. Metcalf (Stockholm: A.-B. Nordiska Bokhandeln, 1979); and B. H. Sumner, *Peter the Great and the Ottoman Empire* (Oxford: Blackwell, 1949). A collection of scholarly articles on various Petrine topics is in *Canadian-American Slavic Studies*, vol. 8, no. 2 (Summer 1974): this is a special issue devoted to the reign of Peter the Great.

Among general works in English, the classic is Eugene Schuyler, *Peter the Great, Emperor of Russia: A Study of Historical Biography*, 2 vols. (New York: Scribner's, 1884; reprinted New York, 1967), which is still valuable for its detail, much of it drawn from Russian sources. More recent efforts include B. H. Sumner, *Peter the Great and the Emergence of Russia* (London: English Universities Press, 1951; frequently reprinted), which is generally considered the best short survey in any language; Ian Grey, *Peter the Great, Emperor of All Russia*

(London: Hodder and Stoughton, 1962); and M. S. Anderson, *Peter the Great* (London: Thames and Hudson, 1978). Robert K. Massie, *Peter the Great: His Life and Work* (New York: Knopf, 1980), while massive in size, is novelistic in style and based mainly on secondary sources (notably, on Schuyler); similarly popular, in French, is Henri Troyat, *Pierre le Grand* (Paris, 1979; English edition, New York: Dutton, 1987). The most comprehensive scholarly work in any language is Reinhard Wittram, *Peter I Czar und Kaiser: Zur Geschichte Peters des Grossen in seiner Zeit*, 2 vols. (Göttingen, 1964). Władysław A. Serczyk, *Piotr I Wielki* (Warsaw, 1973), offers a Polish perspective as well as a survey of Peter's reign as a whole.

Two outstanding textbooks with substantial sections on the Petrine period are Michael T. Florinsky, *Russia: A History and an Interpretation*, 2 vols. (New York: Macmillan, 1953; see vol. 1), and Nicholas V. Riasanovsky, *A History of Russia*, 4th ed. (New York: Oxford University Press, 1984). Other general works in which Peter, his reign, and his legacy figure prominently include Richard Pipes, *Russia under the Old Regime* (New York: Scribner's, 1974); Paul Dukes, *The Making of Russian Absolutism, 1613–1801* (London: Longman, 1982); and Marc Raeff, *Understanding Imperial Russia: State and Society in the Old Regime* (New York: Columbia University Press, 1984).

The following specialized works in English deal in considerable part with major aspects of Peter's reign: Paul Avrich, *Russian Rebels, 1600–1800* (New York: Schocken Books, 1972); Valentin Boss, *Newton and Russia: The Early Influence, 1698–1796* (Cambridge, MA: Harvard University Press, 1972); Robert O. Crummey, *The Old Believers and the World of Antichrist* (Madison, WI: University of Wisconsin Press, 1970); Gregory L. Freeze, *The Russian Levites: Parish Clergy in the Eighteenth Century* (Cambridge, MA: Harvard University Press, 1977); J. G. Garrard, ed., *The Eighteenth Century in Russia* (Oxford: Clarendon Press, 1973); Arcadius Kahan, *The Plow, the Hammer, and the Knout: An Economic History of Eighteenth-Century Russia* (Chicago, IL: University of Chicago Press, 1985); J. L. H. Keep, *Soldiers of the Tsar: Army and Society in Russia, 1462–1874* (Oxford: Clarendon Press, 1985); Gary Marker, *Publishing, Printing, and the Origins of Intellectual Life in Russia, 1700–1800* (Princeton, NJ: Princeton University Press, 1985); Brenda Meehan-Waters, *Autocracy and Aristocracy: The Russian Service Elite of 1730* (New Brunswick, NJ: Rutgers University Press, 1982); Andrew Rothstein, *Peter the Great and Marlborough: Politics and Diplomacy in Converging Wars* (New York: St. Martin's Press, 1986); Harold B. Segel, ed. and trans., *The Literature of Eighteenth-Century Russia*, 2 vols. (New York: Dutton, 1967; see vol. 1); Orest Subtelny, *The Mazepists: Ukrainian Separatism in the Early Eighteenth Century* (New York and Boulder, CO: Columbia University Press, 1981); and A. P. Vlasto, *A Linguistic History of Russia to the End of the Eighteenth Century* (Oxford: Clarendon Press, 1986).

Of course, the bulk of the historical literature on the life and times of Peter I is in Russian, and readers of Russian are urged to consult, first, the surveys by Nicholas V. Riasanovsky and by Hans Bagger cited above. Among the more recent works published, representative titles include: T. V. Alekseeva, ed., *Russkoe iskusstvo pervoi chetverti XVIII veka* [Russian Art of the First Quarter of the 18th Century] (Moscow, 1974); E. V. Anisimov, *Podatnaia reforma Petra I* [The Tax Reform of Peter I] (Leningrad, 1982) and Anisimov, *Vremia petrovskikh reform* [The Era of the Petrine Reforms] (Leningrad, 1989); V. I. Buganov, *Moskovskie vosstaniia kontsa XVII veka* [Uprisings in Moscow at the End of the 17th Century] (Moscow, 1969); N. B. Golikova, *Politicheskie protsessy pri Petre I* [Political Trials under Peter I] (Moscow, 1957); G. I. Komelova, ed., *Kultura i iskusstvo petrovskogo vremeni* [The Culture and Art of the Petrine Period] (Leningrad, 1977); S. P. Luppov, *Kniga v Rossii v pervoi chetverti XVIII veka* [The Book in Russia in the First Quarter of the 18th Century] (Leningrad, 1973); N. N. Molchanov, *Diplomatiia Petra Pervogo* [The Diplomacy of Peter I] (Moscow, 1984); N. I. Pavlenko, *Petr Pervyi* [Peter the First] (Moscow, 1975); N. I. Pavlenko, ed., *Rossiia v period reform Petra I* [Russia in the Period of the Reforms of Peter I] (Moscow, 1973); A. N. Robinson, ed., *Russkaia literatura na rubezhe dvukh epokh* [Russian Literature at the Crossroads of Two Eras] (Moscow, 1971); and V. E. Vozgrin, *Rossiia i evropeiskie strany v gody Severnoi voiny* [Russia and Europe in the Years of the Northern War] (Leningrad, 1986).

The life and times of Peter the Great have been dramatized in several outstanding, more or less historically accurate, full-length Soviet films: *Peter the First*, in 2 parts (1937, 1938); *The Blackamoor of Peter the Great* (1978); and *The Youth of Peter the Great*, in 2 parts (1980, 1981). All three are available (in Russian with English subtitles), for purchase or rental, from Corinth Films, 410 East 62nd Street, New York, NY 10021; (212) 421-4770.